THE REST OF THE ICEBERG

AN INSIDER'S VIEW ON THE WORLD OF SPORT AND CELEBRITY

by
Robert Smith

Edited by John Wiebusch

DEDICATION

This book is dedicated to Jerry Zovko, Pat Tillman, and all the other true heroes who have given their lives for our freedom and safety.

TABLE OF CONTENTS

Dedication v

Acknowledgements ix

Foreword xi

Introduction xiii

PART ONE
THE MAIN SEQUENCE xvii

    Chapter One: Humility 1

    Chapter Two: Messiah 33

    Chapter Three: Pariah 49

    Chapter Four: Sea Change 71

    Chapter Five: Sisyphus 102

    Chapter Six: Serendipity 127

    Chapter Seven: ? 161

    Chapter Eight: King Cornell 174

PART TWO
SERAPHIM 181

    Chapter Nine: The "Giant" Myth 183

    Chapter Ten: The Have$ v$ the Have Not$ 191

    Chapter Eleven: Pros or Cons? 202

    Chapter Twelve: The Race, Creed, and Color Cards 212

ACKNOWLEDGMENTS

I would like to thank all my friends and family, especially my brother Scott, my mother Emilie, and my father Emmitt for sticking with me and encouraging me through the good times and the bad.

I would also like to give special thanks to Hattie Webb and Jennifer Smith; I couldn't have gotten this done without you believing in me and this project.

FOREWORD

Retrospect is just a word, but it has a lifetime of meaning. Do you have any regrets? Would you change something in your past? What would you do differently? *The Rest of the Iceberg* is a brutally honest collection of thoughts from Robert Smith, a friend who has never been one to back down from either his opinions or thoughts.

Let me assure you that this is not your typical professional athlete "fluff" book. This is a book based on the real-life adventure of an athlete who took a meager and typical (for a professional player) upbringing and brushed off stereotypes and media scrutiny to become a successful, articulate, intelligent man.

Robert's athletic accomplishments speak for themselves, so there is no need to highlight them here. By the end of his book, you will get a pretty good insight into his thoughts, but as someone who has known him for roughly 15 years, I would like to point out a few things about Robert that won't be covered. Robert is hard-headed, thoughtful, honest, tough, trustworthy, dependable, self assured, never wrong (at least in his mind), funny, passionate, non-diplomatic, caring—basically, he's human.

Could you give up millions of dollars in the prime of your career? Could you give up adulation, notoriety, and fame? Could you do it all at the ripe old age of 28? The theory that all athletes play for money took a "shot in the ass" the day Robert retired. He had just come off his best season ever and was arguably the most sought-after free agent on the market. Instead of looking for a new "crib," he contemplated what was next. As you will see by reading this book, the NFL has given Robert a platform, but it's not written to take advantage of the NFL affiliation. Robert has never been one to boast of his accomplishments. You never saw him in commercials; hell, he never even spiked a football! So as would be expected, this book is REALLY not about him or his playing but about his thoughts, both on and off the field.

If you get anything out of this book, I hope you get an understanding that not everything you read or hear is exactly what you think or want it to be. When an athlete/celebrity is "high profile," they often are put in situations where the "facts" get in the way of the truth. Robert has made mistakes, the media has made mistakes, and we've made mistakes in assuming we know the answers. One thing I think you'll get out of this book is that maybe, just maybe, we never knew the truth. After reading this book, maybe the next time you read about an athlete, you won't make a judgment until all of the facts are known.

Mike Gutter

INTRODUCTION

Errors like straws on the surface flow;
He who would search for pearls must dive below.

——John Dryden, *All for Love*

What do we really know about the world around us? Many of us believe we have a firm grasp on reality and what constitutes fact. But who is to say what is right or what is true? We may receive information about various topics and events, but information is only as good as its source. Another problem is that we base our determinations on our own biases and pre-conceived notions. It is difficult to separate what we believe or, more pointedly, what we want to believe, from objective truth.

For a long time people believed the world was flat. Why wouldn't you? It sure looks flat, doesn't it? Many people claim the Great Wall of China is the only man-made object that can be seen from outer space. But here, once again, myth fails to pass the test of truth. But our distorted and incorrect views are not limited to the realm of urban legend.

Many people read the Bible and think they know the story of Noah's Ark. They will say that the Bible tells us that Noah took the animals two-by-two onto the ark. But the Bible clearly says that Noah took two each (one pair) of the "unclean" and seven pairs (14 total) of the "clean" animals. How could one of the most popular stories in history be so often distorted? The simple answer is that we are conditioned to believe things we hear from what we consider to be reliable sources. How long did you believe in Santa Claus? The real challenge is finding a credible source of knowledge, especially in this era of instant, if not always completely accurate, information. Even the most powerful people in the world must deal with the possibility that the information they receive is incomplete or even false.

Our current problems with intelligence agencies have highlighted these issues. Recent news coverage has also shown how one-sided the presentation of information can be. Many news outlets have clearly decided that showing one side of issues is sufficient in presenting today's events. But we must understand that news outlets can be as fallible and biased as the individuals who run them. We see the world they choose to present to us through their filters. This is why it is so important for us to seek an understanding of topics by intelligently examining all sides of an issue. We need to remain open-minded and diligent in our efforts if we are to achieve better understanding. We still may be incorrect, but we will be closer to an objective truth.

Seeking primary sources is an important first step in this process. If you want to understand war, you shouldn't go to academics who study it or to news outlets that cover it. Rather, you should try to get information from the soldiers who live and fight it. This is where my book comes in. I would like to make it clear that while I make the comparison of being a football player to a soldier for convenience, by no means do I consider the two to be equal. I know what it's like to face imminent danger and pain on a football field, but I cannot fathom the horror and anxiety soldiers must feel as they face death on a daily basis. We must never forget that soldiers like the late Pat Tillman (killed in Afghanistan) and Jerry Zovko (a friend of mine from high school who was brutally killed and then dragged through the streets of Fallujah in Iraq) are our real heroes and deserve the utmost respect from our society. Without them, we wouldn't have the freedom we take for granted.

Understanding people can be extremely difficult. It takes years to get to know people in our personal lives and yet some try to accomplish this feat with celebrities from interview segments and sound bites. So I've tried to be thorough. I wrote this book by myself because I feel that you can't really touch raw emotions by dictating a story for someone else to write. It was a struggle to accomplish, but I felt it was necessary to convey my message accurately.

This book has two main sections. The first, "The Main Sequence," is autobiographical and focuses on the transition one goes through to become a star. The Main Sequence is an astronomical term that refers to part of the life cycle of a star like our sun. Our society places a heavy emphasis on athleticism. It treats athletes differently in good and bad ways. I try to show how difficult the stresses of this life can be and how it can affect one emotionally.

The second section, "Seraphim," discusses what I characterize as the "fall from grace" of modern athletes, celebrities, and other public figures. Our society's fascination with the people they watch and read about has turned into obsession. The public tries to find out everything about its idols. This has been made easier by the Internet and constant news coverage of celebrities. People become disenchanted when they find out that their heroes are nothing more than ordinary people in extraordinary circumstances. I also offer other reasons I feel people often turn so dramatically against the heroes they used to blindly admire.

I hope this book helps explain some things to you. I hope this book entertains you. Most of all, I hope this book teaches you to see things from different perspectives—to not just focus on surface issues, to see the rest of the iceberg.

PART ONE

THE MAIN SEQUENCE

It's so easy to laugh at yourself, when all those jokes have already been written.

—Beck

CHAPTER ONE

HUMILITY

If I claim to be a wise man, it surely means that I don't know.

—Kansas

It didn't take me very long to figure out I was different than most other kids. In my kindergarten year at Thomas Jefferson Elementary, we were sitting in a semi-circle around the teacher. She was going over a topic she had gone over one too many times. In one of those great moments of indiscretion, I decided to raise my 5-year-old voice and protest the teacher's waste of our precious time: "Yeah, yeah, we know, we know!" This unwelcome comment left the teacher less than pleased with me and she responded with a quick smack to the top of my head with a rolled up magazine. Next thing I knew, I was sitting in the hallway crying my eyes out. My mother later said that the teacher had claimed she had offered me the opportunity to return to the room if I would apologize for what I said. I insisted that I was right (hardly a shock to anyone who knows me). I decided to wait in the hallway until my mother got there.

That was my major early attempt at anarchy. From that time on, I decided that making a point against a teacher wasn't worth the embarrassment I would get. However, my fledgling smart-ass mouth was not the only thing that separated me from my classmates. At times in our society, we long to be like everyone else, or, failing that, at least fit in. But, at the same time, we are also ultra-competitive and long to stand out from the rest of the crowd—not to be different, but to be special. It almost sounds silly, but being "special" helped me stand out from the beginning. For one thing, I had the gift of speed.

It's not that I wasn't a bright or charming boy. In fact, I was considered to have both of those qualities. But when you're a kid, athletic prowess is considered the best of all talents. Sure, singers and actors are cool when you're older, but when you're in school, those kids are considered geeks. No, being the athlete is the way to rise above the crowd.

I was only five or six years old when my gift was discovered, so the benefits were few, but important. It gave me bragging rights as the fastest kid in my class. I've never felt the need to show others up, but it's always nice to know that you can shut people up when they brag about being the best at something. I was like a sideshow performer during recess or gym. We would set up races and when some loud-mouthed kid wanted to race me, I'd give him this huge advantage…and still win. It was my introduction to the pure joy of running.

Animals feel a genuine joy when they use the physical gifts they possess. A monkey gains pleasure from swinging on branches. A dolphin feels elation as it springs playfully from the water. An eagle feels a sense of pride and purpose as it soars majestically or cuts through the wind with its powerful wings. For me, the moment of genuine joy came when I ran at full speed. I could feel the wind racing by my head and my feet barely seemed to touch the ground as I glided along. All of my internal energy flowed out of me and the slightly blurred surroundings gave me a sense of the speed at which my legs carried me. My entire being was immersed in the sensation of movement.

It felt great to win the races, but the sense of self-awareness and completeness I felt with the simple act of running would have been enough reward. The second benefit of my gift—schoolyard respect—is a prize every child desires. In some sense, we all want to be accepted, especially in the brutally honest environment of elementary school. Kids have no sense of political correctness. Every parent in the world has dealt with the embarrassment of their kids throwing out one of these types of gems in public: "Why does that man walk so funny?" "Why is that lady so fat?" Or "What's the matter with that man's face?"

2

The slings and arrows cast at perfect strangers are no match for the salvoes of embarrassing scrutiny and painful insults kids reserve for their classmates. Some kids spend their days at school looking for ways to call out other children for their imperfections. No wonder so many of our youth fail to behave the way we want them to. Many of them are either mounting verbal or physical attacks on their fellow students or they're trying to defend themselves from onslaughts. I can honestly say that I never had to distract myself with either of those tasks. Even at a young age, you're almost immune from such attacks when you're athletic.

I suspect I would have gotten along fine without my athletic gift, however, because I have always been a well-rounded individual. I had a fascination with the world around me, and learning about it was a constant joy. I got along with my teachers. Except for the outburst in kindergarten, they had no reason not to like me. I was pretty much a quiet kid who always did as I was told. On top of that, I did well in class. But school was never enough to completely satisfy my appetite for understanding. I hate not knowing how something works. Everyone knows that a plane works, but I've always been the type who wanted to know *how* it worked. I always had a lot of questions. I always wonder how so many people go through life without questioning the world around them. Part of it is laziness, but part of it has to be a sad lack of curiosity.

My mother is a very bright person. As a registered nurse, she could tell early on that I had the need to learn. Because of this—and I'm sure because she kind of got tired of fielding so many questions—she bought me a book called *Tell Me Why*. It was perfect for a kid like me. It had answers to the types of natural phenomenon that dominated my interest. Why does thunder make noise? (It's the expansion of the superheated air that results from lightning.) Why are there rainbows? (It's the splitting of light into its constituent wavelengths and corresponding colors.) These were the kinds of things I felt I had to know. I've always believed that to understand the world around you, you need to know as many things about it as possible. I wanted things to make sense and for that I felt I had to learn about all the things that I didn't know.

So there I was—a young man with a thirst for knowledge, sitting in an average public elementary school. My mother was too smart to allow me to stay there. My grandmother and her sister lived very close to our Euclid, Ohio, apartment in a place of their own in nearby Richmond Heights. They knew of a Catholic school near them that seemed a better alternative than the public school system. Forget the fact that I had never been baptized or that none of us really went to church. It's sad that so many people feel the need to go to alternative schooling in America, but our public school system just doesn't provide students with the same level of education. Parochial schools not only give their students a better education, but they also teach discipline and respect, something public schools rarely seem to instill. "Please" and "thank you" have been a big part of my vocabulary ever since. It wasn't going to be easy for my family to afford sending me to the school, but they wanted this for me and they did whatever it took for me to go there.

I was excited about the new school, but I was also apprehensive about the adjustment to a different environment. As I already mentioned, I had never been baptized so I thought I would be looked down on. I also knew that the school I was going to attend was predominantly white. I'm from a mixed marriage—my mother is white and my father is black. I thought that this might be a source of friction between me and my fellow students. The public school I had attended was pretty racially diverse and I never had any problems getting along with white or black children. I guess it has always been easy for me to get along in different crowds because of my mixed race. I never saw people in color because black and white people both were family to me. American society has a pretty simple way of deciding the issue: If you're not white, you're black. But it never came up as an issue until I arrived at St. Felicitas.

I remember standing out at the bus stop with what, if I remember correctly, were the only two other black kids going to St. Felicitas at the time. I felt kind of funny out there in my Buster Browns and clip-on tie (I never once wore a "real" tie in the four years I went to St. Felicitas). I could see other kids walking to other schools in jeans, tennis shoes, and T-shirts and I thought of how much more comfortable I would feel in those clothes. Oh, well, I thought, time to get into character: *You're going to be a good little Catholic school boy now...forget about what those public school kids are wearing.* There were a few other kids on the bus—all of them white—as we made our way to St. Felicitas.

When I first visited St. Felicitas, Sister Bruce, the school's principal, made it a point to emphasize the large gym that the school was built around. It was as if the school itself was an extension of the gym. Clearly, this was a place that focused on sports and athleticism. Sister Bruce saw me as a model citizen who wanted to develop himself even more in the environment of Catholic school. I was convinced that all of these kids were "angels in training" and I was on my very best behavior at all times so I wouldn't stand out any more than I already did.

Anyone who has ever gone to a parochial school knows how wrong I was. Sure these kids wore ties and dressed nicely, but, beneath the uniforms, they were the same loud, rambunctious kids I had left behind at public school. I almost felt as if they were trying to test me to see whether I'd start acting like the hooligan that they were convinced I must have been. Stereotypes exist in all of our minds to some degree and kids are no exception. We just don't feel as comfortable around people who talk, look, or act differently than we do. It was clear to me once I got there that these kids were really no different than I was, but it would take time for them to make the same realization about me. I wasn't accepted immediately, but my athleticism came to the rescue.

The Robert Smith Sideshow was back in business at recess! I was far advanced in strength and speed over these kids. Once you start getting picked first for all the teams and out-perform everyone in all of the contests, people automatically take notice of you. They talk to you. They stop seeing you as just some black kid and start seeing you as a person.

I'm sure many Americans wrestle with the notion that their favorite athletes or singers are black, while they themselves harbor ill feelings or prejudices against black people in the general population. But that's the key: Black athletes and entertainers aren't viewed in the same way as other blacks.

There's a great scene in Spike Lee's *Do the Right Thing* that covers this subject perfectly. In the movie, there's a white pizza shop owner (Danny Aiello) who has his shop located in the Bedford Stuyvesant area of Brooklyn. The area has a mostly black population and the movie deals with the problems that arise from the racial and ideological differences between the shop owner and the majority of his customers. His sons also work at the store alongside a black employee named Mookie (Spike Lee). One of the sons, Pino (John Turturro), is talking with Mookie about how he doesn't like black people. Mookie asks him who his favorite basketball player is and he responds Michael Jordan. He then asks him who his favorite singer is and he says Prince. Mookie asks him why he doesn't have a problem with these people based on his feelings towards blacks. Pino replies that "they're not....you know.... black, it's different."

I think most sports fans that harbor prejudicial feelings make this distinction as well. A person's not considered to be black in the same way if they're a celebrity. Part of this is simply that people begin to feel a degree of closeness with public figures that they continually see or read about. You see someone interviewed on television enough and you begin to think you really know that person. That's why media relations can be so important for athletes (much more on that later). You often are judged by the way you appear and sound on TV.

In a more cynical sense, I feel some people make an exception for celebrities. They retain their prejudicial feelings in private but have no trouble cheering for their favorite black athlete or black celebrity. They use the public persona of a celebrity to rationalize their feelings of admiration for a person they might not even talk to on the street. These people stand up and cheer on game day or at a concert. But they would disown their daughter if she came home with one of them.

The only other black kid in my class wasn't as good an athlete (although he was better than the other kids) but he always seemed to find a way to get himself into trouble. Some kids are just less well-behaved, but in their minds he was confirming every stereotype that these kids had about blacks. He didn't study, he would act up in class, and he made a general nuisance of himself. He wasn't the only kid doing those things, but he stood out because of his race. It's not that I was trying to be some goody-two-shoes or, to be more blunt, some kind of house-nigger. I wasn't "acting" white—I was *behaving* with common sense.

I was embarrassed—and my third grade teacher was shocked—when it was revealed I hadn't learned to write in cursive. It sounds like an insignificant matter, but it's another example of how the public school system lagged behind parochial schools. Part of the problem is a lack of funding. Public schools just become too crowded and teachers are unable to give students the personal attention they need. This neglect can lead to students who fail to learn required skills but still are passed into the next grade where they fall even further behind. Well, I wasn't going to let anything like that happen to me. I studied hard to catch up with the other students and I began to excel.

Things were going well at school, but the picture at home was far from rosy. My father had become disabled and could not work because of emotional problems. The stress of his life had become too much for him and he broke down mentally. My mother put him in various treatment centers. She did her best to shield my brother and me from the problem by telling us that our dad was working for the government. "Cool…I won't say anything" I said. *Yeah, right.* Of course I had to share this news with some of the kids at school. But it soon became painfully obvious that my father was suffering from major problems as he started to abuse drugs. It was hard enough for my mother to support us on her salary, but now she had to deal with supporting his drug problem. If he couldn't get money out of her he'd fly off into a rage and just take anything he could sell—a TV, a radio, anything to support his habit. He would come home with a few thousand dollars of drug money for us to help him count and yet we couldn't even afford to get by on our own. He told us that he had the money from operating a game room and that it wasn't his. He became increasingly abusive and disruptive to the household. It would have been impossible for us to deal with these issues on our own. Fortunately, we didn't have to.

The apartment of Aunt Ruth and Nonny, my great aunt and grandmother, was our sanctuary. There were times when my father would fly off into a drug-induced rage and we were left with no choice but to go to stay with Aunt Ruth and Nonny. They loved us in a way that words fail to convey. They would have done anything to make my mother, my brother and me happy. It's not that they had unlimited resources or anything close to that. They just dug as deep as they could to try to comfort us. There's a feeling of desperate hopelessness you experience as a child when your father is threatening your mother. It's an awful mix of terror and useless anger—a desire to fly away—to capture for any brief moment a piece of tranquility from the terrible night-time mayhem and soothe the ones you love that you know are hurting so deeply. You feel like your whole world is poisoned—impossibly jolted, that things will never be normal. But then we would get to Aunt Ruth and Nonny's place ... and the world would be made right again by these two angels. A hug, a kiss, some candy, soothing words. They were an inspiration to us. I knew I wouldn't let our lives stay like that. I told myself I would make a difference. They had shown me the way—my mother, my grandmother, my great aunt. They showed me how to be strong, to persevere, to never stop believing. Love is the world's strongest weapon.

My father ended up going in and out of jail a number of times while I was growing up. It was tough to have to go down to jail to visit him. We still loved him, but we were mad at the things that he had done to make our lives difficult. And we knew that, despite his actions, he loved us. It's the problem with drugs; it makes people seem like something they're not—and sometimes that can have dire consequences. It's like what Hunter S. Thompson wrote in *Fear and Loathing in Las Vegas*: "You can turn your back on a person, but never turn your back on a drug—especially when it's waving a razor sharp hunting knife in your face." Well, people on drugs can become possessed; they become more of a drug/person hybrid than a person. I was angry for years at the way he made us suffer. But even at what seemed the cruelest of depths, I knew that my father loved us. He had lost control of his life, but he deserved the chance to prove that he could reform. You never should give up on family.

I'm proud to say that my father has made a change in his life. I recently spoke at a correctional facility and shared my father's story with some of the inmates. Some of them wanted to know how they could reconcile their family situations. I told them that you can't make people believe what you say, but you hope that with time they will realize that you truly want to be different and, most importantly, that you are. Only you can make the changes in your life that will help people regain their trust in you. My father is living proof that it's never too late to try to make a change in your life. He's fortunate to have had as many chances as he's had. He's got a bullet entry wound in his chest and a bullet exit wound in the middle of his back. I'm tired of our culture glamorizing gangsters and thugs. He was a real-life gangster—and he's glad that dead-end life is behind him. He's a very happy person now and he wears a genuine smile that belies all the years of abuse that he both took and gave out. He's a survivor in the truest sense of the word. I owe him for my independence and resilience.

I must say that my transition also was made easier by a friend I made named John Parsons. John lived fairly close to me and we took the same bus to school. He was one of the first kids I talked to at school. As I said, most of the other kids kind of kept their distance for a while, but John was there from the start. We found out quickly that we were both Pittsburgh Steelers fans (a sacrilege worse than blasphemy in Cleveland) and we just kind of hit it off. John and I ended up going to the same high school as well and I speak to him to this day. It's rare in life to find real friends and I can honestly say I feel blessed to have the few that I do. I remember John bringing up the race issue. He sounded just like Pino from *Do the Right Thing*. He would say that I wasn't really black. He may have meant it in more of the mulatto sense, but I think his perspective was also based on the fact that we were friends.

Even though I was a Steelers fan, I never really watched them much on TV. I really never watched much of any sports on TV. It was always more fun for me to be outside playing it with my friends. I would pretend to be Franco Harris on offense or Jack Lambert on defense. If the Steelers hadn't been winning Super Bowls about that time I probably wouldn't have even known those guys. I also admired Terry Bradshaw, Mean Joe Green, John Stallworth, and Lynn Swann. I loved seeing those guys win. I bet my dad $20 bucks (I had no way to pay him, of course, if they had lost) the Steelers would win Super Bowl XIV against the Rams— they came through for me! I don't remember exactly what I spent my winnings on but I'm sure it involved candy and video games.

Up to this point, my only "real" competition was on track and field day at St. Felicitas. They would take an entire day of school in the spring and run events for the students to compete against one another. It was my introduction to the thrill of real competition. Sure, we had played games on the playground, but those dramas couldn't come close to the organized events. For one thing, there's the build-up to the event itself. You prepare yourself mentally and physically to perform—and then the day finally arrives. For some it's a desire to show-off, but for me, it was always a time to compete against myself. Of course, it's also a time to try and capture the greatest reward in competition: victory.

I competed in four events in my first track and field day. I won four blue ribbons. Mr. Rico, the gym teacher, suggested that I go out for the track team at St. Felicitas. The track team would compete in the C.Y.O. or Catholic Youth Organization. It consisted of Catholic schools throughout the Cleveland Diocese. I remember we practiced in the gym at St. Felicitas for most of the season with occasional trips to Richmond Heights High to use their track. I don't know why, but we only competed in one meet that year and it was the city C.Y.O. championships.

Competing in track and field day was pure fun, but the city championship was plain nerve-racking the first time. The anticipation and nervousness actually made me feel sick. I think it was because I assumed that I wouldn't be head and shoulders above these kids like I had been with my classmates. I was scared to lose. It turned out my fears were unfounded. It was clear that I was one of the fastest kids in my grade throughout the entire city—at least in the Catholic school system.

That summer I got a chance to test myself against the best around. Frank Lipold, our track coach, realized that I was a special talent and convinced me to try the city-wide AAU (Amateur Athletic Union) track meets. This would be a test against kids from all over Cleveland. Frank used the term "inner-city" kids to describe what he thought would be my toughest competition. He was right. I've often wondered how many of these "inner-city" kids never get the chance to compete in organized competition and miss out on the chance to earn a scholarship later. Organized athletics also give children a sense of belonging and a better understanding of cooperation and discipline.

These kids were fast—real fast—but I was still proving to be the fastest. We ended up going to one of the regional meets that brought kids together from the tri-state area. I met my match in some of the events, but ended up being nationally ranked. It was an unbelievable sense of accomplishment and pride to know that out of all the thousands of kids in the nation, I was one of the best at something. I was driven more and more to compete and be competitive in general. I've always felt that all things in life are transitive—that is to say that different aspects of your life shouldn't be thought of as completely separate. People who are competitive have an advantage in life. My competitive nature in sports has helped me in other areas. I've wanted to be good at everything I try. I don't like not understanding things. I don't like not winning (subtly different from losing)but I've always been gracious in defeat, because I don't blame my opponent for what I perceive is my failure. I've always felt there was something more I could have done to win. I think this stems partially from the fact that I've always been good at whatever I've tried. But there are times when you just have to realize that someone else is better. It's not that you should ever take losing lightly, but you have to be strong about it and prepare yourself for your next chance.

The track coach was good friends with the football coach at St. Felicitas and he suggested that I try out for football that fall. It had never really even crossed my mind to try out for an organized football team. I enjoyed playing football in the neighborhood, but the idea of playing for a team just didn't really excite me. But it seemed to make sense. I remember showing up that first day. Coach Brian Cooper had one of the quarterbacks throw me some balls. I'm sure he wanted to get a feel for how well I caught the ball. With my build, he probably thought I should try receiver, but he must not have been too impressed with my hands that day because he decided to put me at running back—the position I would keep for the rest of my playing days.

Like every coach I've ever had, I'm sure he wondered at first if I would be able to put up with the pounding of football, let alone the pounding a player receives at running back. My trademark skinny legs were that much skinnier then, so I'm sure I must have looked quite unimpressive when I came walking into practice that first day. I've always thought that my legs were too skinny for my body. One of my elementary school teachers actually asked if I was eating enough at home. I've been blessed with phenomenal metabolism, so it's always been difficult for me to gain weight. But the size of my legs has been shocking to some people. I'm definitely built for speed. Anywhere you look in the animal kingdom, you'll see the same thing: thin legs=fast animal. Former Ohio State strength and conditioning coach Dave Kennedy put it best: "Secretariat had skinny legs, too!" The thing about the running back position that has always made it more attractive to me is the fact that runners have a better chance than wide receivers to impact a football game. Apart from the quarterback, they have as great a chance as any player on the field to change the outcome of a game. You can put double coverage on a receiver without greatly impacting the integrity of your defense, but it is much more difficult to keep a good running back from getting the ball into his hands. All you have to do is look at the number of touches a good running back gets in an average contest compared to what a good receiver gets. Obviously, the more touches you get, the more chances you have to make a difference in a game, and nobody but the quarterback will touch the ball more times (barring the center of course) during the course of most games. Even if a defense changes its structure to try to defend against the run, you can still get the ball to your running back by throwing to him. And if the defense changes its structure too dramatically, it simply has left itself that much more vulnerable to the passing game.

The first thing that struck me about football was the pain involved. I didn't like it. Some players truly like the pain involved in football. I definitely wouldn't put myself in that masochistic group. I did develop an enjoyment for the physical nature of the game, and the pain bothered me less and less as my career evolved, but, when I first started playing, it seemed like an unnecessary hassle. Running around in all that equipment during ridiculously humid Cleveland on late-summer days while getting pounded on, wasn't much of a selling tool to me initially. It just didn't seem like that much fun. Sure the equipment was cool—I remember going home and putting the equipment on just to run around outside—and it would impress the girls, but, man, those hits hurt!

But I did start to get used to the hits and once we started playing games it began to seem a lot more fun to me. Just as in track, it didn't take long to stand out. I was the only sixth grader starting on a team of eighth graders, which impresses me now when I think about the size difference between sixth and eighth graders (No wonder it hurt so much). We had a decent season and I scored a good number of touchdowns. Football isn't that complicated at that level—not that it's ever rocket science—so our primary running plays were sweep left and sweep right. They would toss me the ball to the outside; I'd beat the defense to the edge and run up the sideline. I probably didn't have a touchdown up the middle all season.

My notoriety began to increase in school. I remember one player's father would always say something about me getting him tickets to Browns games when I played for them in the future. Quite a few of the kids made similar comments about me one day turning pro in football or running in the Olympics. Maybe it's because I was still a quiet kid, or maybe it's because I couldn't believe that something that good could ever happen to me, but I always tried to keep thoughts like that from my head. I knew things would be better for me and family some day—but *that* much better?

Before my first season of football, my mother had decided that we should move out of our neighborhood in Euclid to someplace a little safer and quieter. It's not that we were living in a slum or had to dodge bullets to get to the store, but it wasn't the nicest place on the planet either. Good old Section 8 had done its work to deteriorate our town home development. It was the first time in my life that I became aware of the struggle that goes on within the black community when it comes to those who have money and those who do not. It wasn't as if we were rolling in money, but we didn't have to depend on Uncle Sam to help us pay our rent. The kids from our old development saw kids from the place we were moving as the more "uppity" type. It was a couple of steps up the ladder, but still very far from the top. It was a struggle for my mother to pay for a place like that, but she felt it was better for my brother and me to live in a place where you didn't have to see kids making drug deals or playing basketball until three in the morning (that damn court was right across the street from us, too!). It's sad, but the same people in the black community who so desperately long to escape the clutches of the ghetto curse those that do as being sell-outs. No community is immune to jealousy.

This move also caused a complication with my continued attendance at St. Felicitas. The closest bus stop was far enough away that I would need a ride there. My mother decided it would be best that I move in with Aunt Ruth and Nonny during the week to attend school and then move home on the weekends. It was kind of strange at first, but I really grew to enjoy it. They didn't have much, but they would try to spoil me the best they could. I remember Tuesday nights the best. Aunt Ruth had become very religious and joined one of the groups at St. Felicitas that met every Tuesday night. Before going to her meetings, she would buy cheesecake and Pepsi for Nonny and me. We would sit there with cheesecake and Pepsi and watch "The A-Team" (Nonny had a thing for George Peppard). It's amazing how such seemingly simple interactions and memories can have such a lasting impact on your life. Nonny would talk to me about life, about growing up, about how she felt the world had become so twisted. Her lessons didn't mean as much to me then, but you come to realize how fortunate you are to have someone with experience like hers as you get older. Once it reached Friday, the good times were over: It was time to go home.

I had things much better than my brother Scott. I would be at my grandmother's place living like a king and he'd be at home where my mother struggled to keep food on the table and my dad continued to do his best to make life miserable for everyone. Scott might have had the same opportunity to attend a private school, but he never asserted himself the way that I did. He skipped school quite a bit and really didn't seem to care much for how he did when he would actually attend. I don't really know why Scott behaved the way he did. Part of it may have been the attention I received and his belief that he was being overlooked. Part of it was the fact that Scott just never was much of a self starter. He's a very intelligent guy, but he just needed to be pushed harder.

I would come home on the weekend and have to deal with those things as well, but it's a lot easier when you know your sentence is short. I loved hanging out with my friends from St. Felicitas. Kids really know how to have fun, but there was always a stuffiness I felt at Catholic school, like it wasn't truly okay to be yourself. The kids at home weren't like that. Sure we all made fun of each other for anything we could, but we all knew that we belonged—even if some of us felt it more than others. I think it's why blacks in America give each other hugs when they greet. Some of us act like fools and punks sometimes—sellin' shit or starting fights—but when it comes to your boys, there's nothing but love. We appreciate what we all have to go through just to live in America. It's not that other minorities or white people don't have to struggle, but it's different for blacks. We've had to put up with a lot of stuff in this country and when we're together having fun—you'll know it. I loved the way I felt being home—even though it was a struggle sometimes. I don't care who you are, what you do, what you own or where you decide to live—there's nothing like home.

As I began to think about my life moving towards high school, it became apparent to me that I wouldn't want to attend a private school. It would have been difficult for us to handle it financially, and I thought that going to a public school would give me a chance to be around a wider range of people. We decided it would be best for me to transfer to a public school before high school. This decision wasn't very popular with my grandmother. She could see how I was excelling at St. Felicitas, and I remember her saying, "Do you want to be a big fish in a little pond or do you want to be a small fish in a big pond?" Clearly, I wanted to be a big fish in a big pond. I was aware of my athletic ability by this time. More importantly, I was confident in my ability to get along with any type of person, and this made me feel at ease with my decision to go back into the public school system.

I'm sure the transition would have been a cakewalk except for one small detail: I decided to continue playing football and running track for

15

St. Felicitas. I was the new kid once again. It's never easy for kids going into a new school. This is especially true when you're in your awkward, early teen years. Most of the kids at the school had known each other throughout elementary school and felt more at ease making the transition into junior high. The job for me was made even tougher by the fact that I was coming in from a Catholic school. I wasn't quite sure what to expect. It's not that these kids were really any different deep down, but they were used to a different type of environment at school and it was something that I would just have to get used to. I had become comfortable and confident at St. Felicitas. Most of the people in the school knew me and respected me. I even hung out and talked to the eighth graders while I was in the sixth grade, an important privilege at that age. It was time to start over.

I remember feeling out of place initially. I had hung out with a few of these kids in the neighborhood on the weekends, but this was in a setting of hundreds of other kids. It was clear who the "cool" kids were, and they were all athletes. I was an athlete, but because I had been at St. Felicitas hardly any of those Euclid Central kids knew it. I just did my best t slowly fit in. Once the Presidential fitness tests rolled around in gym class, my reputation as an athlete began to spread. I was breaking records and turning a few heads with my performances. The coaches at the school were pressuring me to go out for the sports teams there, but I continued on at St. Felicitas for the entire year.

I was amazed at how much more confident I was on the football field in my second year. It was a theme that would repeat itself throughout my career. When you first arrive at a new level of football, you feel a sense of shock and are overwhelmed by the speed and intensity of the game. The longer you play, the more comfortable you become and the game begins to slow down for you. You aren't just out there running around like a chicken with its head cut off. Instead, you begin to feel a greater sense of purpose. I'm sure that part of my comfort came from the fact that I also was growing physically. I was still a very thin kid, but I was very strong and fast for my age. I was now playing against kids who were my age or only one year older than I was. I could still reach the corner and run up the sideline, but I was becoming a much more physical runner, capable of running inside or out. We had a perfect season and advanced to the city championship for our division. We destroyed the other team in the championship game. For the first time in my career, I experienced the unbelievable feeling of accomplishment that comes from winning a championship.

There's no denying the joy that one has after winning a race in track. You prepare yourself for months for an event that may be over in less than 11 seconds. To know the instant you cross the finish line that all that work has paid off is a special moment. It's an internal struggle that you have overcome. You rely on yourself and you win or lose based on how you alone perform. But football is different. It's a totally different way to prepare and it feels completely different when you win. You go through quite a bit as a football *team* preparing for a season. From hot training camp days to injuries and exhaustion, you struggle *together*. And when you've put all of the phases of the game-offense, defense, and special teams, together on game day and come out victorious, you celebrate *together*. You have completely relied on each other. Without everyone working towards the same goal and pulling their own weight, you can't win. And those wins throughout the year are all special, but they pale in comparison to that ultimate victory. By winning a championship, you have accomplished a feat that none of your competitors can claim. You are the last team standing.

I was a champion for another school, but back at Central I was still pretty much just a regular kid. It wasn't that I was obsessed with having these kids know how good I was, but I did long to have their respect—and I knew that the quickest way to do that was through sports. I knew I'd be attending the public high school in Euclid after my eighth-grade year, so I decided it was time for me to start competing in the public school system. I was anxious that summer to get the football season started at Central. I had some anxiety about the transition—anxiety that was exacerbated by the death of my grandmother.

When Nonny died on July 18, 1985, I lost one of my angels. I'll never forget the day my mother and father returned from the hospital and told my brother and me that Nonny was gone. She had been in deteriorating health in the last few years and she finally succumbed to pneumonia. It was the first time in my life that I had lost someone close to me. I never got to know my father's parents well because they lived in Mississippi. Nonny and Aunt Ruth had played central roles in my life up to that point. I had spent two school years living with them…and now Nonny was gone. She would never get the chance to see her grandson become a big fish in the biggest of all ponds. I would never be able to share the excitement of my career with her.

Prince came out with his movie *Under the Cherry Moon* that summer and the soundtrack has a song that still reminds me of Nonny. It's called "Sometimes It Snows in April" and it talks about how life throws curves at you. It's one of the most beautiful songs I've ever heard and it expresses a sentiment that rang very true for me that summer: "Sometimes I wish that life was never-ending, but all good things they say never last." She's gone from this earth, but we were blessed to have known her. I loved her completely and I will miss her until the day I die.

Things got good for me at school once the football season started. The difference in the way the other students acted towards me was astonishing. It felt great to be appreciated and to have people acknowledge my talent. We were playing well and were going to have the chance to play the rival junior high at the high school's stadium. In those days, the Euclid school system had two junior highs that came together to form the freshman class at the high school (all junior high students now attend Euclid Central). The schools would compete against each other in sports. There had been some buzz about a skinny running back from Central. I didn't disappoint in the game, rushing for two touchdowns in a victory. Two games later, I broke my arm in a game and my season was over.

Mr. Anthony Syracuse was my eighth-grade science teacher at Central and he was one of those teachers who literally can change the way you look at life. He had a very off-beat manner using characters such as Talula Tobacco Breath and Dude Dropout to espouse the dangers of smoking and general laziness, among other pitfalls, to reach kids. I was always a fan of science but Mr. Syracuse taught with such a strong sense of enthusiasm that he not only made you want to learn, he made you want to become a better person. I kept in touch with Mr. Syracuse through high school and beyond and he told me how difficult it was to keep up his enthusiasm. It is vital for our youth to become better-educated, particularly in science, and teachers who realize the importance of their jobs and struggle to reach every student are vital tools in reaching that goal.

It was time for me to prepare for the transition to high school, and high school sports. That summer I got a chance to talk at length with a couple of the varsity players who lived in my neighborhood. As chance would have it, they also were running backs (P.J. Allen and Shaun Johnson). I had attended one of the varsity games while I was still in junior high and I was impressed by the entire scene. It was as much a social gathering spot as a sporting event. There were a few thousand people in attendance. Parents, teachers, students, cheerleaders—it was almost overwhelming to someone who had never played in front of more than 500 people. P.J. and Shawn prepared me for what was in store. They talked about the energy and emotion that you can feel when you play in front of large crowds. They talked about the strength and confidence that those cheers can instill in the young players. It defines the home field advantage. When you have the fans' support and belief, you feel you can achieve anything. I had always believed that it was best to block out as many distractions as possible while performing athletically. But there are times when it helps to realize that the fans are on your side. They want to see you succeed. The joy of winning is greatly enhanced by the experience of doing it in front of your home crowd. The feeling that the crowd is against you also can be a huge motivational tool. Playing on the road definitely requires a different mentality. It becomes us against them and their load-mouthed arrogant fans. There was a supreme sense of accomplishment when you went on the road in front of a hostile crowd and won.

As I mentioned earlier, two junior highs fed into the senior high school. We would have to blend together to form one freshman team after spending the previous year as bitter enemies. As we sat in the hallway at Euclid High waiting for our equipment, there was the usual macho talk. I'm gonna do this…I'm gonna do that…y'all weren't shit…the standard fare. I've never been a trash talker. I've always thought it best to let my playing do the talking. I was just anxious to start playing again and see how this team would come together. I would leave the trash talking to my teammates.

When classes started, we had the added stress of adjusting to high school life. Euclid was a big school then (about 2,000) but nothing compared to the class size of its earlier years. Still, it seemed like a labyrinth on the first day of school. I got lost trying to find my classes a couple of times on the first day. You had five minutes to go from class to class, but this seemed grossly inadequate for already overwhelmed freshmen. Most first days of school are pretty informal, and, with the short class time, there's just enough time for the teachers to introduce themselves and the course material that they would be covering during the school year. One teacher asked us to fill out a form and many students didn't have anything to write with. She decided to single me out as I asked around for a pen or pencil. "So Mr. Smith, you showed up to class without a writing implement," she said. "I bet you wouldn't go on to a football field without your equipment!" She was right about that, and I probably shouldn't have shown up without something to write with, but it was the fact that she singled me out that bothered me. Throughout my career I had incidents where people tried to call me out on this or that subject. It's like they feel a need to bring you down a peg, even if you didn't think that you were up on a higher one. Some people get tired of hearing about sports and athletes. They feel that athletes are unnecessarily placed on pedestals an should be regarded as normal people. I agree. But I don't like it when people act as if all athletes think they deserve special treatment, and this is clearly what she thought of me.

The football season went extremely well for both the team and me. We were undefeated going into our last game- against another undefeated team. That week our coach decided to put in a trick play that involved me getting a pitch and then handing the ball to a receiver on an end-around. One day in practice we tried the play and, as the receiver came towards me, he didn't leave enough space for me to extend my arm away from my body. The result was that I handed him the ball with my arm pointed straight towards his midsection, jamming my wrist and breaking a bone in my lower arm. Sadly, that was the end of that season for me and I was sure it would put doubt into the varsity coaches' head as to whether I could endure an entire varsity season. I was beginning to wonder the same thing myself. "Maybe I should just concentrate on track," I thought.

The track season the following spring put me on the Ohio map. I advanced all the way to the state final in the 400 meters as a freshman and ended up finishing fifth. The winner also was freshman and I would have to race him for another three seasons. Most importantly, though, colleges had begun to take notice of me.

For the third consecutive season, I would be entering unfamiliar territory going into a football season. This was the big time—as big as it could get at that point of my life—and I wondered if I'd be good enough to shine as I had at all of the previous levels. I had always been a starter, and as a sophomore the prospects for that weren't good for me. Training camp was brutal. Hot, humid, miserable days on the lake in Euclid, Ohio—what a way to spend a day. And it was a full day; none of that half-day practice stuff for us. The hitting was intense and the speed was incredible. There was nothing in my practices or our initial scrimmages to give head coach Tom Banc the impression that he had anything special in me. But then it was time for my first real game day. There's something special about high school football. It was playing in front of a crowd that consisted predominantly of people I had a real connection to. They were people from my hometown. They were the people I grew up around. They were the people who knew me, who helped me through real struggles in my life. Nothing in my career ever came close to the intimacy of playing in front of that home crowd at Euclid High School's football stadium.

That first night had a great feel to it. I dressed proudly in my gold and blue and prepared to step out onto the field for the first time as a

21

varsity Euclid Panther. There's a sign on the wall inside the locker room that gave an inspiring message, one that sticks with me to this day: Great Success Comes Only After a Commitment To Excellence. I wasn't going to be the starting running back that night, but I also knew that I had committed myself to excellence and I would do everything I could to make my presence felt. As we walked onto the field, I felt as if I were dreaming. The lights glaring down gave the field an eerie glow and served as a reminder that this was not practice: It was time to play…for real.

We were playing against Cleveland Heights High and through most of the first half I stood anxiously on the sideline, waiting for any opportunity to make an impact. I got in for a few plays, but didn't do much of anything. We were locked in a tight game as the second half began. I started to get more plays and I began to feel more comfortable. To be on that field in the huddle and look up into the stands felt amazingly calming. My friends and family were up there cheering me on and I knew that no matter what happened they would be there to support me. It began to feel like every other huddle that I had ever stood in. I belonged out there.

We trailed by 7 points with five minutes to go. The ball was on our 45 yard line. In the huddle, they called a play for me. "*No need to panic,*" "*You belong here…you've been in huddles before…pull up your arm pads…straighten your thigh pads…get the ball and go…run….run…run. Make it happen.*"

I got the ball and cut to the sideline. "*I've got him…he can't get there!….go!…explode!…speed! I've got it!…this is it!…..I've got it! I can't believe this!…GO!*"

I sprinted up the sideline and went on to score. It was better than I could have possibly imagined. A 55-yard touchdown in my first high school game to tie the score! My teammates rushed to congratulate me. I've always felt a great joy in celebrating touchdowns with my teammates. I felt like I scored for them, and that without them it would have been impossible. So why carry on a personal celebration? Why go running off showboating? The people in the stands were going crazy. The picture in the paper showed me receiving a hug on the sideline with a grin that wrapped around my head.

The game went to overtime and Cleveland Heights had the chance to score first from the 20. They were unsuccessful. We would have four downs to try to win the game. The call came in and it was a run for me: *"Are you kidding me?...relax...don't fumble...fix the arm pads...fix the thigh pads... better fix the knee pads too...be special Robert...speed...relax...relax"*

The play was designed to hit just inside the left tight end. As the ball was snapped and I headed in that direction, I just had that feeling: *"Just try it...you can get outside again...they don't have the speed to catch you...get to the edge...make him miss...got him!...go, go!...it's there!...it's there!...finish...I can't believe!...I can't believe!...I!....I!...got it! I got it!!!"*

I had barely crossed into the end zone and turned around when I was tackled by my teammates in a pile-up of youthful exuberance. I could barely breathe but I didn't care. My mind was racing with disbelief as I got up and walked with my teammates back to the sideline. It had really happened. I looked up at the scoreboard in a daze: We had done it—20-14. Even Hollywood doesn't have the audacity to write something that cliché.

The next morning my picture was in the *Cleveland Plain Dealer.* That's big stuff when you're 15 years old.

On days after games, we would watch a tape of the game in the locker room. On this, my first day after, I felt a heightened sense of ease around the guys. I truly had become one of them, even though I was one of the young kids. But after that first game, I became just a player; I was no longer the rookie. More would be expected from me now but that was how I wanted it. That first taste of victory was sweet and I wanted to feel it again. I had nine more chances to feel it that season as we completed the first 10-0 season that Euclid had ever seen. We ended up losing in the first round of the playoffs, but it was a hugely successful season that promised great things.

Throughout my sophomore season, I continued to have big performances and prove that the first game was no fluke. It's amazing how confident you can become when you are successful. The whole world is telling you how good you are, and it's hard not to believe some of it. I'm sure the converse is also true: Kids who are repeatedly told how dumb they are begin to believe it after a while. It's why positive reinforcement is so important for youth. Of course, I've also been told—and I completely agree—that you're never as good or as bad as they say you are. People have any number of reasons for saying what they say to you, and the reasons aren't always good. Many people feel the need to project their inadequacies on other people and this causes them to constantly insult or try to bring down other people. On the other hand, some people feel the need to live vicariously through others. This is how "heroes" get created. Two problems can arise from hero worship. First, the "hero" may begin to believe his own hype and lose the desire and determination that got him there. Second, the person who has created the hero may be crushed emotionally if his "hero" does something wrong or fails in an attempt to win or to accomplish something.

Hero worship aside, I was having a great time just being me. For me, it was just fun to perform the way I knew I could and to continue to get better. My friends still were my friends and I still was me, even if people in the city began to recognize me when I was in the mall or at the movies. I was truly becoming a local celebrity. I've never enjoyed the "fame" part of being a star athlete. For me, it's always been about respect. I never cared if people liked me or wanted my autograph. I just wanted to be acknowledged for my talent and work ethic. I worked hard to be as good as I was, and it was important for me that people knew it wasn't easy. I wanted them to know how good I was without feeling the need to have them come up to me and say it. I've always enjoyed my privacy. I had no idea how difficult it would be to keep as my career progressed.

I made some of the all-city teams and was an honorable mention for the state team. I was pleased to have the recognition, but it still stung me that we had lost in the playoffs. I looked forward to returning to the field the following season. During that off-season, I started to receive letters from colleges. The first letters were basically just generic questionnaires. They came from some small schools in Ohio and didn't really excite me too much. I was honored to have the recognition but I also knew that bigger schools would start looking and this is what I was waiting for. Coach Banc asked me about the types of schools I would be interested in. I mentioned the bigger schools such as Ohio State and Michigan. From that point on, he handled the letters and recruiters, politely telling the smaller schools thanks, but no thanks. I had a great support group of faculty and coaches at Euclid. They shielded me from a lot of unnecessary headaches. Schools would become increasingly aggressive but many of them were turned away before I even knew about it.

That spring I received a note in class one day to go see Coach Banc. I went down there not quite knowing what to expect. I figured it had to be about some college, but normally he would just wait and give me those letters after school. This letter was different though. This letter was from Ohio State. It was the first letter that I had gotten from a major university. I was so excited I could hardly contain myself. The first thing I thought to do was to find my brother. He was going to Euclid at this time as well and I wanted to show him the letter as soon as I could. I found him in the hall between classes. As usual, he was as happy for me as I was myself. I was no longer just a local sports star. I was now on the national stage. Things were starting to get interesting.

There was a great deal of hype moving into that next season, about both our team and about me. I approached the season anxiously and looked forward to improving as a player. I knew that colleges would be looking at me and that I would have the chance to earn a scholarship if I continued to play well. It was exciting to be in that position. I loved the pressure. I loved the challenge.

I knew other teams would be gunning for me and it increased my resolve. It's the attitude you need if you want to be successful in a game like football. I loved the idea of being burned in effigy at their pep rallies. You know you've arrived when the other team hates you. The college scouts were in the stands and we had games to win, I didn't have time to worry about a few jealous punks.

I came into my own that season. I played offense and defense as well as returning kicks and punts. We had another good season, and were on our way to the playoffs again.

Reporters were coming around all season and I was being interviewed all the time. It became increasingly important for me to mention my teammates and their importance to my success. I know it must have bothered some of them that I was getting so much attention. Quarterbacks and running backs get most of the attention on football teams. It seems like the other players only get interviewed when reporters want information about the quarterback or the running back. I genuinely understood the importance of my teammates and I think that they knew that I just considered myself to be one of them. I always played hard at practice and I stayed around to the end even though I had to rush to get to work. Work was causing a problem in another area of my life: my grades.

Like every kid in high school, I wanted to have my own money. My mother could barely keep up with taking care of us, let alone give us spending money, so I got a job at a Burger King. I would leave practice and then go to work there, sometimes even until 2a.mclosing. It was an absolute struggle to keep my eyes from shutting and most days I lost that struggle. I would wake myself up snoring in class and all of the kids around me would be laughing. What wasn't so funny was what this was doing to my grades. I had always been a good student, but this was too much for me. My grades started slipping and my teachers and coaches took notice. Things at home were getting pretty bad and they got worse when my mother lost her nursing job because of some personal demons she was struggling through. Paul Serra, the baseball coach at Euclid and my geometry teacher the previous year, offered to take me into his house, and become my legal guardian. It was a tough decision to leave home, but it was in my best interest at the time. I was able to cut back on my work time and start focusing on school again. Paul was just one of the many people at the school who took a personal interest in my well-being.

We lost again in the first round of the playoffs to eventual state champion St. Ignatius. This time around, I made first-team all-state and was a finalist for the state's Mr. Football award, given to the year's top high school player. I'll never forget receiving the call while I was working at Burger King. Joe Magill from the *News Herald* called and told me that I had won the Mr. Football award. I could hardly contain my excitement. This was big. I was only a junior and I was named the top player in one of the best football states in the country. Schools from all over the country started sending letters. I could barely go anywhere in the city after that and not be recognized. The varsity jacket I bought that said "Smitty" on it started to seem like a bad idea. Of course, back then, the glare of the spotlight still wasn't that intense and it was kind of fun to have people stop me and ask for an autograph. I always wanted to be that good, but I had no idea what it really meant in terms of the attention. You have to be careful what you ask for, even if you don't ask for it explicitly.

It would also prove to be a special year for me in track. Back then, the state finals for track were held in Ohio State's football stadium in Columbus. It gave the Ohio State faithful a chance to see "the next big thing" that might decide to go to Ohio State. I didn't realize it until I was older, but many Ohio State fans (and there are a lot of them) pay very close attention to the high school ranks in anticipation of the players who may one day join the Buckeyes. This gave them an opportunity to see me run in person—not quite on the football field, but close to it. My chances in the 100-meter dash improved dramatically that season when Chris Nelloms (the winner of the 400 the previous two years and the 100 the year before) had decided to run the 110-meter high hurdles instead of the 100.

Track is an under-appreciated sport in the United States. It is the purest of all sports—*mano a mano*. You step into the blocks and you rely on your preparation for one championship race. You have no one to blame but yourself if you lose. If you aren't able to condense an entire year's training into that brief moment of supreme competition, then you have to wait an entire year for another chance to shine—or you might not get another chance at all.

The wait in track can be excruciating. From the moment you get the schedule of events for the weekend, you know what time you'll be tested. Time ticks away mechanically as your mind races, trying to envision the possibilities of the moment of truth. The moment the gun goes off, you begin running. You have trained yourself for that moment and now you must make it pay off.

2:05pm Men's Final, 100 Meter Dash. The time has come. Are you ready? 12:30 and it's time to warm up. *"The short nap was good...almost made me forget...I don't want to do that though...not completely...I know why I'm here."* I jog around the stadium with my headset on and think about the task at hand. Less than 11 seconds. A whole season's training comes down to a burst of energy that takes me over 100 meters in less than eleven seconds. *"Are you ready? This is why you're here. Stretch. Loosen the tension. Tension is the enemy."* 1:45. *"They're making the call for us. Time to get over to the paddock area. This is your day! Make it happen! Explode!....smooth, smooth"* 2:00 *"It's close now...breathe easy, relax..... stay smooth."* Gentlemen, remove your sweats! *"This is it! No turning back. It's what you want...You can see the finish line...here it comes."* 2:05 Runners, take your mark! *"Ease into the blocks...kick out the tension...relax...stay smooth...last look down the track...relax."* Time stands still as 10 runners rise into a sprinter's starting position. Sinews relaxed and ready to flex with all their might to spring the body forward in an awesome display of human locomotion. "Set!" The stadium is silent and mesmerized by the moment.....Bang! You are up and running. You see the finish line ahead of you and hear nothing but the sound of your own breathing. *"Go, go!...I'm out! I can't see them!....I can't see them!....stay smooth!...It's almost here!...Finish!...Finish!...Lean!!!!!"*

Four of us crossed the finish line nearly simultaneously. I hadn't seen anyone until we had just gotten to the invisible finish line. No one knew who had won. We would have to wait for the judges to examine the picture of the finish line. We waited for an agonizing 15 minutes. We looked for some sign from the judges. And then it came. One of the judges whom I had known from previous meets turned and made eye contact with me—giving me the thumbs-up. I sprinted off of the infield and underneath the stadium, hardly even believing what had just happened. I was looking for the one person in the world who would be as happy as I was at that moment and it didn't take me long to find him. My brother and I caught sight of each other and locked in a hug that was a release of all the tension that we had just gone through. I was a state champion in the 100-meter-dash, the mythological fastest-man in high school. I had grown up watching races like that with my brother and now I had the chance to share that victory with him. It was, without exception, the greatest and most rewarding moment of my athletic career.

As my senior year approached, national publications were listing me as one of the top prospects for college recruiting. The college scouts were making regular stops at the school, and my list of favorites was narrowed to five: Ohio State, Michigan, Miami (Florida), USC, and UCLA. I thought these schools would give me the chance to excel both on the field and in the classroom. I had wanted to be a doctor since I was a young boy and all of these universities had highly rated medical schools. My initial interest in medicine developed because of my mother's job as a nurse. To me, it seemed to be the pinnacle of learning and the noblest of all jobs that one could do. My ideas would change somewhat as time passed (as most thoughts do), but at that time, it was very important in my decision-making process.

Things also began to take a turn for the better at home. My mother had put aside her pride and taken a job at a gas station in order to make money while her nursing license was suspended. It's hard to express how proud I am of her for going through what she did. She taught me that there is nothing more important than family and there's no task too difficult or humbling that should keep you from trying to help people you love. She ended up getting her nursing registration back and I moved home for my senior year. My mother is a great example of what people can achieve by determination. She worked hard to get everything she had in life and it served as an example for me in the tough times that I was about to go through.

Now that I was back at home, college recruiters began to visit me there. There's a job I don't envy. College coaches go from spending 12- to 16-hour work day during the season to traveling around the country sweet-talking and kissing the asses of a bunch of ego-inflated 17- and 18-year-old athletes (as if there were another type). It has to be brutal work. I was never very fond of this process because I thought it was degrading to both parties. To them, it must have seemed as if I was some spoiled prima donna who thought my time was too valuable to spend talking to them. (Many people have that judgment of me after their first encounter. I'm a person who likes to sit back and observe and this often comes off as arrogance.) I just wanted to tell these guys: "Look, I appreciate you being interested in me and coming all the way out here, but I'm a big boy now and there's nothing you're going to say that's going to convince me to go to your school. Just let me sit back, make my own judgments and let the decision flow from there." No such luck.

Gary Moeller of Michigan was the worst. He was an assistant head coach to Bo Schembechler then, and I couldn't turn around without seeing him somewhere. It was annoying, but it also got pretty funny. I'm sure they didn't think so. College coaches depend on good recruiting classes to keep their jobs. If you don't bring in the best talent, then you may not win enough games to keep the alumni happy, and you know what that means. So you have a bunch of grown men relying on the recruitment of young men for their livelihood.

We had another great season and won our third consecutive conference title. For the second year, we were heading into the playoffs with one loss at the hands of state championship winner St. Ignatius. Earlier in the year we had played them in the first-ever nationally televised high school football game. They embarrassed us 55-10 in that game and we knew that we would have to try something different this time around if we were going to have any chance of winning. Throughout that year, I had taken some snaps at quarterback and we felt that with our depth at the running back position, we could effectively employ a wishbone-type offense against St. Ignatius. It was a bold move by Coach Banc: Take one of the country's highest rated running backs and put him in at quarterback in the most important game of the year. We almost pulled it off.

We went into the final 10 minutes of the game leading 30-19. Then the unthinkable happened; they returned a kickoff for a touchdown. Our offense went in and took the field and had a three-and-out. No problem, we'll just hold them on defense. They faced a third-and-17 near midfield and the game appeared to be ours. Their quarterback threw the ball up and it was caught for a first down after bouncing off of several of our players (the quarterback was Joe Pickens, one of the highest rated quarterbacks in the nation, who later became one of my roommates at Ohio State). The luck of the Jesuits! We ended up losing the game 31-30 and Ignatius went on to win its second straight state title as well as the USA Today's national title. We had fought valiantly but lost. It was one of the toughest losses I ever had to take, but I took consolation in knowing that we had lost to one of the best high school football teams of all time.

Now it was time for me to get down to the business of choosing a college. I had about three months until national-letter-of-intent-day, but I wanted to get this decision out of the way as soon as possible. I was named Gatorade national high school football player of the year and Dial scholar athlete of the year. More importantly—when you're 17 at least—was the fact that I would get to visit the schools on my list, which included a stop in Miami and two stops in California.

You weren't allowed to fly first class on recruitment trips, but they were allowed to take you to some great restaurants and have your hosts take you to some great clubs. You did have to sit down and listen to the coaches tell you how they felt their system was best for you and how you had a great shot at moving right in to their systems and being successful. At UCLA, the running back coach went into this long discussion predicated in the belief that his job was to prepare me for professional football. I was insulted. Who did this guy think he was dealing with? I wasn't some average jock who only went to college to get a shot at pro football. I was a serious student who wanted to go to medical school and become a doctor. How dare he talk such nonsense to me! Turned out the guy was absolutely right. College coaches are there to teach you many things, but being a position coach at a major university like UCLA, he was right to want to prepare me for professional football. It's not like the guy was saying that school was unimportant, he was just saying that it was also important for a guy with my talent to prepare himself for the next level. Part of my indignation was based on the simple, ignorant ideals of youth. I still had trouble believing that I was actually on the way toward

31

professional football. At the time, I didn't even think it was right for players to leave college early (it's hard for me now to believe that I *ever* thought that!). Big-time college football is partially about preparing players for the next stage. There's no good rationale against it. I was too young and naive to understand it at the time, but it wouldn't take me long to figure out what this guy was talking about.

All of the schools had positive qualities, but in the long run I knew the decision should come down to comfort. There was one place where I felt most comfortable and where I knew I'd have all the comforts of home. It was time to make up my mind.

CHAPTER TWO

MESSIAH

Brian: "I am not the messiah!"

Woman: "Only the true messiah would deny his divinity!"

Brian: "Well what chance does that give me then?"

—Scene from *Monty Python's Life of Brian*.

T he principal of Euclid High school at the time, William McGuiness, was aware of the fanfare surrounding my decision and suggested that I hold a press conference. He knew that news media from all over would want to interview me following my announcement. In the interest of time, he felt it made more sense to get them all out of the way at once. I'm sure that many people thought "Who does this kid think he is, holding a press conference at his age?" I'm sure they felt I was just an egomaniac who wanted to maximize his time in front of the camera. Well, for one thing, it wasn't my idea. Principal McGuiness was looking out for my best interests and he realized that for my life to return quickly to some level of normalcy following my announcement I'd be better off getting it done this way. Secondly, I never thought the announcement itself was very important; to me, the decision mattered most. It's not as if I felt the need to proclaim to the world that I had made up my mind. I had decided which college to attend and I knew the decision would impact the rest of my life.

The final choice came down to Ohio State (now *The* Ohio State University) and USC, but I felt that in the long run it would be better for

33

me to stay in Ohio. I've always loved living in Ohio, and I don't think that ever will change. Don't get me wrong, I'm glad to be able to travel and be away from there on some of the many dreary and cold days, but I even enjoy some of those. More than anything, though, I like Ohio people. There's not a lot of pretension them. I can't stand pretentious people and I would have had a lot of them in Los Angeles. Everyone there seems to be in the "business" and no one seems to work. Those types of people long for attention and don't have anything "real" to show those who do pay attention. Of course, not everyone in L.A. is a jerk and not everyone in Ohio is cool, but I think Ohio just has a better and truer vibe to it. Also, my friends and family would be able to come see me play. It's always nice to play in front of a true home crowd.

I knew that people were recognizing me more, but it never occurred to me the level at which fans in Ohio pay attention to football. I've had former Cleveland Browns players who played in the city when I was in high school tell me that they would go to games and watch me play. People from all over the city were going to our games just to see me play. It's flattering that people thought so much of me as a player, but it also points to how obsessed some people get with sports. Ohio loves its football. And if Ohioans are mildly neurotic about football, then they are raving psychotics when it comes to Ohio State football. Ohio State fans study recruiting classes as if their lives depend on it. I didn't even realize how wild some of the fans were until I started spending more time in Ohio after my retirement. I'll have people come up to me and ask, "What do you think about such-and-such player." I'll almost always answer "who?" because I don't really pay much attention to any level of sport, let alone high school sports in some other area of the state.

They'll continue to run off the player's stats from the previous year and all of the other schools the kid is considering. It's borderline excessive.

It was big news for those fans that I was going to Ohio State. I was one of the top recruits in the country and I had decided to stay home and become a Buckeye. A news crew came up from Columbus to record the event. It was the first time that I met Dom Tiberi and Paul (Moose)

Spohn, from Channel 10 in Columbus (a couple of years later I did some work with those guys and I still make occasional appearances on one of their programs). These guys had driven 2 ½ hours from Columbus to cover the press conference of a 17-year-old kid. A publication called *Buckeye Sports Bulletin* did a story on me and featured me on their cover wearing a doctor's jacket and holding a stethoscope. The headline read "The Doctor Is In!"

A couple of weeks after signing my letter of intent, I attended the Columbus Touchdown Club and received its national high school player of the year award (I wondered if I would have received it if I had decided to attend USC). I was an instant celebrity in Columbus and everyone there wanted to ask me questions. "You excited to come down and play?" "You really gonna be a doctor?" "You think we can win the Big Ten?" It was a whirlwind. The storm had been coming for a long time, but its intensity still shocked me. I wasn't sure how I would do the following season, and all of the attention just made me more anxious to get started.

I returned to Euclid with two national player of the year awards (the second came from the Atlanta Touchdown Club) and a burning desire to start my college career. It was difficult for me to concentrate on my schooling and track in those final few months at Euclid High. I lost my state title in the 100-meter dash and ruined my perfect school year by getting a B in math. I had "Buckeye" on my mind!

My best friend, Bill Laurenson, was also going to be attending Ohio State and walking on to the football team. We worked out that spring in our big, red Ohio State-issue Pony turf shoes with the pride that only the Scarlet and Grey can know. I spent that summer working for a construction company on the other side of town. I would go to work, then go work out—and come home exhausted. My excitement about the months ahead carried me through and, at the beginning of August; it was time to make the move to Columbus.

My mother wasn't crazy about saying goodbye to her baby boy, so she made the trip with me. Bill and his parents drove us down to the dorms we would be staying in for training camp. It felt great to finally be leaving, but I also felt a great deal of anxiety from all the pressure that people were putting on me.

Ohio State's usually bustling campus looked like a ghost town. Summer session had ended and students were gone. It was surreal. All of the other freshman football players were arriving as well and we sized each other up. The upperclassmen wouldn't be arriving for a few days.

The first thing that strikes one about the football facility itself is its overwhelming size. You walk in there after just arriving from high school and you feel small and insignificant. I'm sure that's what they were going for with the design of the place. They want you to know that you're no longer that high school "superstar;" we don't tolerate players who think they're bigger than this place because nobody is bigger than *this* place. You walk into the huge locker room and get a chill from the silence of this dormant room so soon to be filled with young men on a mission. You can't help but feel the nostalgia of the school's history. You are no longer on the outside looking in. It's your turn to become a part of the mystique and legend of Ohio State football.

We received our schedules for camp and I was instantly impressed with how well they could occupy a person from wake-up to lights-out. Meetings, meetings, meetings, practice, meetings, lunch, meetings, practice, meetings, meetings, lights-out. Of course, by the time you reached the end of the day, you wouldn't want anything but lights-out. We were so busy with everything that the significance of what we were going through never sank in. We were freshman football players preparing for a season with one of the great college teams. Thousands of kids from all across the nation dreamed of being where we were.

The practices weren't that bad, but we knew that the upperclassmen would be in soon and that would change everything. Up to that point we had been wearing shorts and practicing only against each other. When the upperclassmen arrived we'd have to face experienced players longing for the opportunity to test first-year guys unfamiliar with their level of play. Just about every recruit who comes into a school like Ohio State has received a lot of accolades and awards in his high school career. Some players shine in the high school environment only to be revealed as lumps of coal when they play the college game. You can look at a player's height, weight, and forty time. You can watch them dominate their opponents on high school football fields. One thing you can't see on film is a player's heart.

It was a bit intimidating in the early days with the upperclassmen. There's no doubt in anyone's mind that they are there to play and to win. But in order to play you have to compete against and out-perform all the players at your position. You have to appreciate and work with players at your position while realizing that if they win the job, then you don't have one. Every year there's a new set of recruits chomping at the bit to go out and prove themselves. This means trying to take the job of upperclassmen. They're also very aware of your desire to take their job. These older players have spent hundreds of hours in that facility and they're accustomed to the pressures at this highest level of college football. All they've heard about for the last few months is how some kid is coming in to take over. I knew that people would be gunning for me. I was trying to take the job of one of their friends, someone they had already gone through camp with, someone they had already struggled through conditioning with, someone familiar. I was now their teammate, too, but it would take time to earn acceptance.

Shocked, stunned, and amazed is how I felt when I saw the first live-contact drills at practice. The ferocity of the hitting and the lightning speed of the players really made me wonder if I was in the right place after all. Bodies moved in a blur of motion, crashing into each other with a sound that seemed almost certain to break something—or someone. The size difference between high school players and college players is very pronounced. You may have a couple of guys approaching 300 pounds on a high school football field, but even these are in no where near the shape college players are. Some of these players are on the verge of their pro careers and there you are, put out there against these beasts, wondering if your body will be able to take the pounding. They yelled and jumped around with a vigor that seemed almost intoxicating to them. Things happened so fast that I felt I couldn't do anything to adjust. I felt embarrassed and devastated. I was going to be one of the greatest college flops of all time.

37

Ohio State has long been known for its strength at running back. That year was no exception. Carlos Snow, the previous year's starter at tailback, was out for the season with a knee injury he sustained in spring drills. But Dante Lee and Raymont Harris were strong second-year players who had performed impressively. Raymont had been red-shirted the year before but was slated as the starter for the upcoming season. There was also another freshman, Butler By'no'te, who joined me and the others in the battle for the starting job. Bobby Turner was our position back and he had every intention of giving each of us a shot at the starting job.

I don't think I've ever had as much fun playing for a coach as I did for Bobby Turner. He was knowledgeable about the game and worked us hard, but he also had a way of making us feel comfortable that made our jobs that much easier. Coach T. was funny without even knowing it. We would laugh so hard at some of the things he said that it almost made us forget that we were in heated battle against each other. His voice had this way of going into a high pitch that just made his comments that much more entertaining: "Dante! You're attention span is shorter than a chicken's dick!" "Will! You're too soft! You're a St. Bernard! You want to lick people! You don't want to bite 'em! You need to be more like those dogs that pinch. Robert! What's the name of those dogs? (Coach T. always had a way of singling me out whenever he needed some piece of trivia.) You know, the ones that pinch?" "A Doberman Pincher, Coach?" I said. "Yeah! That's it! You gotta be more like them!" He once told us a story about how he lived with his brothers in a house about the size of our 12'X 20' meeting room. He said that they didn't have anything to eat but moldy bread: "So we toasted the bread" and then he turned and gave us this deathly serious look and said, "But it was still fucking moldy bread!" We roared with laughter. We knew he was trying to be serious and we could appreciate his point, but that couldn't stop us from reacting. He really brought us together as a group and was responsible for us being the strong, effective unit we were that year.

The playbook was far more than we were used to from high school. In fact, we really didn't have a playbook in high school; we'd pretty much just show up, go over a couple of plays, and then go out and practice. College football was far more intensive. You had to learn much more complex defensive schemes and be able to protect your quarterback. The failure to master protections has kept more running backs out of the lineup in college than any other factor. The plays themselves are more complicated than in high school, but it really just boils down to terminology. Most teams run basically the same plays; they just have different names. You need to get used to being in the huddle and absorb the formation, play, and direction quickly enough that you can concentrate on the play itself by the time you get to the line to run it. It all sounds pretty simple, and people who haven't played at that level wonder how players are "dumb" enough to ever make mistakes. Well, drawing up a play and understanding it in the classroom is a universe apart from executing the play when a motivated and talented group is lined up on the other side of the ball. Those players have a job to do, as well, and they want nothing more than to keep you from doing yours. For running backs, this usually comes down to a direct confrontation with a linebacker.

I've always felt that linebackers are a bit off-center. It takes a different breed to play that position. Along with running backs, they have the most dangerous job on the field. Linebackers need to take on players of all sizes from all directions and they must be able to react quickly in order to avoid taking too many direct hits. They were always the players I took note of first when I left the huddle because they had the greatest potential to disrupt a play. You could always see them back there blowing snot bubbles (that was Coach Banc's phrase) and looking around wildly like animals in anticipation of an attack. You almost wanted to avoid making eye contact lest you provoke some atavistic tantrum against you. It was pretty awful when the defensive linemen broke free because of the weight you gave up to them, but it was worse to see a linebacker come charging up the middle at the snap of the ball, completely untouched. You may chop them at the knees and send them toppling head over cleats. One of the linemen may come off of a block and ear hole them, sending them crashing to the turf. But no matter, on the next play, the linebacker still wants to get to the quarterback and he is completely insulted and enraged by the running back that is standing between him and a quarterback sack.

It's one thing to try to block a linebacker when he knows that you might chop him down with a block below the waist. It's also easier to block him when he knows that there are other people who may peel off to block him. In one-on-one blocking drills, however, it's an entirely different ball game. The linebacker can charge full-force and try to bull-rush you and all you can do is lower your center of gravity and try to dig in to withstand the hit. You can try to deliver a blow, but you have to be careful not to lunge and miss the hit, which allows the linebacker to have a free hit on your quarterback. For the most part, you have to expect to take some punishment. Coach T. would tell us that it only took one punch to the throat to forget all about home, and truer words were never spoken.

On the first day of one-on-one drills, I got matched up against this guy named John Kacherski. He was a poster boy for wild linebackers. John was one of our most physical linebackers and I felt that I should be able to show that I could withstand a bull-rush from the best if I was going to prove my mettle. He came rushing full-speed, fully believing that he'd be able to run over this skinny kid who was in his way. I dug in, lowered my hips and prepared to strike with my hands. "Pow!" There's a moment of confusion following hits like that in which both players are trying to figure out what happened. I recovered my senses and found myself locked up with John with my hands in perfect position underneath his pads. Coach T. blew the whistle and said, "Good job, Robert! Way to stand in there!"

These words of encouragement combined with the taunts from the other running backs and linebackers did nothing but make John mad as hell. In drills like this, it's all about who puts on the best show, and players love to instigate increasingly violent confrontations. I went up against John again; once again, I stood my ground. It was a great confidence builder for me and it showed the other players that I was willing to mix it up and be physical. Coach T. told me that they made a big deal about that drill on the radio that afternoon. It was hard for me to understand how they could have cared about some drill at practice, but that's the way things work in Columbus. When you play football for Ohio State, you live in a fishbowl, and every swish of your tail or movement of your gills gets watched and scrutinized. People tune in to news about the Buckeyes like their very lives depend on it. To the rabid Ohio State fans, this simple drill in one practice was further proof that they were right about me: I was every bit the player they had imagined.

As training camp came to a close, it was time for media day. It was the first day that we got the chance to wear our game day uniforms. I was finally wearing the Scarlet and Grey. The snug fit of the game day uniform was very rejuvenating. We had been struggling through our rigorous two-a-day practices and it was time to show off our battle garb. Media day is open to the public in Columbus and hundreds of fans show up to get autographs and have their picture taken with some of their beloved Buckeyes. Fans cluster around their favorite players and leave the lesser-known players conspicuously unattended. I felt bad for these players that had to deal with 10-year old kids walking up to them and asking, "Who are you?" Some of these players had to walk-on, meaning that they wouldn't even be receiving money for school. They would work their butts off in practice and many of them would never even see the field. I have a great deal of respect for anyone who goes through what those players have to go through.

It was a busy and interesting day for me. I was signing autographs and taking pictures constantly. People were handing me babies to pose with for photos. I felt like a politician. Some people just came up and said things like, "I used to watch you play in high school!" I've never seen myself as a big deal, and it's embarrassing for me to have people come up and ask me to sign something. We are all just people, and it's hard for me to understand how a person could derive so much pleasure from having someone else's signature. Now I do think it's different for kids, but even kids looking up to people just because they play a sport is a bit strange.

The 1990 season was quickly approaching and we were going to have an intra-squad scrimmage in the stadium as a tune up. They normally would have held this game at the end of spring practice, but they had to stay off the newly planted grass field at Ohio State Stadium. We were going to be the first Ohio State team to play on grass at the stadium. I'm guessing about 40,000 people showed up at the stadium for our exhibition. I was beginning to realize how fanatic Ohio State's following was. The game would mark John Cooper's third season and they expected this team to be able to return to greatness with the help of a new potential "star." It was an incredible feeling going out and warming up in front of such an enthusiastic crowd. I could hear them calling out my name and the adrenaline flowed through my system until I could barely contain my excitement. It didn't take long for the fans to see what I had. The opening kickoff came sailing to me on a high arch that seemed to carry it a mile high. *"No way!...here it comes!...secure it...no mistakes...moving forward...get it and go...now!"* You have to instantly shift your focus from the ball to the blockers and potential tacklers in front of you. *"Fly!...secure it!...go!—you gotta be kidding!...I'm gone!...just the kicker!...no chance!... I'm there!...it's just a scrimmage."* The crowd roared its approval. I had returned the opening kickoff all the way for a score. I didn't even know if we were supposed to return it all the way, but I also wasn't told to stop. It was almost too perfect. But it was also just a tune up. The rest of the game went well for me, but there would be no more spectacular plays. I had proven that I could play, but I had not done enough in the eyes of the coaches to prove that I deserved the opportunity to start the first game. We headed into the final week of preparation with me listed as the third back. The time had come for our first test.

The day before a game, the entire team meets at the practice facility and then loads onto buses to go to dinner at the university golf course. Everyone was supposed to dress for the occasion. No one was immune to a barrage of insults for wearing something that seemed less than appropriate. Shoes were always a favorite target. We would sit together by position at dinner, be led in team prayer by one of the captains, and then quietly (mostly) enjoy our dinner. Inevitably, someone at the table would crack a joke and you'd have to do your best not to laugh. If things got too noisy, one of the captains or coaches would admonish us to be serious and think about the job ahead of us. It wasn't very difficult for me to be serious at that first dinner because I couldn't get my mind off the next day's game. I've always been a pretty serious person anyway, but when it came to games, my mood became even more intense. I just wanted to focus on the task at hand. This was going to be my first venture into college football, and I wanted it to be special. I knew I wasn't going to start at running back, but I knew I had to be ready to go in at any time. Coach T. always said to us that luck was when preparation met opportunity, so I wasn't about to let a lack of preparedness interfere with my ability to perform at my peak level. When I got to my hotel room that night I just took out my playbook, trying to calm myself as much as possible. There wouldn't be much sleep for me that night.

The next morning I got up and went into the bathroom to brush my teeth. I looked into the mirror, hardly believing that the person staring back at me would be playing in a nationally televised college football game that day. This was really it. There was no turning back now.

I walked down to breakfast and tried to act like my stomach wasn't twisted into knots. I had to look cool. From the way he scarfed down his steak (they served breakfast steaks at the college and pro level, and I never understood how anyone who had to play could eat one of those things before a game) and two of ours, it was obvious that Coach T. was not bothered by the same nervous stomach. Some of the other players joked about his appetite and that helped calm my nerves a bit. After breakfast, the offense and defense met separately. Jim Colleto, our offensive coordinator, showed us film and then called out plays and had us sit there and think about our assignments. I just wanted to get to the stadium and get started. It seemed like an eternity before we actually loaded our buses and headed for the stadium.

It was a perfect late-summer day for football. The route to the stadium took us by fraternity row, which was already lined with faithful fans. They either waved their arms wildly or gave silent salute with their Saturday morning pre-game beers. It was strangely calming to know that these people were on our side. As we approached the stadium, we saw the thousands of fans who already had arrived to begin their football

Saturday with the time honored tradition of tailgating. The parking lot was filled with Scarlet and Grey RVs and people eating brats and drinking beer. They all cheered loudly as we approached. As we exited the bus, we walked through a gauntlet of fans who were held back by security. They shouted encouragement as we passed.

As I entered the stadium and walked to the freshman locker room, a sense of calm started to come over me. It was time to get to work now, and that was all I could think about. We had separate game day and practice helmets then, and I felt a sense of pride as I looked into the locker for the first time and saw the pristine Scarlet and Grey helmet. Now I was a "real" Buckeye. I could barely wait to take that helmet out and feel its tightness on my head for the first time. Game day equipment was never used during the week, so it had a different feel to it. The fit was tighter and it gave me the feeling that I was more in control of my body when the time came to play. It's kind of like a kid who feels he can run faster with new shoes on. I put on my shorts and t-shirt and walked upstairs to get taped. "You ready, blood?" shouted Billy Hill, the team's head trainer. "You know it," I replied, still not feeling too uptight yet. *"Ahh...tight tape job...now I'm ready...well...almost...here it is!...you wanted it...you still do!...be special!...finish getting ready...I can't believe how calm these guys look...I wonder if I look that way?"*

I put my shoulder pads in my jersey and my thigh and knee pads in my pants. I then finished getting ready with very deliberate movements, trying to ensure the tight fit of every aspect of my uniform. "All right returners, let's go!" I got up and moved slowly out of the locker room, making sure not to embarrass myself by slipping in my cleats. As we stepped out into the bright air of the stadium, I felt a chill run up my spine. This was Ohio State Stadium. Jim Marshall, Archie Griffin, Les Horvath...so many others. They had all played there before me. It was an awesome responsibility to carry the torch for greats like them. If you aren't willing to carry this responsibility, you don't belong at Ohio State.

I jogged onto the field with a vigor that comes from a huge rush of adrenaline. My footing felt sure and my body felt secure with the tightness of a perfectly fit uniform. It was that old feeling again—as if my feet weren't touching the ground. *"This isn't even fair!...nobody should feel this good!...I can't believe this... this is really happening... playing in your own backyard now...I wonder where my mom is... concentrate... relax..."*

After our warm-up, we headed back into the locker room for what seemed like the longest half hour of my life. You sit there in the locker room with your mind racing in anticipation of the game, and there's nothing you can do to make the clock move any faster. *"Let's go!...Let's go!...why do we have to wait?...calm down...you can't change it...Let's go!"* I sat there with my elbows on my thighs and my head down. *"I wonder if these legs and feet are good enough?...they have been up to this point...they had to be right about me... I know what I can do!...Let's go!... relax... concentrate... smooth... relax."*

Then Coach Cooper shouted, "All right men, let's go!"

I felt light headed as I stood up. It felt like I was walking in a dream. We stopped again just short of the entrance to the field. *"You gotta be kiddin' me!...let's go!...man these guys are big...you're fast...no substitute for speed...relax."* We all began to hop in unison as our bodies relented to nervous energy. I don't remember hearing a call to start, but all of a sudden we were running wildly on to the field. We ran out to the far end of the stadium to the thunderous roar of the sea of Scarlet and Grey that filled the stands. Every person in the stadium was standing and it seemed as though every heart in the venue was beating in unison. We were one. The excitement was nearly overwhelming. But now it was time to play.

The captains went out to the middle of the field for the toss...and we won it. I was one of the primary kickoff returners, so I would be taking the field for the game's very first play. As I walked back to retrieve the kick, I started waving my arms up and down to incite the crowd. The response was amazing. They instantly began to cheer more enthusiastically. It gave me an exhilarating sense of power. I felt as if I was the conduit for the energy of 95,000 fans. I had never experienced any feeling like this. *"All right, all right...time to get ready...mouthpiece in...this is really happening now...full speed...don't hesitate...here it comes!"* The kicker approached the ball and sent it soaring high and in my direction. I caught the ball and starting running towards the middle of the field. I cut to the right and then ran up the sideline for a 40-yard return.

For the rest of the first half, I just stood on the sideline, longing for the opportunity to get in the game. I was amazed at the energy and enthusiasm of the crowd. We were locked in a tight struggle and all I could do was root for my teammates; it was a helpless feeling.

At halftime, the position coaches talked to their players about what had happened in the first half and the rest of us just kind of sat there feeling a bit out of place. Then Coach T. came up to me and told me I'd be starting the second half. I don't know what my face showed him, but on the inside I was ready to explode. I was happy and, at the same time, shocked. I checked the tightness of my gear again and tried to prepare myself mentally. *"Relax...it's still just football...still a game...smooth....I wonder how it's gonna feel...make it happen, man...be special..."*

I stepped into an Ohio State huddle for the first time and was almost overcome with the excitement of the moment. I hadn't been in a huddle in a real game for 10 months. Now I was in a huddle at the Horse Shoe. A lot of people had said I would make an instant impact. Well, none of those people were in the huddle to help me. I was there on my own. On my very first touch, I caught a pass over the middle and gained about 20 yards. I got up off the grass as fired up as could be... *"yes!... more!...let's go!...let's win!"* We were down 7 points, but momentum was now on our side. Our offense had started to move the ball. We moved the ball to their four yard line and we were ready to move in and tie up the score.

"Give me a chance...I got this!...let's go!...I wonder what the play is?...man, this is cool!...here it comes." One of the receivers ran in a play from the sideline. It was an option play. "I'll be ready for the pitch, Greg." Greg Frey had been the quarterback at Ohio State for a couple of seasons and I'm sure he was used to running backs giving that little reminder before they got to the line for an option play. Of course, I was going to be ready; it's what the play called for. It was really just a different way of saying, "Come on, man, pitch me the ball!" I'm sure he was thinking, "You better be ready! I'm not getting my ass knocked off if you're not!" We got up to the line and Greg went through his cadence. As soon as the

46

ball was snapped, I looked to the end and saw that he was going to take Greg. *"This is it!...pitch it!...pitch it!...catch it...go!...got it!...got it!... reach!!!...I'm in!!! I'm in!!!!"* I was flooded with adrenaline and a crowd of jumping teammates. I could barely breathe. I just wanted to get to the sideline. That corny Hollywood writer was at it again. How could it happen this way? It was too perfect. I took my helmet off as I jogged to the sideline and could feel some Gatorade welling up inside me, ready to make an unwanted visit. *"Don't do it!... don't throw up!...you know the camera's on you!...breathe...relax... breathe."* I squatted down near our bench and then completely lost it. It looked like a couple of gallons of Gatorade made its way back out right then and there. So much for not throwing up on national TV. I had pulled this little puking stunt in games before, but never on national television. It became kind of a calling card for me.

"We better win this game!...what a waste if we don't...first game, first touchdown...I'm getting laid tonight!...concentrate!...game's not over...stay ready!!"

We ended winning the game and I jogged off the field feeling as if my life had changed. I had made it to big-time college football and had made an instant impact. I knew I was a good player, but I had no idea that things would happen that quickly. It almost felt as if I was back in high school; the game was on the line and I had come through for the team. I had moved into a spotlight whose intensity can burn those who fail to realize its power. You have to watch what you say and watch what you do, or the spotlight can expose you to an unforgiving world. There was one thing that my first game made very clear: I belonged.

I didn't start the second game, either, but I did play most of the game and had my first 100-yard rushing game. I made my first start the following week against USC, of all teams. It was only three weeks into the season, and I was already facing the school that had been my second choice. When I got tackled near our sideline on the first play of the game, the USC players had some choice comments such as, "You should'a brought your punk ass with us!" The game was played at Ohio State and I'm sure it wouldn't have been a very warm homecoming greeting for me if I had decided to go to USC. College fans hate defectors. They really see those kids as traitors—and recruiters try to sell it that way, too. I was playing in my home state and I was starting to feel more comfortable as each week passed. School had started and I got a real taste of what it meant to be an Ohio State football celebrity.

Everywhere I walked on campus, people would stare. It was tough to get used to. I was used to receiving attention in high school, but this was something completely different. Someone would notice me from a distance and then yell, "Hey, Robert, let's kick some ass this weekend!" It was embarrassing. When they did roll call in class, people would turn around and look at me when I responded. It was tough for me as a person who didn't like being in the spotlight. It was hard enough just trying to do my job in the classroom and on the field. College football demands a great deal from a student-athlete. You spend your entire day in the classroom, and then you're off to practice. After practice, they shuttle you to dinner. Then, for the freshman, it was right to study table. Until you've got your GPA up, you have to stay on morning and evening study table to ensure that you get some quality time in a study environment. This was definitely one of their better ideas. It would have been difficult to manage the time if they had not put those study tables aside for us. It's tough enough to handle the adjustment to college without the rigors of a college football season. You are being tested physically, mentally, and emotionally. You drag your butt out of bed in the morning and begin to wonder if it's worth it. "I help make the university millions of dollars, and all I get is a $20,000-a-year scholarship! The head coaches get houses and the assistants get cars and I get a scholarship. Something's not right here." Don't get me wrong, I was thankful to have the opportunity to play for a school like Ohio State and to be getting an education out of it, but I was definitely re-thinking my attitude about not leaving early. Why stay here and do this virtually for free when I could make great money and be able to pay for school whenever I wanted to go back? It didn't make any sense for me to stay in college football any longer than I had to. Up to that point, the fans at Ohio State loved me. I was everything that they had asked for. Talented, smart, a good kid—the model Buckeye. But like most marriages these days, mine with the Ohio State fans was about to end. It all started (or ended) with one article.

CHAPTER THREE

PARIAH

So I'm not your pearl, to this I am resigned but, to an outside world, I
will not be defined.

—Terrance Trent Darby

If everyone likes you, you're probably lying to somebody.

——Robert Smith

The question seemed harmless enough: "Do you think you'll be here for four years if the opportunity to play pro football arrives before then?" Tim May, the Ohio State beat reporter for the *Columbus Dispatch*, asked me if I thought I'd stay at Ohio State for all four seasons of eligibility or if I'd decide to turn pro if the opportunity arose. "No," I said, "it seems to make sense to take advantage of that opportunity if it's there." It never occurred to me to answer the question dishonestly. I had been doing interviews since the tenth grade and I considered myself to be pretty savvy at them by this point. I had no idea how swift and negative the response from the fans would be.

Most of the interview that day had focused on how successful the season had been for me and how I was closing in on the freshman rushing record held by Archie Griffin. The response for that one question became the focus of the entire interview. Controversy sells. The headline for the article said something like: "Three Years at Ohio State May Be Enough for Smith." The article portrayed me as a poor soul,

49

suffering beneath the yoke of oppression placed on my neck by the cold, unfeeling world. I did talk about what I saw as the disparity between what a college player receives as compensation and what he earns for the university. And I did question whether it was really worth it for the player in the long run. All some people heard were the ramblings of an unhappy prima donna.

I rarely took much of a look at the newspaper's sports section in those days (and even less now) but on Sundays there was a "Letters to the Editor" section. I took an interest in this section because it offered some insight into the community pulse.

There was a lot of talk in that town the following week about me breaking Archie Griffin's freshman rushing record. I really hadn't thought much about it up to that point because I was more concerned about us winning games and staying in the hunt for the Rose Bowl, and I was never happy after a game if we didn't win, regardless of how I may have played personally. Well, we did win that week and I did break the record. Afterward I talked about what the record meant to me. I started off by saying that I knew there was a possibility that I would break the record that week, so I'd thought about my response quite a bit.

It's impossible to overestimate what Archie Griffin means to Ohio State. He's the only player in college football history to win two Heisman trophies. He holds the career rushing record at Ohio State. He was a part of two Rose Bowl championship teams. He works as an assistant athletic director at the university and is one of the most well-respected players and people in school history. After the game I talked about how humbled I felt to even be mentioned with a man like him. This was not a speech to please The Ohio State brass; I still truly believe that no one, regardless of how many records of his they break, can touch the legacy of this man.

Instead, I took another beating in the *Dispatch*. "Who does he think he is to prepare an answer before he even broke the record?" This was from an actual letter. Instead of acknowledging the thought that went into answering the question, this person attacked me for being presumptuous. And the editor thought this was an appropriate letter to print.

Once people think a certain way about you, there's nothing you can do. They either completely ignore the positive things you do and say or they twist them to justify their feelings. I was truly taken aback by the negative comments. I thought I was doing everything the right way. At that point in my life it was important for me to feel that people liked and accepted me. But I was quickly learning that you need to focus on the people inside your circle. Family and friends are the important people in your life.

Before I got to college, my position was simple: the university is committing to me so I will commit to them for all my years of eligibility. But as I came to realize, you start to see situations much differently when they affect you directly. It is true that the school is committing to pay for your room and board, but they aren't just doing this out of the kindness of their hearts. Large division I schools make millions of dollars off of their football programs. The coaches and athletic directors see plenty of this money, but the players are not as fortunate. Players would even scrounge up tickets after home games just so we could get the coupon for a free Wendy's hamburger.

The average division I football coach makes more than $500,000 a year. The average among the top 10 percent is more than $1 million a year. This latter average represents more than 5 percent of the total money the school brings in annually from its football program. The average athletic director at these schools makes more than $230,000. These numbers don't even include perks such as vehicles and houses. Even the assistant coaches can expect to make more than the average, tenured professors. And the student-athlete is left with a scholarship package that is worth maybe $20,000. Sound fair? This doesn't even consider the toll that football takes on the body and the fact that players have no insurance to cover surgery they might need after leaving school. Something needs to change in this system.

Not long ago, a bill was introduced in Nebraska that would mandate some sort of pay for athletes. I think this may go a bit too far, but maybe some sort of trust fund, as suggested by columnist John Feinstein, would be a good idea. At least players could have some money that compensated them more fairly for what they have contributed to the university. This money could be divided from a pool derived as a percentage of the total monies generated from the football program. There's also been talk about Title IX that mandates an equal opportunity for female athletes. While I do think it's important for women to have opportunities in sports, it's not fair for all of this money to be diverted from the programs that make the money. What do you think the NFL would say if it were asked to set aside money to fund professional female sports?

And does it make any sense for a player to risk injury in a sport as dangerous as football for virtually nothing when they could earn hundreds of thousands of dollars a year for doing the same job as a pro? Why do people even go to college in the first place? Some purists may say to receive an education. But I've learned far more on my own than I ever learned in a classroom. What about getting a good job? Being a professional football player is a pretty good job. Sure, you get the hell knocked out of you sometimes, and your body pays a hefty price, but you're well compensated. You can earn enough to go back and get your degree if you want. Some would say that these players are just using the college system as a stepping stone to the league. So what? Anybody outside of sports would leave school early if the right job opportunity came along. Do you think Bill Gates is upset he left school early? Do you think anyone at Harvard is upset with him? It's not just about money, it's about common sense. What would you tell your child to do in the same situation?

The problem here is that people get emotionally charged about certain issues and fail to realize the most salient points. Emotion shapes perception. Unfortunately, their perceptions become so distorted that people come to incomplete and unrealistic conclusions. They may complain about loyalty and fairness or give some other reason for why they feel players should stay in school, but I think it boils down to one simple issue: jealousy. It's hard for someone who works his butt off day in and day out to hear some 18- or 19-year-old kid talk about getting a job that will earn the kid as much in a year as he would in a lifetime. They hate the fact that people can make so much money "just" playing a game. But it's not fair to blame players for the way the system works (see Chapter Ten). These people wish they had that decision to make—and I don't blame them. I consider myself fortunate to have had the opportunity. But I didn't feel sorry for using a system that used me right back. And I didn't feel sorry for saying so.

The way the rule stands now—and it will be defeated in the courts in the near future—a player must wait until his graduating high school class has been out of school three years before he becomes eligible to enter the NFL draft. At that time, the player may forgo his final year or years of eligibility and enter the draft. Unlike prospective NBA players, there is no turning back for a football player; once they have declared eligibility for the draft, they can no longer play college football. College basketball players can enter the draft and then go back to play college ball if they are not satisfied with their draft position. After that, I didn't take the time to care about what people on the outside thought. School and football were plenty for me to worry about. We were also in Michigan week, and that meant that there was no doubt where everyone's focus was.

From the day you arrive at Ohio State as a football player, you know that the Michigan game is the primary part of your focus. There are signs around the football facility that say things such as: "What Have You Done Today to Beat Michigan?" It is one of the most heated and storied rivalries in all of sports. All of the other games are important, but this one is something different, something special. The coaches even refrained from pronouncing the name Michigan at times—as if the very act of saying it somehow cursed you and your chances against them that season. "That team up North is coming to town," they would say. If you want to get dirty looks and choice comments in Columbus, wear a blue hat with a big yellow "M" on it. It's a battle royale intensified by years of close games that often decided the winner of the Big Ten. This year was no different.

If we win, we're in. There's no better position in football. You control your own destiny—no waiting around for some other team to get things done for you… you're in charge. If we won this game, we were going to the Rose Bowl in Pasadena. It's what everyone wants when they get to Ohio State (at least back then, before the BCS). If we lost, we would have to play in the Liberty Bowl, in Memphis. Obviously, the two options were as far apart as any could have been for us. We didn't need any added incentive to play hard in this game, but the prospect of playing in Pasadena instead of Memphis certainly provided one. It was tough to think about anything else the week before the Michigan game. You go to class and go through the motions, but you can't help but think about the task facing you on Saturday. The game was in Columbus that year and I passed the stadium on the way to class, so there was no way for me to escape my thoughts about "The Game." As if my own thoughts weren't enough, it was all everyone around campus talked about as well. The yells came: "Let's kick Michigan's ass!" And then you get to hear it from the reporters all week: "The Buckeyes haven't won in blah-blah-blah." "So what—this is a new team. What other teams have done mean nothing to what we're doing now." Reporters love coming up with streaks, stats, and reasons they feel something is going to happen. The national media trucks began lining up outside of the stadium days before. I just couldn't wait for game day to arrive.

And then it was Saturday. There's just a different energy… an undeniable excitement. The long buildup makes this energy an inevitable part of the day. It's like you've been shuffling your feet on the carpet all week and you're filled with electricity that longs to be released. Even the students on Fraternity Row step things up a notch. You get to the stadium and wonder how you'll be able to contain yourself until kickoff. I went through my preparation routine and walked out into the stadium for the warm-up. This was not the same kind of crowd we had all season. You could sense the tension. This was big for them, too. Bragging rights for an entire year.

As I prepared to take the field for my first Michigan experience, Bill Myles, a former Buckeye line coach, said something to me that immediately calmed me and changed the way I approached games the rest of my career. "This is big, Robert," he said. "But there are a billion

Chinese people who don't even know this is going on right now." Truer words were never spoken. This was important, but the future of the world did not hang in the balance. This was the same game that I had been playing since I was 12 years old. I knew I was good at it and I knew I was prepared. It was time to do my job. Players let off some steam by jumping around a bit more or by making more noise, but when it all boils down, you're just out there playing a game. If you need to step it up to play a game, then there's something wrong. It's like the old line about giving 110 percent. You can't give more than the 100 percent you should have been giving all year. I think a lot players mess themselves up by trying too hard in big games. They get themselves so worked up that they get flustered and make mistakes. You need to have poise as well as intensity to be successful in a game like football.

My first Ohio State-Michigan game was a classic: hard-hitting and closely fought. Near the end of the first half, I took a helmet to my left thigh and had to leave the game. I could barely bend my leg. It was the first time that I had a serious injury since my freshman year in high school. I jogged up and down the sideline as my thigh continued to tighten. At halftime, I went to the locker room certain that there was some way I would get to play in the second half.

I came back out in the second half and jogged out to the huddle to try and run a play. It wasn't going to happen. Coach T. told me to come out. He was right, but I didn't want to believe it. There are times when you need to realize that it's better not to play. Apart from risking further injury, you also can do your team a disservice by playing at less than 100 percent. We had a stable of good backs, and I wasn't close to full strength. We fought to a 14-14 tie and, with the clock winding down, went for it on fourth down. We ran a quarterback-option. Greg kept the ball and was stopped for a loss. Michigan moved the ball into field goal position and lined up for a game-winning kick with three seconds remaining. Everyone in the stadium drew in a breath and watched silently as the ball sailed through the uprights. The gun fired and the game was over. We had lost 17-14. The team walked solemnly towards the locker room. A few fans lined the tunnel where we entered the locker room, clapping and cheering for their fallen heroes. It made me want to cry. The loss was tough for these people to take, but they still felt they should show their support. I felt I had let our team and our fans down. I wasn't there when they needed me and it stung me to the core. It may not have been the end of the world, but it felt like my place in it was impossibly damaged.

The loss was devastating to the team, especially the seniors. They talked about boycotting the bowl game. Of course the University wouldn't have any of that. The bowl game may not have been the most prestigious, but it still meant money for the school. I worked on getting my leg healed up and had a chance to concentrate on the end of the school quarter. The adjustment in class had been easy for me, except for one math class. I got a D on the first test in the quarter, but battled my way back to a final grade of A-. I was proud of my comeback, but the A- did cost me a place on the Dean's List. I was also happy that I was able to maintain my classroom focus throughout that whirlwind first quarter. I was finally starting to believe that I would have the ability to play pro football, but I still realized that I needed to have my education to fall back on. Any day of football can be your last—it's the nature of the game. I wanted to prepare myself for medical school, and I wasn't going to let the demands and pressures of college football get in the way.

We had missed out on the chance to play in the Rose Bowl, so we were headed to Memphis to play the Air Force Academy. Nothing against Memphis, but it sure isn't Pasadena. Our attitude about the trip was horrible from the beginning and you could smell the letdown coming all the way from Columbus. We got into the game and completely embarrassed ourselves. We tried fighting back in the fourth quarter of the game, but our flat start had doomed us. We ended up losing and had to go back to Columbus totally humiliated.

After the game, we only got a couple of weeks off before winter conditioning started. Being a college athlete really is a year-round job. John Cooper had a relaxed style of coaching. He hired good assistants and let them do most of the hands-on work. He had never beaten Michigan at this point in his tenure at Ohio State and he had not won a bowl

56

game. He must have felt that it was partly due to a relaxed atmosphere and lack of discipline among the players. It was time to get tough. Instead of taking on the role of tough guy himself, he decided to hire a drill sergeant of a coach named Elliot Uzelac. This guy was straight out of *Full Metal Jacket*: "Why is private Pyle out of his bunk!…Why are you not stomping private Pyle's guts in?" His lines were slightly different but said with same gung-ho bravado: "First, we're gonna hit! And then we're gonna hit some more!"

Elliot never liked me. Loud coaches who try to intimidate players never like the cerebral types. They know that we're aware of their attempts to play head games. They try to scare or belittle players to accomplish their goals. I'm not scared of any person on this planet. Sure, there are some I would rather not tangle with—guys like *Pride Fighting* champions Kevin Randellman and Marc Coleman, or boxer Mike Tyson, to name a few—but I'm not scared of them. I'm certainly not scared of some person who does nothing but yell. I've always found coaches like that amusing. Some people need that type of motivation, but for me, it was unnecessary. Elliot thought that I was being babied (he later told me this) by the coaching staff, and he was right to a degree. I think all of my football coaches treated me gingerly because they saw my frame as making me somehow fragile. But what I needed was more opportunities to touch the ball in games, not some Neanderthal trying to put the prima donna in his place. I was never given special treatment by the coaching staff—I worked as hard as anyone there. But people believe what they want to believe, and Elliot believed I needed to be brought down a few pegs.

He started in on me almost as soon as he got there. He brought us all together after a winter conditioning session and gave us a little pep talk. He talked about how important it was for us to be focused on football and how we couldn't let outside influences get in the way of us being successful players. Then he said: "Like Robert there, he wants to be a doctor, but he's taking that school thing too seriously." He added a little laugh for good measure and everyone kind of turned and looked at me. I didn't think it was funny and I'm sure my face showed it. There was a clear challenge in my eyes because I know that many serious notions are said in jest. He moved on quickly, but the gauntlet had been thrown down. This guy had it in for me and he wanted to be sure I knew it.

I decided not to run track that spring so I could focus on football. Spring ball went well for me and I was excited to get the summer started and begin preparations for the season. In order to stay on track within the pre-med curriculum, I needed to sign up for a summer class that would interfere with training camp. I got permission from the coaching staff to sign up for the class, but the situation quickly came to a head once we reported for our first practices. We were down to the last few weeks of class and I needed to miss most of the first two practices (we had three a day) in order to attend the class. I had been goofing off and missing class all summer and was in danger of failing my chemistry class. If I failed this class, I would have to wait until the following fall to start my organic chemistry series, leaving me a full year behind. I needed to bear down those last few weeks to get through the class.

Camp was being run like a prison. Lights out usually meant that you had to be in your room when curfew rolled around. Well, this year they actually had you turn out your lights and get in bed. Are you kidding me? Grown men being told that they have to be in bed for football practice? Well, I wasn't turning my God damn light out! I had to stay up and study. When the coaches came around for bed check I told them I wouldn't turn the lights out. It was my own fault for being in trouble in the class, but I wasn't about to fall a year behind in school because some megalomaniac thinks he can rule the world. Well, Elliot had some different ideas. He wanted to assert himself a bit more. He came to me at my locker one morning and said: "Hey, we need you here at least two days in the morning next week." The implication was clear: Don't go to class, come here and practice instead. I was shocked and mumbled something like, "I'll see what I can do." This guy was trying to run my life, and I wasn't having it.

I thought about it overnight and decided the next day to tell Coach Cooper that I wasn't going to play that season. It was a tough decision, but I thought it was the right thing to do. Coach Cooper and I have talked since that day and he says that I didn't mention what Elliot had said to me about missing the class. I was pretty flustered that day, and there's no reason to believe that Coop is lying about it. Maybe things would have turned out differently if I had said something to Coach Cooper before I went public. But I was a frustrated and angry 19-year-old and I had no desire to enter into calm discussions at that point. I stormed out of his office and back to the dorm to grab my things. I went back to my apartment and was confronted by throngs of media anxious to get the story behind my departure.

I remember turning most of them away, then giving an interview to my old friends Moose and Dom from Channel 10. I struggled with my emotions in the interview and basically said that I would refuse to return to the team until two of the coaches were removed. I was referring to Elliot and Coach Cooper. My mind was such a mess at that point that I barely even remember giving the interview. I felt betrayed, but I was incorrect to think that Coach Cooper was really against me.

This was huge news in Columbus. In late summer '91, the Soviet Union was on the verge of breaking apart, but my story led off the news and dominated the papers the following week. Reporters were lying in wait whenever I returned to my apartment. It got so bad that I ended up moving in with the family of one of my friends. Dom and Moose got word of where I was staying and actually showed up one day. Luckily for me, this family has a lot of pull in the area and their request for privacy kept those guys from revealing my location. Even the national papers and media outlets were all over it. There I was, the national freshman of the year from the previous season and a potential Heisman candidate for the coming year, and I was saying that I wasn't even going to play. The smear campaign from the university began almost immediately. They wasted no time noting that I had missed "at least 23 classes that summer." The teacher of the class obviously had been checking to see whether or not I was present even though it was a class that didn't take attendance. There were also (true) stories about me hanging out late night and drinking on campus. It reminded me of the way in which rape victims are attacked during trials. I had not been taking care of business in the classroom that summer, there's no question about that.

And I knew I was wrong to have been running around the way I was that summer. But the reason I was struggling in the class didn't excuse Elliot's request. It was inappropriate, but the more I thought about it, so was my response.

I should have taken the time to talk things over with Coach Cooper. He was willing to listen throughout the ordeal and the entire situation could have been handled internally. Once I went public, I embarrassed the university and Coach Cooper on the national stage. *Sports Illustrated* jumped all over the story and portrayed me as a poor, tortured student athlete fighting the good fight for college players everywhere. I also put Coach Cooper in an almost no-win situation. If he got rid of Elliot and I came back, it would look as if he were pandering to the prima donna. If he wouldn't have me back, he would have been skewered by the media. I knew I wasn't done playing football, but I also knew I wouldn't be playing for Ohio State that season.

I wasn't sure what I was going to do next. I felt as if I were on an island. But it was my choice to be there, and, having gone through it, I learned a great deal about both people and life. The most important thing I learned was that you can only rely on yourself and your true friends and family in times of struggle. Everyone wants to be around you when you're scoring touchdowns and setting records. Only the people who care about you will be there when you're down. People were calling me a quitter, saying I wasn't good or tough enough to play in the Big Ten and saying that I would never be able to make it back. But the important people in my life were there for me the whole time. With them behind me, I knew I'd be back, one way or another.

I also learned that you're better off staying inside of a system if you want to effect real change. Rabble rousers don't have much credibility if they're on the outside; they look as if they have an axe to grind. I had assurances from Coach Cooper that his door would always be open for me so I knew that going back the next season was an option. But I also looked at the option of going to another school to play.

The way I understood the rule, I would be able to transfer, attend school for three quarters, and then play for the new school. Unfortunately, I didn't read the rule carefully enough because it also stated that the summer term would not count as one of the three required quarters. So if I transferred to another school, I would lose the following football season as well. This rule only applies when you are transferring to another Division I school, but I had no intention of transferring to a smaller school. It's just another one of the delightful ways in which the NCAA restricts student athletes. The coaches have no such restrictions; they can move about freely to whichever school they choose. By the time I learned of this rule in its entirety, I had committed to taking a couple of recruiting trips. At least I got a couple of free trips out of it. And it was on one of these trips that I met Denny Green. He was the head coach at Stanford at the time and had invited me out to visit. It was like paradise out there: great school, great team, great coach. I wondered why I hadn't thought about the place when I was in high school. I also ended up meeting Ty Willingham, who was Denny's running back coach that year. Denny became the Minnesota Vikings head coach the following year.

Meanwhile, I transferred to a track scholarship at Ohio State and began training with the team. It had been a couple of years since I had run, so it was pretty refreshing to get back to my first love in sports. I had known the track coach, Russ Rogers, since high school and had looked forward to training under him. He was the Olympic sprint coach in 1988 and had turned Ohio State's track program into a national power. Running for Russ was a nice change of pace for me. I was able to escape the spotlight for a while and also dedicate more time to my class work. It was a good thing, too, because I needed all the time I could get for organic chemistry.

My teacher for organic chemistry was named Harold Schecter and the students called him "Hannibal the Cannibal" Schecter because his six-hour tests tended to devour students. Organic chemistry is a true test of a student's commitment to his schooling. You spend an entire five-hour lab to make banana odor! You spend six hours on a test just naming molecules! It's a bear. But it was a good opportunity for me to recommit myself to my studies. I felt as if I was in control of my life again. I was confident that I would be able to return to the football team, regardless of who was coaching. Getting along with Coach Cooper would be no problem; Elliot would be a completely different story.

61

I talked to Coach Cooper and told him that I wanted to come back to the team if there were no objections. He put it to a vote on the team and they unanimously approved. He also talked to Elliot and decided that the three of us should get together to talk things over. We had our meeting at the St. John Arena football offices. It was the first time that I had seen Elliot since our little talk about missing class the previous fall. I went in with a positive attitude and promised myself that I would act unemotionally. I shook both of their hands and sat down on the opposite side of a large wooden conference table. Coach Cooper spoke first and basically said that it was in everybody's best interests to get along because we would all be working together. He said we might disagree but that we shouldn't be disagreeable. I stated that I was sorry for handling the situation the way I did and that I looked forward to playing for both of them. Elliot said that he agreed but that he wanted to speak with me alone. Coach Cooper left the room and then it was just old Elliot and me. He pulled out a tape recorder, put it on the table between us, and said, "Why did you lie to *Sports Illustrated* about me?" I looked him in the eye and said: "I didn't lie to *Sports Illustrated*." He repeated the question, "Why did you lie to *Sports Illustrated*?" I said, "Look Coach, I don't care if you have a tape recorder, it doesn't change what you said to me—you know it and I know it." He shot back again, "Tell me why you lied." I got up from the table and left the room. Coach Cooper was standing outside in the hall and I said to him, "This is pointless. That guy's got problems."

A few days later, Elliot was fired. Apparently, he had been trying to build some defamation case against *Sports Illustrated*. The university had warned him not to continue with the case, but he refused. They say you should never attempt to sue people who buy ink by the barrel. Apparently Elliot had never heard that adage, and it cost him his job. Regardless of the university's official reason, it appeared as if Elliot had been fired to make room for my return. The prima donna had gotten his way. Of course, I had already agreed to come back to the team with Elliot as the offensive coordinator, but, people being people, the untrue, but far more interesting story stuck. I would be going back to the team with the ever-increasing legend that I was a spoiled brat who always got his way.

That was unimportant to me, however. I knew the team wanted me back—and that was all that mattered.

I did genuinely feel bad for Elliot. Apart from what I felt must be some serious emotional problems, he felt pressured to win, and that makes people do some outrageous things. The NCAA claims to be on the side of players, but it needs to do more to take the pressure off of coaches who inevitably end up pressuring players. The NCAA could make universities honor contracts and forbid buyouts. This would give coaches some peace of mind. I know it would be tough to try to tell universities what to do, but something has to be done. It doesn't make any sense that a coach with a winning record could be fired for a lack of performance. The pros are completely different. An owner can fire anyone he wants for any reason; after all, he owns the team. But college coaches need more security. It's the only way they won't get pressured into leaning on players for performance and time.

I finished up a great spring in track by qualifying for the Olympic trials in the 400 meters. I knew I had an outside shot at making the team, but my chances weren't good enough for me to justify taking the extra time away from football. It had already been a year and a half since I had played in a game and my chances of making the Olympic team were slim at best. This is a strong track country; to make the Olympic team here, especially in the sprints, you need to be among the top ten in the world. I wasn't nearly that fast, so it seemed to make more sense to concentrate on getting back to the football team.

I entered the summer preparing for what I figured would be my last year of college football. I spent the summer working in the hematology/oncology lab at the Arthur James Cancer Research Center in Columbus. I was working with Jas Lang, a brilliant Scottish research scientist who was working on isolating a cancer-causing gene. I did the grunt work of the cloning and sequencing of the gene. It was amazingly interesting work. I got a chance to see and work with the cutting-edge technology that would be used in subsequent years to map the human genome. I would go in to work at this lab during the day and then work out with the football team in summer drills. My excitement about the upcoming season was growing rapidly. I had been away from the game for a long time and I had a renewed sense of vigor to get out and show that my first season had been no fluke.

About a month before reporting to camp, I was stunned by the loss of another loved one. Aunt Ruth's health had been declining since the death of her sister. She didn't have the money to stay in the apartment she had been living in and we didn't have the money to help her. She ended up having to move into a nursing home. I had hoped to turn pro after that season and move her into her own place with nursing assistance. She suffered a heart attack early that July and never recovered; she died about a week later. I was devastated. I couldn't help but think that if I had played the previous season and turned pro that I would have been able to keep her in her own place. I think she gave up on life when she moved into the nursing home. She had loved watching me play for the Buckeyes. Losing her was very difficult for me. This woman had done so much for my family and me. She taught me the importance of helping other people, that no amount of effort is too great for you to spend on the ones you love. I wish that she had had a chance to see me return that season. I also know she would have gotten a real kick out of seeing me playing for the Minnesota Vikings.

When I decided to donate some money to The Ohio State University, I thought it would be a good chance to pay tribute to this wonderful person. I've always thought that it's tacky to name donations after yourself. It reminds me of the tale of Ozymandius. In that Percy Bysshe Shelley poem, he talks about a traveler who sees a pair of legs and a large base that once belonged to a long-destroyed statue. The base has an inscription that contains the words of the person whom the statue represented. His name was Ozymandius and he spoke of his greatness and his immortality. The point here is that no matter what you think of yourself, you're not that big of a deal. And you will someday die like everyone else. *Sic transit gloria!* Glory is transitory! When you give money for a project or a charity it's a great opportunity to honor someone else from your life. That's what I decided to do for Aunt Ruth. The football team wanted to redesign the atrium in its football facility. Having impressive structures is a great way to impress recruits. I gave them some money to complete this project but turned down the suggestion to have my name attached to the project. Now, when I walk into that beautiful atrium, I can see a plaque that honors a truly special person. It says: "Dedicated in memory of Ruth C. Cole, a true Buckeye fan." It makes me smile every time.

And then it was time for football again. It was an unbelievable feeling to be back preparing for a season. I had missed the camaraderie of the locker room and the intensity of practice. I woke up every morning of training camp, enthusiastic just to be there. I felt like a new person—and in many ways I was. I wasn't willing to let other peoples' plans for me interfere with my own. I wasn't going to let other peoples' words affect me. And most of all, I wasn't going to obsess about what other people thought of me and my actions. When I stepped onto the field, I felt a sense of power and control that mirrored my feelings for my life in general. It was this notion of responsibility that gave me the confidence of independence.

I stepped onto the field for the first game and felt a rush of joy that had been missing in my life for the previous year-and-a-half. I was alive. The roar of the crowd, the excitement of game day, the nervous tension before kickoff—I had yearned for them all. It didn't take me any time at all to get back into the flow: It was like riding a bike... and crashing into a wall at 40 miles an hour! Coach Cooper had more confidence in me as a player now and he used me in more situations on the field. I was even out there on the kick block team. I just wanted to win games. I would have played nose tackle if they had asked me. I wanted to win for Coach Cooper as much as anything because he was the one who maintained his faith in me throughout our ordeal. I felt I owed him. On one of the kickoffs in the second half of the opening game, I caught the ball and headed up the left sideline. One of the defenders was coming from my right and I raised the ball over him thinking I would be able to move by him untouched. Well, he did a very good job of touching me. He caught me in the ribs with his right forearm and I instantly went down on their sideline, writhing in pain. I had broken the tenth and eleventh ribs on the right side. To make matters worse, some of their players decided to jump on me after I was already down. A little scuffle broke out and the resulting additional players to the pile-up made it even more difficult for me to breathe. The players who jumped on me were flagged for a penalty, but that wasn't much of a consolation to my ribs. I had to sit out the rest of the game. We won, but I had to concern myself with getting healthy again.

You don't realize how many activities affect your ribs until you have the displeasure of breaking one. Walking, breathing, laughing, sneezing—they all remind you of your injury. I think it had been a couple of years since I had the hiccups before I broke my ribs, and then—you guessed it! I got them while I was in the hospital getting x-rays. I couldn't help but laugh, which made the pain worse. The bad part about a rib injury is that you pretty much just have to wait for it to heal; there's not much you can do to speed the process. I ended up sitting out the next game. It was the first game that I missed since the eighth grade. They thought it would be better to sit out that week and have me back against Syracuse, one of the top ranked teams in the nation that season.

My ribs weren't feeling great that week of practice, but there was no way I was going to miss that game. They gave me a special flak jacket to help protect against direct blows to the ribs. The jacket wasn't the most comfortable thing in the world, but I knew that if I took a clean shot that I'd be glad I had it. I'm sure the Syracuse players were well aware of the fact that I had been out the previous week with broken ribs and they wouldn't hesitate to take a few extra shots at the bottom of some piles.

The game was played in the Carrier Dome in Syracuse and it marked the first time in my career that I'd be playing at an indoor venue. You just can't imagine how loud these places get until you step inside one during a game. The home crowd knows how big an impact it can have, and the amount of noise it makes is impressive. All of the yelling and whistling blends into a deafening white noise that makes it almost impossible to hear the quarterback cadences and audibles. From deep in the backfield, you just kind of watch his head and count the bobs to at least get a clue as to when the ball is going to be snapped. The quarterback will turn around to tell you directly if he's going to audible, but you'll usually see the running back step up to get the signal in these situations; it's just too loud to hear what's being said in most cases. That place was fired up for this game. Syracuse was undefeated and picked as one of the early favorites for a national title. Our fans and players were the only people in the nation who thought we had a chance.

You feel an extra sense of motivation when you know that people think you can't do something. It's insulting. What do these people know? They don't sweat with you in camp. They don't struggle with you in practice. Many of the "experts" have never even stepped onto a football field to play. We didn't need anyone else to believe; we had each other. Road games can be tough if you go in with the wrong attitude. You need to stick together and fight until the fight is done. We did both that day. We posted a victory and returned to Columbus with strong momentum heading into the Big Ten schedule. My ribs held up well underneath the flak jacket, but my post-touchdown puke made its triumphant return for the national television audience. It was embarrassing, but well worth it.

The next week had us back on the road against Wisconsin. The last trip I made to Wisconsin two years earlier had been very productive. We won the game, I rushed for 100 yards, and I went over 1, 000 yards for the season to break Archie Griffin's freshman rushing record. This trip was quite the opposite. We lost the game and I was knocked out of the contest early with what is now called a "high" ankle sprain. "Normal" ankle sprains refer to ligament damage that occurs at the junction of the foot and leg, which is commonly known as the ankle. "High" ankle sprains refer to a classic ankle sprain combined with damage to the connective tissue that helps hold the two bones of the lower leg (the tibia and the fibula) together. Ligament damage is difficult enough to heal on its own. They often say that you're better off breaking bones in your ankle than damaging ligaments. It all depends on how much damage has been done to the ligaments. Any sprain denotes some degree of tear and the more tearing there is, the longer it takes to heal. The process becomes even more difficult when you try to heal the extra tissue involved in a high ankle sprain. Every time you put pressure on your feet, you stress that tissue, so you need almost complete immobility to allow it to fully recuperate. Of course, during the season, you don't have that luxury of time.

I wanted to get back out on the field as soon as I could. We had another important Big Ten battle against Illinois the following week, and I knew I had to do whatever I could to get ready for that game. You're torn between trying the ankle out and resting it. It was still extremely sore on Saturday, but I felt I could still contribute that day. We put it in a sturdy brace and I played sparingly in the game. I had a couple of big runs to put us in scoring position, but we just couldn't overcome our turnovers that day (one of them was mine). We had lost two consecutive Big Ten games, and the city was starting to get impatient with the team—especially Coach Cooper.

During the week of preparation for the next game, one of the reporters said something to me along the lines of: "Back in Woody Hayes' days," or "Well, Woody would have..." Whatever it was exactly that he said, he was trying to say that Coach Cooper wasn't doing enough or that he wasn't adequate for the job. I lost it. I said, "Look, I don't give a shit what Woody Hayes did, it's not going to help us win games now!" I might as well have called the Pope a pedophile. People in Columbus went nuts! One thing you don't do in Columbus is make disparaging remarks about Woody Hayes. I was just trying to say that we needed to carve out our own place in Ohio State history and that people needed to realize that the past was gone. It didn't matter though; the damage was done. I remember standing on the sideline next to strength coach Dave Kennedy that Saturday. They had decided to rest my ankle that week, so I wasn't even in uniform. He came up to me with a big smile on his face and said, "Mr. Controversy strikes again!" I hadn't seen the paper yet, so I didn't even know what he was talking about. I was trying to defend my coach and these people made it out to be some attack on Ohio State history.

In another interview, someone asked me how I compared to Georgia's Garrison Hearst, one of the top backs in the nation, and I replied: "Is he better than me? I don't know. Am I better than him? I don't know that, either, but I think we're both right up there." In the

Sunday "Letters to the Editor" section, someone wrote in and said, "If he's supposed to be so smart, why doesn't he use proper grammar in his sentences? He should have said Is he better than I am? And am I better than he is?" And once again the editor thought that this was a point worth making.

We ended up tying Michigan in the final regular season game and finished with an 8-2-1 record. We missed out on the Rose Bowl again, but at least this time we were headed to a New Year's Day bowl game—the Citrus Bowl in Orlando. We would be going up against Georgia, and that meant that the nation (and professional coaches) would get a chance to compare Garrison Hearst and me first-hand. I was almost sure that this was going to be my last college game. I wanted to win, but I also knew this would be my last opportunity to show NFL teams what I could do. I had missed two complete games and parts of two others that season, so pro teams didn't have many games on which to base their evaluations of me.

It was a beautiful Florida day for football and those in attendance saw a great match-up between two talented teams. The day was going well for us as a team and for me personally. The game was tied 14-14 in the fourth quarter after I scored my second touchdown of the day. We got the ball back and starting heading down the field for the go-ahead score. I caught a pass on the right sideline and cut across the field for a 45-yard gain. We were in great field position and were pretty well assured of at least getting a field goal out of the drive. A play to the fullback came into the huddle. We broke the huddle and lined up in an I-formation. Our quarterback, Kirk Herbstreit, noticed a defensive alignment that called for a change of direction on the play. He called out the audible twice and then called for the snap. I know that Herbie announced the audible loud enough for everyone to hear because I was the deepest in the backfield and I still heard it. Only he knows whether or not he heard the audible, but the fullback (Jeff Cothran) ran the wrong way and knocked the ball from Herbie's hands. Georgia recovered the ball and its offense moved down the field to score the winning touchdown. It was a crushing defeat.

I sat in front of my locker after the game and cried. We had fought so hard. We had come so close. I had done all I could, but it wasn't enough. My college career was over. No Big Ten championships. No Rose Bowls. No victories over Michigan. No bowl game wins. No Heisman trophies. I felt an insurmountable emptiness. I had accomplished none of the things that I felt would have made my college football career successful. I still felt that it was time to move on. Your football clock is always ticking, and I felt it made more sense to have that clock run while I was being paid.

I talked to Coach Cooper before making my announcement, and he also felt it was the right thing for me to do. I thanked him for the opportunity to play for him and for allowing me to come back to the team. I would be leaving Ohio State football on good terms with the coach. The same could not be said for the fans.

After the game, the letters section had some pretty interesting comments. Apart from the usual calls for Coach Cooper's head, one of the fans decided to take another shot at me. He basically said that it was my fault for losing the game because I was caught on the 45-yard screen play that preceded the fumble. It was a pretty odd spin on the events, but once again, the editor thought it made enough sense to put this letter in the paper. The fans had been hearing for a couple of months that I would be turning pro after the season. They had become angry with me and my viewpoints. I'm sure they didn't lose much sleep when the official announcement came. Many of them shared (probably with slightly altered language) the sentiments of the person that sent me an anonymous (no surprise) letter that read: "I hear that you're turning pro. Good riddance, we don't need uppity niggers like you here at Ohio State!"

CHAPTER FOUR

SEA CHANGE

Put your hands on the wheel, let the golden age begin.

—Beck

People are strange, when you're a stranger...

—The Doors

There was no turning back. I had declared myself eligible for the draft, and, in doing so, had made myself ineligible for college football. You don't like your draft position? Tough! You declared yourself eligible. You didn't get drafted? Tough! You declared yourself eligible. I knew that I was good enough to play in the NFL, but the finality of the decision was a bit disconcerting. I now realize that more players get drafted than deserve to be. Or that you're more likely to get drafted and not be good enough to play than you are to be good enough and not be drafted. Of course, there's also the money issue. You earn far more money in your first years if you're drafted than if you're not. You never know how long you'll play if you do make it, so your first contract is vital.

But the draft was another four months off, so my focus shifted to the NFL Combine. Any doubts about the fact that football players are considered pieces of meat disappeared from my mind when I arrived at the NFL Scouting Combine in Indianapolis. The Combine brings together prospective NFL players to be poked, prodded, and tested by NFL coaches, scouts, and trainers. Experts from around the league show up to evaluate college players in mental and physical examinations as well as in various agility tests to try to determine which players they feel would make good additions to their teams.

You show up at the hotel and they give you a bag at check-in that contains the schedule of testing as well as shorts and a T-shirt that has a number and your position on it. Every step is watched in the next couple of days, and how you perform could make or lose you millions of dollars. The chatter among players in the hallways of the hotel sometimes releases and, at times, increases the level of anxiety. Stories circulate about how a particular test is extremely difficult and confusing or about how a certain team doctor gives a particularly brutal physical examination. Many players ease their nerves by talking about their accomplishments and victories over other players who are present. Like most sports talk, it's mostly just friendly banter. It takes your mind off the tasks at hand.

The first day consists of physicals and written exams. The most dehumanizing part comes early as you are told to enter a room wearing just shorts and stand in front of a group of coaches, general managers, and trainers. "Number 37, running back, Robert Smith. The Ohio State University. Turn to the right. Now turn to the wall. Face the other wall. Please step onto the scale. 198 pounds, six foot one and three-quarter inches. Please place your hand on the table and spread your fingers. Maximum width: eight and a half inches. Length: same. Thank you, you can leave now." It was impossible not to imagine a prison scene: "Where do I pick up my stuff and meet the people who posted bail?" You even had a drug test that looked more like a body cavity search. You walk into the bathroom and grab a cup to pee in. Then you walk over to one of the stalls accompanied by a testing representative. Then you drop your pants and raise your arms, do a 360 and pee in the cup. They're trying to make sure that you don't bring in a "clean" sample to get away with something. I understand it's necessary and worthwhile in the end, but it feels pretty dehumanizing.

The next step is to get examined in the physical room. This is the step that most of the players dread. The team doctors have files that contain your medical records from college. Any injuries you had during your college career have been scrutinized intently (knee injuries are the worst; doctors and trainers are on the exam tables leaning with all their weight on the suspect knee). Luckily, I had no really serious injuries in college so the exam process was less painful (literally and figuratively) for me than it was for some of the other players. I had suffered an injury to my left quadriceps muscle early in my college career that left a large, somewhat grotesque, lump. The site of this thing created quite a stir among the doctors. They called to each other to come over to look at it; some of them even took pictures. "Wow, I've never seen scar tissue move like that!" They were all impressed that I hadn't missed any time with the injury, so all the attention was worth it, I figured. Some of the players were so sore after their physicals that they couldn't participate in the agility tests the following day.

Damaged goods would be no good to anyone and teams wanted to make sure that their prospective draftees were not damaged mentally, either. They figured this could be determined by a series of written tests. The questions on the exams ranged from the pointless to the downright absurd. One of the questions asked, "Have you ever lost your temper for no reason and gone into a fit of rage?" Put another way: Do you want to make sure we never draft you? The Wunderlick test, which is a general purpose intelligence exam, was also given. Many players found it to be particularly frustrating. Some years later we saw the results of some other players' Wunderlick tests. The football profession has plenty of dumb people in it (just like most professions). Of course, I know that all players aren't dumb but there were some pretty low scores. We had some good laughs in the Vikings locker room over some of them a number of years later.

At the Combine, you were also expected to make yourself available for interviews by members of coaching staffs. This was a particularly important aspect of the trip for me because I figured many of the coaches probably thought I was a head case. So it was an opportunity for me to show how normal/accommodating I could be. One of the Kansas City assistants asked if I would speak with head coach Marty

Schottenheimer "Sure, no problem." I never thought much of Marty, but I went into the room and calmly took a seat across from him. Anyone who thinks NFL players have ego problems needs to try talking to a few coaches to see what arrogance really is. These guys are in charge of all the players. They're responsible for whether or not players get a job. They're basically in charge of running a high profile, multi-million dollar NFL team. Do you think that would send a guy on an ego-trip? It does—and you can sense it with Marty the moment you sit down with him. He asked me if I was a Browns fan. I said, "Only when you were there." I've seen that comment re-run on an ESPN special on the Combine. The trick to dealing with people like that is to let them think you realize their power: "Of course you're great, Coach, and I know it!" Let them have their power trip... so long as you get the job.

The next day was the real stuff: running, jumping, and football drills. I knew it would be my time to excel. The testing took place in the Hoosier Dome, with hundreds of NFL personnel watching. The pressure was intense. Most of the players present would sign an NFL contract, but how well you ran on the notoriously slow Hoosier Dome turf could mean the difference between mid-first round and early second—or hundreds of thousands of dollars in bonus money. Track guys definitely have an advantage in this type of setting. Some people just aren't used to performing on their own. You step up to the starting line for the 40-yard dash and each tenth of a second could mean thousands of dollars difference. There's no starter giving you commands-you just step up, crouch down, put your hand on the line, and think speed. You start when you're ready. Explosive, but smooth. That phrase is tough for non-track athletes to comprehend. Tension is the enemy in sprinting. You need to be coiled at the start, ready to accelerate with all your power. You also need to transition smoothly into sprinting stride. This isn't as important in a sprint that short, but it still comes into play.

I could see the coaches crowded around the finish line with their stopwatches raised in front of them in the classic track-timing pose. It was a scene that I had witnessed before and it made me feel even more at ease. I crouched into my start and exploded off the line. I could hear a murmur from the coaches that convinced me I had done well. From there it was on to a vertical jump, a horizontal jump, and some other change of direction drills. Individual position coaches also had the opportunity to put you through drills. It was a rewarding couple of days for me. Whatever my draft position was before the combine, I'm sure it was higher afterwards. I had shown that I wasn't a head case—that I could perform under pressure. Now all I could do was wait to see which team was willing to take a chance on a guy who had played only twenty college games.

I really let my schooling fall apart before the draft. I was focused on that last college season and the draft; I didn't take much time to do anything else. I did need to maintain full-time status to remain eligible for track, but I ended up taking some failing grades just to stay above the required hours. I wasn't in danger of being on probation at the school, but my GPA dropped below 3.0 for the first time. I felt bad about this, but I knew that I'd bring it back up, after I turned pro. I always knew I'd get my degree no matter what happened in my pro career. I hoped I wouldn't need my degree anytime soon, but it would be nice to know that I had it to fall back on.

So I went on running track, skipping class, and preparing myself mentally for the transition to professional football. On the weekend of the NFL Draft, I found myself on the road traveling with the track team to Philadelphia for the Penn Relays. The draft didn't begin until Sunday back then, so I had the time to compete in Philadelphia on Saturday and make it back to Columbus on Sunday.

I didn't get much sleep that Saturday night and when I got out of bed my stomach was twisted in knots. It was hard enough making the decision to enter Ohio State three years earlier. Now I had to wait around for some team to choose me. The next years of your life will be spent in an unknown city with an unknown team. You have no choice. You'll go where they tell you to go. All you can do is wait for that phone call—and hope it comes.

I went to Bob Evans to grab some breakfast but I was too nervous to eat much. I just wanted to get back to the apartment and sit by the phone as I watched the draft on TV. Teams have 15 minutes to pick in the first round, so it takes a long time to get through the opening round. I sat there and watched as player after player seated in New York at the draft had their NFL dreams fulfilled. Garrison Hearst was the first running back taken as the third overall pick. Eight picks later, Jerome Bettis was drafted. I didn't expect to go any higher than those guys, but I did expect to be the next running back taken. Where was I going to end up? It really started to eat at me now. The phone rang. It was for one of my roommates. I had given instructions to my roommates not to tie up the phone that day, but apparently the message had not made it to all of their friends.

Word was that the Raiders and Dolphins were particularly interested in drafting me. They were picking fifteenth and twenty-fifth, respectively. After the Raiders didn't pick me, I thought I'd take some time away from the draft and do what any intelligent adult would have done at the time: I turned on "Ren and Stimpy." The phone rang again. It was Neil Cornrich, my agent. He had caught word that Minnesota was interested. I turned the television back to ESPN and the phone rang almost immediately.

"Hello, may I speak to Robert?" "Speaking." "Hey, Robert, Dennis Green." I could barely think straight. He said, "I'm not gonna let you get away again," referring to the trip I had made out to Stanford. I couldn't wait to get off the phone and get on the plane to go up to Minnesota. It had really happened. I was a first-round draft pick, twenty-first overall. I was part of an NFL team. All I could do was think about how different my life was going to become. I got on the phone with Neil again and he started filling me in on some of the details of the organization. He told me the names of the pro personnel people, some of the coaching staff, and the team's record the previous season. Before talking to Neil that afternoon, I didn't even know which division the Vikings were in.

I went upstairs, packed a bag, and headed to the airport. It was pouring rain in the normal April-in-Columbus way. As I sat on the plane for the hour and a half ride, I struggled over the information Neil had given me. I was going to a new home that had just been determined a couple of hours before. I was about to begin one of the most high-profile jobs in the world. The pressure would be immediate and intense. "Don't forget to smile," was the last piece of advice that Neil gave me. He was right; I would be starting over and making a good first impression was important.

As the plane approached the Minneapolis/St. Paul International Airport, I was amazed at how beautiful the area seemed. I had been there before, but now I was seeing it in a different light. The sky was perfectly clear and the sun glistened off of the lakes in the line of our approach. It seemed like a dream. I stepped off of the plane and was greeted by running back coach Ty Willingham. He handed me a Vikings hat and said, "Welcome to Minnesota!" "Thanks, Coach," I said. "It's great to be here!" It was one of the greatest understatements of my life. As we left the jet way, we were immediately surrounded by a large group of cameras and reporters. Having a first-rounder was news in itself in Minnesota at the time. Because of the infamous Herschel Walker trade, I was the first first-round pick for Minnesota since 1988. The barrage of questions began instantly: "Are you happy to be in Minnesota, Robert?" "Ever think the Vikings would draft you?" "What do you think of Denny Green?" "Do you think you'll compete right away for the starting job?" The Vikings weren't actually hurting at running back. Terry Allen, who had set the team's single-season rushing record in the previous season, would be returning. They also had a very experienced runner and receiver in Roger Craig. So why pick me? Well, the philosophy on draft day is that you never pass up certain players if they're available. I was one of those players for Denny. I was his pick, and I wanted to make everyone realize that he was right about me.

Two weeks after I was drafted, I flew back to Minnesota for my first mini-camp. Teams hold these camps in the spring each year to bring their new and old players in for some work together. You learn right away that you're a second-class citizen when you're a rookie. Veteran players have their own lockers with nice plastic placards above them with their name and number. Rookie players (and some free-agents) have to share lockers and both names are written in with markers on a piece of masking tape. No sense wasting all that plastic on a guy who might not be around that long.

All rookies are in the locker room early for fear of being late. They just sit around talking to each other nervously or staring at their playbook, which seemed like it was written in Greek. When the veterans start coming in, the rookies really start getting nervous. A guy you watched growing up may sit right next to you. "What's up, Rook? Shit, they'll let anybody in here, huh?" Players take their locker room very seriously. The area around a veteran's locker is his neighborhood and you better not get in his way when he's trying to move around there. All of the veterans are catching up on old times and sharing stories about their kids, wives, and/or girlfriends (some have both, of course). They feel at ease in these surroundings that at first seem so foreign to rookies. The conversations are pretty amazing to young men fresh off of college campuses: "What kind of car did you end up buying, the new Porsche or the new Benz?" "I couldn't decide, Dog, so I got both!"

At this time, few drafted players have signed their contracts, so most of the rookies are still broke. I stared around the room at these other athletes and thought, "Man, there's a lot of money in here!" It's hard enough for people to start a new job in a new city. New professional athletes have to deal with the whole country watching them while trying to accustom themselves to an entirely different lifestyle. Boohoo, right? It's not easy to do, though. It's not like most jobs where everyone in the same office makes about the same money; there's a big difference between the top and bottom dollars in the league. And many players spend themselves into a hole while trying to keep up with everyone else in the locker room. Wearing jewelry was never my style, so I didn't have to worry about buying any to try to fit in. On the flight into Minneapolis, I sat next to Cris Carter and he shared with me one of the ultimate truths of life, "The only difference between men and boys is the price of the toys." With jewels of logic like that, it's no wonder he's a reverend now.

The locker room is a very colorful place (and I don't mean that as a reference to the fact that the league is 70 percent black). A lot of different personalities come together to make a football team. You have guys from schools all over the country and from all different types of families. It's more diverse than most work places. I spent as much time laughing in that football facility as I did learning. You bring together natural characters as diverse as Jim McMahon and Cris Carter and you know you're going to have some pretty entertaining days. One of Denny Green's strong points is that he is able to join such diverse elements into a cohesive unit. You were never scared to be yourself in Denny's locker room. Diversity wasn't just tolerated by Denny; it was encouraged—even celebrated.

In my first team meeting I sat next to Roger Craig, one of the few football players that I had actually taken the time to watch when I was a kid. He was one of the greatest backs ever to play the game and here I was joining him in the backfield. I knew before I got there that I'd be seeing him that weekend, but it still struck me when I first saw him. It's not that I was in awe or anything like that; it was just strange to be sitting in the same room with him, preparing for the same job. We flew through the information that first meeting and my head was spinning. There was so much to learn. With all the other adjustments I knew were coming, it seemed like learning it all would be impossible.

When I finally stepped onto the practice field for the first time as a Viking, my heart raced. I looked to the sidelines and all of the cameras were focused on me, the first-rounder. *"Stay loose, stay loose.....just relax...it's practice....yeah, your first... ...nice good stride."* We got into our lines and stretched. During the stretch players yelled to each other: "Hey 68! Ya' lookin' kinda' heavy! You know this is a professional team, right?" Another yells from the other side of the group: "Yeah, he better be careful about eatin' at Big Jim's Grease Shack!" Jim Muse was the team cook and we referred to his cafeteria as his "Grease Shack." Many players were overweight on weigh-in day because of eating too much of Big Jim's food. Cris Carter says, "I don't know, Denny [he was one of the few players who actually called Denny by his name when Denny was around], this group looks kinda soft!" Denny replies, "Don't worry, Cris, we'll get 'em ready!" Steve Wetzel, the strength and conditioning coach, finishes his call of the stretch: "One more time on your toes!" Randall McDaniel, a perennial all-pro offensive lineman who weighed about 270 at the time, sprinted off to one side of the practice field, closely followed by Roger Craig. It was a pretty good race but Randall won, as much because he started a few seconds early as anything. Despite his "competitive edge" in the race, Randall showed me early on just how fast big men can move in professional football.

The beginning of each practice started with the stretch and then the offense would get together and run a few plays against air. We called it "team get off" and it helped set the tempo for each day's practice. I stood close to the huddle to see if I could figure out how to run the play called, "Spread right, 60 outside. On one. Ready? Break!.... 60 outside, 60 outside...." *"Easy...run to the right side tight end, read his block and the tackle's block, get the ball....run...piece o' cake."* The running back took the ball and ran about 20 yards down the field, with the rest of the offense following. I could see Denny standing in front of the drill watching us. *He wants to see my "burst"—it's why he brought me here. People watching it can almost feel the acceleration.* "Robert, take the next rep! Let's go, number one!" Some of the players just call you "number one" when you're a first-round draft pick. It's not a compliment; it's just another way of saying, "Show us what you got!" *"Relax, relax...it's football...my first carry as a pro, though!....still just football, though...don't look nervous..."* "12 trap on two, ready, Break!" *Perfect!....straight up the middle!....got to burst...get the ball and go..."* "Blue fifteen, blue fifteen Hut!!!!" *"Get it, get it...Go!"* I could hear the astonished "wooos!" from the players who weren't in on the play. I knew they were impressed—this kid can really go. I stretched out my stride and got that feeling I loved so much...the wind racing by my helmet...the freedom...the exhilaration of fast movement. I could almost sense the smile inside Denny as he watched. He was probably thinking, "That's my man, he's gonna make me proud."

And I hoped that someday I would.

I made it through my first day of practice and thought, "I did it...it really happened: I'm a professional football player now."

Before any of that, though, I had to get back to Columbus and finish out the quarter at Ohio State. There was a marked change in the

80

way that people approached me. Before that time, I was "just" a college star. Now I truly was on a world-wide stage. The NFL is one of the most recognized symbols of sport in the world. People began to treat me with a kind of deference. To them it was as if I were a different person. I felt the same and I thought the same of myself, but people just made it seem as if it was now a big deal to meet me. I had had a taste of this playing for Ohio State, but it now took on a whole new dimension. I've always felt uncomfortable in those types of situations. I mean what do you say when a grown man comes up to you and says: "It's a real honor to meet you, sir?" There's this uncomfortable silence in which you fish for the words to fill in. It's not that I didn't think that what I had accomplished was impressive; it's just that it's still hard for me to believe how impressed some adult fans are to meet players. It's not as if I had cured cancer or rescued a baby from a burning building. We're just people, people with extraordinary athletic talent, but people nonetheless.

I headed to New Orleans with the track team for the NCAA championships. I had qualified once again in the 400-meter dash and as part of the 4x400 meter-relay team. I decided to concentrate on the 4x400 meter relay. The meet was being held at Tulane University and the meet organizers mercifully scheduled the running events later in the day to try to avoid the most oppressively humid hours. Ohio State was one of the favorites in the event that night, along with perennial track power Baylor. The wait for the start of the event was nerve-wracking. When they finally called us up for the race, we headed for the starting line, silently contemplating the next few minutes. It was going to be over in about a three minutes, and one team would be national champion. I would be running the third leg of the relay and handing off to our fastest runner on anchor. Baylor had decided to put its fastest runner on third leg to try to build an insurmountable lead heading into the final leg.

My stomach dropped as the gun went off. You haven't witnessed excitement until you've seen a world-class 4x400 race. The 4x100 is exciting, but it's over before you really have a chance to take in the experience. In a 4x400, you can recover from mistakes that are irrevocable in a shorter sprint. Each runner makes a complete lap of the track, then hands off the baton in a state of near-exhaustion. The athletes are pushed to the point of breaking and you can see the tension in their bodies and faces as they struggle down the home stretch. As Aaron Payne, our second leg runner (Rick Jones led off the relay), came off the final turn in first place, my mind had already taken the baton. *"This is it, it's up to you...if he doesn't move ahead of you, we win...we got it!"* I took the baton and sprinted as smoothly as I could. Now 400 meters is slightly longer than you can run at absolute full speed, but it's still a sprint. You have to train yourself to run at maximum speed, with minimum effort. It's a delicate balance.

I raced down the backstretch, seeming to barely touch the spongy, rubberized surface of the track. As I moved into the final straightaway, I could see Chris Nelloms ahead, frantically waving me on and the Baylor anchor doing the same for the runner who was creeping up to my outside. *"Finish!...this is ours!...this is you!...get it to him!"* I could hear the crowd getting louder. I knew the Baylor runner was getting close. My legs stiffened from the buildup of lactic acid and my lungs burned as they fought feverishly to supply my muscles with oxygen. As I leaned to hand the baton to Chris, the Baylor runner was handing off as well. Their anchor got off first and moved ahead of Chris. I stumbled to the infield and collapsed into an exhausted crouch. I was nauseated and weak, hardly able to even get my cheer out: "Let's go Chris!"

Chris was the fastest 400-meter runner on the track that day, so I felt good about our chances. But this was going to come down to the wire. Chris stayed in position behind the Baylor runner and then moved along side him as they came down to the finish. Chris started to pull ahead in the final 50 meters and I knew it was over! He crossed the finish line and the other two runners from the relay team and I joined him on the track. We shouted and hugged. We had won the national championship in 3:00.84 seconds, the fastest time in the world that year up to that point.

As the school quarter ended, I went to Minnesota for the Vikings' June mini-camp. This is a time when the offensive and defensive units work separately to develop their schemes. It was a much more relaxing atmosphere than the previous camp and I began to feel comfortable with the offense. I headed back to Columbus and continued to prepare for my first training camp. It was just a month away. We were reporting earlier than most teams that season because we were playing in one of the overseas games in the preseason.

In Columbus, I received my first NFL rookie football trading card. It had a picture of me from Ohio State. This is one of the most exciting times for an NFL rookie. These cards are a permanent reminder that you actually made it. I bought a few packs of cards when I was young, but I never collected them. I wouldn't lose these cards, though. I proudly distributed them to friends and family. Having a card transformed the experience of turning pro into reality. I had my football card now, but I still didn't have a contract; we had still not come to terms with the Vikings.

I took a trip to Disneyland with my girlfriend, but I still had to be extremely careful about what I spent. I didn't even have a credit card yet. I had always thought that I would never hold out of camp but, once again, facing the situation in my own life changed my perspective on the issue.

This becomes a very contentious issue for people outside of sports (see Chapter Ten). They wonder how you can hold out when you're offered all that money. The problem here is that people have no perspective on the problem. They don't understand the player's point of view. If they applied similar rationale to their own lives and jobs they'd have a better grasp of the situation. What would you say if your boss hired you at the same position as one of your co-workers but said that he was going to pay you a salary 5 percent lower? Let's say your co-worker gets paid $50,000. So your boss is offering you $47,500. Would you accept it because it's better than not having a job? Would you accept it because it's better than getting paid $40,000 or $10,000? Would you accept it because your boss said that he had hundreds of other less-qualified applicants willing to accept the job? Wouldn't that last remark be particularly insulting?

The problem is that people get lost in the numbers and forget the principals involved. The market dictates the value of any job. And if the market dictates that a running back is "worth" $500,000, why should he accept $475,000? It's hard to do, but to understand you have to try to forget about absolute dollars. Whether or not you feel a running back is "worth" $500,000 is irrelevant; it's the percentages that matter. Like any other business owner, people who own sports teams try to keep employee costs at a minimum. This is what contract negotiations are all about. Fans and outsiders seem to feel that pro athletes should accept "high" offers just because they're high in relation to other more important jobs. "Hell, I wish I could make $475,000!" Well, you can't!—not playing football at least. This is where the less-qualified applicant issue comes up. Sure, there are millions of people in the country who would accept $475,000 to play running back, but nobody wants to watch them. Professional athletes represent a unique workforce. They are in a high salary marketplace and they deserve to maximize their dollars within that framework. It was looking increasingly likely that I was going to be reporting to camp late in an attempt to get the best possible contract. The issue was more complicated than usual because it was the first year of the rookie salary cap. So, I would not only be making less money than the player picked at my position the previous season, but I'd also be taking less of it home because of the new tax laws. As I was soon to find out, missing a few days of training camp isn't the worst thing that can happen to a player.

Neil was getting closer to reaching a deal with the Vikings. One of the big sticking points was that Neil only wanted me to sign a two-year contract. Most first-rounders sign multi-year contracts to try to get the most money up front. However, with the new rookie salary cap, the amount of money you could make in later contract years would be greatly diminished with a long-term contract. Of course, the risk for the player is that he will get hurt or not perform well and be out all of the money that he would have received as a bonus. We thought it was a risk worth taking. The other first-round choice he was representing that year, Dana Stubblefield (49ers), and I were the only first-rounders to sign two-year contracts. I was still in Columbus the day the Vikings reported to camp. But the next day, Neil called me to give me the news I had been waiting three months to hear: "We're in agreement!" I was on my way to camp.

This time I was flying in coach. The team wasn't springing for first-class tickets anymore. It was like they were saying, "Wake up, rook, it's time to return to Earth."

I arrived to find that in one of the drills at practice the previous day, Terry Allen had sustained a season-ending knee injury. This obviously changed the complexion of the running back situation. We would be going into the season with only one back, Roger Craig, who had played in a regular-season game. The pressure on me to adjust quickly had increased dramatically.

I got to the dorms in Mankato, and took my stuff up to my room. A "rarefied atmosphere" is the way Denny Green described the environment at camp. Football is all you think about all day. It's similar to the way camp is in college except for the length of camp itself. You only spend about a week and half in camp in college. In the NFL you can spend up to five weeks in those grueling multiple-practice days. Thankfully, Denny was known to run one of the "kinder" camps in the league. We would never wear full pads twice in the same day. Some teams around the league wear full pads twice a day and pound the hell out of each other. Denny has always been considered a players' coach, and the description fits him well. He believes in conserving players' bodies. He understands the way your body gets worn down during those long summer days.

The thing that strikes you immediately when you walk onto an NFL practice field in the morning is the number of people who are there. Some of them are there just to get an early look at the team, but most are there to try to get autographs or a photo. These people get pretty crazy about this. They line up along the path where you walk in and out for practice pressed against a fence and they lean out with markers, desperately trying to get signatures. Some of the adults can get a little out of hand. They literally press these kids into the fence in order to get at their favorite players. "Robert! Sign this!" "Robert! Robert! Over here! This way! Buckeye fan here, Robert!" (That one always worked.) Sometimes you'd have to step back to ask the adults to stop pressing forward. Of course, the kids weren't always very polite, either. "Hey! Sign this! Smith! Smith!" And then they wouldn't even thank you. There would always be some shy kids standing silently with pens in their hands and their arms raised in the air. You'd feel bad for these kids and try to take care of them first. Poor kids, they'd probably never get one signed if you didn't just grab their pens and take care of it for them. Then you'd have the kids who were taught properly. "Would you please sign this for me, Mr. Smith?" It was refreshing to hear this. The autograph seekers were very persistent. They'd even follow you as you walked back towards the dorms. You'd be walking along the sidewalk and have this swarm of autograph-seekers blocking your way. As rookies, we were expected to handle the brunt of the autograph signing duties. Of course, as rookies we were expected to do a lot of things.

The veterans don't go out of their way to make you feel at home when you're a rookie. You basically do your best to stay out of their way. You're expected to be in the locker room and get taped before they even arrive, so you find yourself hurrying around most of the day. You're also responsible for providing some lunchtime entertainment with your best "American Idol" imitations. You're uncomfortable in this environment to begin with, and they give you the added anxiety of standing up at lunchtime to expose your weak singing voice. You do get to choose your own song, but this hardly eases your nerves. For my first song, I thought I'd deliver a little message about what I was thinking at the time. I chose "People Are Strange," a Jim Morrison classic. The white guys loved it, but I got a few puzzled looks from the black guys. I've always had very diverse tastes in music, and I had the widest range of songs for the veterans that camp. I sang everything from the Doors to Heatwave ("Always and Forever"). Practice itself went well. Of course, before you get to the practice field on a hot summer day, you have to make a stop to apply some bug spray. Some people say that mosquitoes should be the state bird in Minnesota. They were brutal and it was an especially bad year because of all the floods in the state that spring. Some of the players just considered the bug spray to be like salad dressing for the mosquitoes, but it helped a little.

I was adjusting to the speed and violence of the game. You don't really get hit any harder in the pros than you do in college, but you do receive a greater number of hits. The defensive players are so fast and agile that more of them get to the play than in college. You end up getting hit with a great deal of force from multiple directions. This gets you pretty sore.

The training room starts to fill up pretty quickly after a few days of camp. There's always a group of players waiting to get into one of the cold tubs. The cold tub was a very special experience. You crouch down into one of these tubs that have water at about 50 degrees (you realize what real shrinkage is all about!). It could be shocking for the first couple of minutes but it helped with the soreness. It's good that there was something to help because getting out of bed after a few days of practice was quite a task. They have these kids who volunteer to help out during camp that go around pounding on the doors starting at 6:30. You wanted to strangle them! Then you have all these players shuffling gingerly towards the bathrooms trying to get the sleep out of their systems. Everyone starts to get tired of just practicing against each other. We were ready to take out our frustrations on another team. We didn't have to wait too long… it was time to play.

People often use the phrase "words cannot describe." Of course, what they really mean is that an event or experience is so rich and colorful with vivid detail and emotion that words cannot do it justice. Game days are one of those events.

As we approached Texas Stadium near Dallas for what would be my first taste of NFL football, it really began to sink in for me. This had been the stomping ground for a long list of NFL legends. This had been the site of championship games that sent "America's Team" on its way to the NFL's biggest and brightest stage. I looked around the bus. I could tell that all my fellow rookies felt the same way I did; it was like a scene from a movie. When I first caught sight of the stadium, it occurred to me that in a couple of hours I would be doing something that millions of people could only visualize in their wildest dreams: I would be playing professional football in one of the most storied athletic venues in the world. To the veteran players on the bus, it was just another pre-season game. To me and the rest of the rookies, it would be the first opportunity to prove that we were worthy of being considered among the best players in the world.

The bus pulled up to the stadium, passing scattered groups of fans—Vikings' faithful holding up thumbs and Cowboys' faithful holding up middle fingers. A collection of security guards pointed the driver towards the visitor's tunnel. The players and staff rose to exit the bus. We filed slowly off towards the locker room. My legs felt as though they had no intention of carrying me towards my locker, let alone run, once I got on the field.

Game time was still a couple of hours away so I just put on some shorts and a t-shirt. I walked into the vast emptiness of Texas Stadium, and it struck me how small the field seemed. When you're sitting at home watching a game on TV, the field seems to stretch for miles. When you stand on the field in an empty stadium, it is dwarfed by the stands that rise like canyon walls on all sides.

When I got back to my locker, I began to put on the rest of my gear. It fit tight. But then, it had to. Whether you're on offense or defense, you don't want the opposition to have anything extra to grab. I found myself continually looking over towards the clock, fully aware that the time for us to go on the field was approaching. I thought of a story one of my history teachers told me about soldiers preparing for battle. They busied themselves with such menial tasks as shaving and shining their shoes. They did this to keep themselves from going crazy thinking about the peril they soon were to face. As I looked around, I could see players involved in diversionary actions. Some listened to music on their headphones, some read, some just quietly stretched. Very few spoke or laughed and these few stopped as game time approached. The emotions one feels in the locker room prior to a game range from nervous anticipation to frenzied excitement. The silent preparation is then broken by intermittent shouts and hoots as players release some tension.

Coaches also can be seen pacing silently and nervously. Of course, coaches must deal with the fact that they cannot directly impact the course of a game. You've heard them blamed for what transpires on the field, but in all my years of playing, I never once saw them on the field during a play. A referee poked his head into the locker room and said, "Two minutes, Coach." Coach Green then walked towards the center of the locker room and began to tell us one final time about the task at hand: "You're all here for a reason. If I didn't think you had a chance to make the team, your ass wouldn't be here. Know your role, accept your role and be the best at your role! Let's go out and play Minnesota Vikings football, because when we play, like we play, when we play, nobody can touch us! Let's get a prayer…" Then we took a knee in the center of the room and held hands. We recited the Lord's Prayer and then sat motionless as some continued to pray. Coach Green then said "Let's go men!" and we were on our way.

As we walked down the tunnel towards the field in a tightly packed group, the noise in the stadium began to rise. I could feel the energy and exhilaration flowing down from the stands and into each and every one of us. Then came the moment of magic that I wish everyone in the world could experience. I'll never forget the first time I jogged into the light of the stadium with all of the spectators in the stands. You are almost overwhelmed by the explosion of light, color, and sound. Even being on the road, with the fans booing us, was an awesome spectacle. All of the sweat, all of the hard work and preparation came down to the moment when the reality of the game was suddenly upon me. This was the game I watched as a youth. This was the game that thousands of college players wished they could be a part. This was the game that millions of Americans watched. It was actually happening to me.

My nerves calmed down. This was, after all, the game I had been playing since I was 12. I stood on the sideline and watched the first half, never once getting into the game, but impressed by the violent action nonetheless. After halftime, it would be my turn…and my nerves began to unsettle once again. Ty Willingham, our running back coach, said, "Robert, you're in the next series!" I could barely think straight.

All right, remember your training—wait a second, it's just a game—a game I'm good at…hell, they drafted me in the first round…they must've known what they were doing… get out there and do it…OK, OK, here we go…be calm… get to the huddle—wait, which side of the huddle do I line up on?—opposite the quarterback....man I wonder if everyone feels like this?" The quarterback called out the play, "Spread right, scat right" *"That's all I need to know—protection first, protect the quarterback...if no one blitzes I'll release."* The huddle broke and for a moment I had the sense that I was back at Ohio State. *"No big deal, man, you know how to do this."* "Green twenty-four, green twenty-four....seeet hut!" The snap of the football also snapped me into the realization that this was not Ohio State anymore! The players moved with impossible speed and incredible agility. Their movements blended into a rapidly changing tapestry of color, and that was the key—color! Although it is difficult to distinguish individuals in that blaze of motion during plays, you could immediately differentiate color—avoid hitting your color if you're blocking and avoid their color if you're running. It's definitely an oversimplification of the issue, but it helped. When they first called a running play with me in the huddle, my stomach instantly dropped. *"Okay, step with my left foot, get downhill, read the block of the tackle."* It happened so fast, I couldn't even remember if I had done it right when I got back to the huddle. All I know is that I was hit quickly—and hard. We had live drills during camp, but this was different. They were shooting real bullets now and defenders came at you with an insatiable desire to knock something loose from you—either the ball or your head.

I settled down and started to feel more comfortable. This wasn't so bad after all.

We flew back to Minneapolis after the game and prepared for an overseas trip to Berlin. This was going to be my first trip out of the country. I had been a history major in college and this trip was going to give me an opportunity to see one of the most important historical cities of the twentieth century. I felt amazingly at ease when I got off the plane in Berlin. My mother's father was a first generation German and I spoke German, so it was almost a homecoming. We were all tired after the long flight but the rookies were responsible for the entertainment at breakfast. I think I sang a little Temptations tune. Denny wanted us to stay awake to get a practice in before we all went to sleep. We practiced in an area right next to Olympic Stadium. Hitler had marched his troops on those same fields.

The sense of history was overwhelming. It had been almost 60 years since Jesse Owens had run in that stadium. He took on Hitler's "master race" before the rest of the world even opened its eyes to the cruel intentions of that madman. Hitler took power with his propaganda that told the apocryphal tale of a great Aryan race that had once occupied Germany. The 1936 Olympics were going to be the showcase for his "master race" of athletes. Jesse Owens went on to win four gold medals.

In the game that weekend, I got the opportunity to showcase my speed. I broke off a couple of long runs and began to feel like I was making a good case to become the starter. While watching one of the long runs in film study, Cris Carter said, "You can't coach that!" I wasn't much of a physical specimen for a running back, but I had the speed that few players in the league could match. I was showing that I could take hits, but the question was, could I handle it during the course of a regular-season NFL schedule? I was going to have the chance to show it soon enough; the regular season was only a few weeks away.

The roster cuts opened my eyes to how brutal the competitive world of the NFL could be. These guys had worked their butts off in camp the previous weeks and their thank you was a pink slip. I never got cut during my career, but it must be an awful feeling. Some guys get their hopes dashed after having given so much of themselves. The sad look and slow walk of these players displays their feelings of rejection. Some of them will get another chance, but not all of them. There just aren't enough jobs for everyone in the NFL. For some of them, the NFL dream is over, but they have made it farther than most ever do. Among the cuts that year was a quarterback named Rich Gannon, who later went on to start for the Oakland Raiders. Rich is proof that you just have to keep believing in yourself, and that even the best coaches sometimes don't make the best personnel decisions.

As a send-off to training camp, the rookies put on a show the last night. You get together that week and plan little skits to entertain the rest of the team. Everyone downs a few beers before the show, so the atmosphere is pretty lively. The show is always fun to watch because it's a time when the rookies get to take some shots at the other players and the coaching staff. Of course, you don't want to get too out of hand with the way you poke fun at the people who decide your future. Players usually end up using this opportunity on stage to imitate their position coaches. Ty Willingham is known to have a classic case of the Napoleonic syndrome. He's a pint-sized general who can drive just about anybody to madness with his meticulous attention to detail. I got together with a couple of the other running backs and we did a skit in which Ty was grading the way in which we ate our breakfast. "Alright, Robert, watching this film I see that you only chewed your cereal an average of fifteen times! That's a critical error! You could have choked to death and cost us a game!" We got some good laughs! We decided not to bring in any strippers and it's a good thing, because some rookies tried it a couple of years later and got an earful!

It was tough being a rookie, but the transition was also liberating. It was the first time in my life that I was really on my own. Even though I had a roommate in the dorm, I was responsible for setting everything up by myself. I had to get my own place, and pay my own bills. I was earning a living and in control of the path my life took. It was the independence that I had always wanted—and there's no greater feeling in the world than to know that you're in charge of your life and that you're happy with what you're doing with it. I don't care how much money you make, if you're not happy with what you're doing, then you won't be a happy person.

The atmosphere in the locker room is so much different than what you experience in college. There's a mutual respect between players and staff. Even something as simple as calling a coach by his first name makes you feel as if you're on equal footing. In college there's a separation between players and coaches. They're in charge and you do as you're told. In the NFL, you're all operating on the same level; coaches and players are all trying to accomplish the same thing. Denny was always different for me, though. A few players called him Denny, but I wasn't one of them. I'll be calling him Coach until the day I die. It's a tough mentality to change.

Our first regular-season game was against the Raiders in Los Angeles. My mother and brother flew out to watch. This was the real thing now…no more pre-season tune-ups. College football is big, but making it in the NFL represents one of the biggest achievements in all of sports. I was proud of what I had done, but I knew that I had work to do. My first real game had arrived and I couldn't help but think about how well things had gone for me in my high school and college debuts. Just like those games, I wouldn't be starting but I would have a chance to get in before the day was done.

We won the toss, which meant that I would be out on the field for the game's first play. I'd be back as one of the two kickoff returners. *"You're in it now…get something done!"* The kicker raised his hand and nodded to the other members of the kickoff team. He started towards the ball, and my world seemed to shift into slow motion. He kicked the ball and it floated slowly in my direction. *"Here it comes!"* I yelled out: "Me! Me! Me!" to the other returner. It was a short kick and I had to run forward to get under it. It seemed as if I was either going to come up short or be at a full sprint to catch the ball. I thought it seemed like a better idea to just let the ball bounce and then field it. Kickoffs are live balls, so I needed to make sure that I got it quickly after the bounce. But it hit the grass and bounced forward into the leg of one of the up men and there was a mad scramble for the ball. The Raiders had recovered. Welcome to the NFL, Robert! So much for a shining debut!

The Raiders took the ball in for a score. So there it was: I had misplayed the ball on my first NFL play and it caused us to go down 7-0 on the road in the first minutes of the game. It was a pretty inauspicious debut. They did trust me enough to put me back on kickoffs, but I didn't get in at running back until the game was pretty much out of hand. I didn't light the world on fire at running back, but I didn't play poorly, either. The damage had been done, though. We lost. Denny must have thought I wasn't ready because of my early miscue. Needless to say, it was a long flight home.

That next morning, Denny walked in for film review looking like a father who was disappointed with the behavior of his children. I felt like

93

a kid again; I wanted to keep my head down to avoid making eye contact. Denny is the kind of coach who always commands the respect of his players. He seems to be the type of guy who would gladly step right out on the field to struggle right alongside you. Players want to win for a guy like that. It's part of what makes him such a successful coach. The first thing we did in those team meetings was watch the special teams film from the previous day. The entire team watches this film together before breaking up to study as offensive and defensive units. And there it was! "All right men! We know we got to get those! We can't afford to make mistakes like that!" I felt like I had let him down. I felt like I had let the whole team down.

There's nowhere to hide when you screw up in professional football. The reporters have free reign of the locker room for most of the morning, so they just kind of hover around the lockers like vultures ready to swoop down for a piece of carrion. "Do you think you should have tried to get the ball?" "I thought it was a bad idea to catch it in a dead sprint, but I screwed up!" People call athletes temperamental when they see these kinds of outbursts. You have all these people second-guessing an action that you needed to decide in a split second. Sure, it's part of your job, but you get sick of hearing people tell you "you should have done this, or that" when they've never had to make those types of decisions. It's real easy to use hindsight to make the "right" decisions.

To make matters worse, I received a notice in my locker that week from the league that warned me about my socks. It said that I had too large a section of purple on my socks and that I would be fined $5,000 if I repeated the offense. The socks you wear are one-piece and are supposed to have a certain proportion of white showing on them. I think the rule states that you need to have white up to your calf and then your team color up to your knee. I didn't pick the socks that I wore and I certainly wasn't aware that they weren't up to standard. I made a trip to see the team's equipment manager after receiving the letter. The NFL has a strict uniform policy, but it gives you a warning before it takes your money. It's pretty crazy sometimes, though. There's a rule that you need to have your jersey tucked in at the start of plays. During the course of some drives, my jersey would pull out in the back and the ref would come over and warn me. You're out there sucking wind and some ref is telling you that you don't look neat enough.

All I could do was go home and think about how I had messed up my first opportunity to show my readiness. It was strange to go home after practice and not really have anything to do. It's not like they assign you homework. My girlfriend lived back in Columbus and I really didn't feel like running the streets, so I just ended up staying at home and reading most nights. I think I read about 10 books that first season. This is where a lot of players get themselves into trouble. All of a sudden they get all of this free time and money and they just kind of go nuts. It's the first time that most of us had so much time to ourselves—and the money to make that time really interesting. Some of the rookies end up staying out all night trying to make the most of their celebrity. And the groupies find you real fast. They know more about you than most of your teammates. I wanted to concentrate on my job. Being out late getting chased by groupies wasn't going to help me on the field.

Staying in and reading certainly didn't help get me on the field those first few weeks, either. I only played sparingly and that was mostly in third-down situations. It could have been worse for me, though; at least I had a job. Our offensive coordinator wasn't so lucky. Denny fired him after only two games. He also decided to bring in some experience at the running back position by signing Barry Word. My chances of getting playing time weren't looking good. The 1993 season was the last NFL season to have two byes. Both of our byes came in the first six weeks of the season. Bye weeks are a nice chance to heal yourself and get away from football for a few days. It was a little early in the season for any of us to be too banged up (especially me), but it was nice to get back home for a few days.

Even though I hadn't been playing, I still was treated like a celebrity when I got back to Columbus. I felt embarrassed because I hadn't been playing and, yet, these people still thought it was the coolest thing in the world to meet me and get my autograph. It was flattering, but I didn't think I deserved the attention. This was the first time in my career that I wasn't a major contributor to my team.

Still, my weekend at home left me energized and it was a good thing, because Denny felt it was time to give me a shot at the starting job. I was the only first-rounder that year who had not seen significant playing time and the local media made sure I knew about it. "I'll be ready to contribute in any way I can," I said. It's easy to be humble when you haven't done a thing. There was nothing I could do to take back the mistake I made in that first game. You have to put things like that behind you if you want to be successful in sports. I think the same applies for other walks of life, as well. You can't worry yourself about the things you may have screwed up in the past. And you can't be successful if you paralyze yourself with the fear that you may make mistakes in the future. We're all going to make mistakes. It's how we respond to them that determines whether or not we succeed. Ty told me that the upcoming Monday night game against Chicago was going to be my coming-out party.

Monday Night Football is an America tradition. It's a television event. Year in and year out, week in and week out, it's one of the most highly rated shows on television. All of the other games for the week are finished and the entire focus of the league turns to that week's final contest. The world is watching and you want to be at your best.

As our bus approached Soldier Field that night, I could sense the history of the place. Soldier Field looks like the Coliseum in Rome. The stately columns surrounding the field add to the feeling of history— Gale Sayers, Walter Payton, Dick Butkus; they all called that field home.

As I sat in the locker room, I struggled to control my racing mind: *"Just a game, just a game...this is why you play...this is what you've dreamed about...know the plays...no mistakes...Ty says there's no such thing as an accident...get it and go..."*

As we stood in the tunnel waiting to take the field, a strange calm came over me. I began to realize that this was natural for me—big game, bright lights. It was time to distinguish myself— not just as a player, but as a great player. The great ones always find a way when it matters most. I knew I wasn't going to start the game, but I also knew it wouldn't be long before I got in. Once the game started I couldn't wait for my chance… "Get ready, Robert, you're in the next series." My heart began to race… *"don't lose it now…settle down!"*

I jogged onto the field and joined the huddle. There I was: 21 years old, in the huddle of a professional football team on Monday Night Football in Soldier Field. I stood in the huddle and looked over at our quarterback, Jim McMahon. He had won a Super Bowl with the Bears, but now he was facing the team he had led to victory. On the first series, I almost broke one… a six-yard gain. There was a rush of adrenaline I felt when I would break free that gave me an almost overwhelming sense of exhilaration.

On the next series, we advanced the ball to the Chicago 21 and the call came in. "Spread right, 12 trap on one, ready? Break!" It was for me. Time slowed down. I saw the best angle to take. I knew what my speed could do. *"Wow! They're coming to congratulate you! Gotta keep this ball!"* I had broken through the line, cut to the left sideline, and outrun the safety. My first game on Monday Night produced my first touchdown.

I sat on the sideline receiving congratulations from my teammates, wondering if everyone at home saw it…wondering if I had set the VCR. In the end, we won 19-12. I felt so relieved on the plane ride home. That weight had been lifted. I was no longer a first-round bust. I would score 31 more rushing touchdowns in my career. But none of them were as special as that sprint to the corner on that cool and crisp October night in Chicago.

My mother still has that ball sitting in her library. I didn't spike that one or any other ball in my career; it's not my style. I understand that players get excited after scoring, but spiking the ball always seemed an unnecessary taunt to our opponents. I had a great deal of respect for the other people I played against. It's not that I liked all of them personally, but I felt they deserved a little respect.

Whenever our quarterback threw an interception, we'd try to take their heads off on the tackle. It was like a personal affront. I'm sure defenders felt the same way when they were trying to tackle me, so I didn't feel the need to fuel their primal rage. The game is rarely over after a touchdown anyway (except in overtime) so why not wait until the end of the game for a big celebration? I would look to celebrate with my teammates after a touchdown. They are the ones who got me there in the first place. It kills me to see players running around acting foolish after touchdowns. I'm not saying don't celebrate. I just think they should act like what they are—professionals. Act as if you've been there before and you'll be there again.

A locker room is a completely different world following a victory—as you might well imagine. Everyone's smiling and laughing and talking about the previous day's (or night's) action. The coaches are just as transparent with their feelings. They bounce around the facility and tell jokes, just like the players. It's a festive atmosphere. Denny would come in all smiles, with a bag of goodies for the offensive, defensive, and special teams players of the game. After the Bears game, I sat there cautiously optimistic that this would be my first game ball. "Okay," Denny said, "Offensive game ball. Made some big plays for us, scored his first NFL touchdown [I must have looked like a five-year-old at his birthday party], "Robert Smith!" I walked up and shook his hand. I felt like I had finally arrived.

Denny decided not to start me the following week against Detroit, but I got a lot of playing time. It was clear that Denny wanted to allow me time to adjust to a starting role. I'm sure that it was the same old fragility issue. He obviously thought enough of me as a player to draft me, but he probably still wondered if I could withstand the pounding that a starting running back must endure. At a shade under 6'2" I only weighed 197 at the time. I was plenty strong, but I definitely did not fit the standard mold for running backs. Some in the media even referred to me as a "dinosaur," claiming that my body style had become extinct for running backs. Dinosaur or not, it didn't seem to bother me much against Detroit. I had my first 100-yard game and scored another touchdown in a losing effort. I was exhausted after the game. I didn't feel right. I thought something had to be wrong with me. I was right.

I went in to see the trainers and team doctors and they discovered that I had chicken pox. I never had them when I was a kid and I had recently visited Children's Hospital in Minneapolis. Bingo! Getting the chicken pox is much more dangerous for adults. It can lead to severe complications, even death. Sure enough, by the middle of the week I was in the hospital. I was supposed to make my first start that weekend, but things weren't looking good for me by the time Friday rolled around. I got out of the hospital and headed to the facility, but I was still very weak. Of course, my teammates thought the whole thing was extremely funny. They would stop walking and stand close to the walls whenever I walked by.

When Sunday arrived, I was still feeling pretty lousy. I also still had some pox marks on my face. To keep some separation between the pox and my helmet, they had me wear a cold-weather mask. The added heat from the mask made me even more uncomfortable. I tired very quickly that day, despite playing only sparingly in the first half. I didn't play at all in the second half. I was embarrassed that I wasn't able to contribute because of something that seemed so trivial. We ended up losing the game, and we faced a tough road challenge the following week against Denver.

I started to feel much better that week and looked forward to getting back on the field at full strength. I woke up that Saturday morning excited to get on the plane for Denver. As I turned to look at my clock, my head suddenly began to spin. I had to run to the bathroom to keep from throwing up on my bedroom floor. Now what? I couldn't keep my head in a vertical position without feeling nauseous. I got dressed and drove to the facility with my head held at a slanted angle. I must have looked pretty funny driving down the road. I got to the facility and ran to the training room to throw up. I laid down on one of the training tables and stayed there for a couple of hours. They ended up taking me to the hospital again, and I missed the team plane to Denver. I remained in the hospital overnight for observations. I had developed an infection in my inner ear that was causing problems with my equilibrium. I got up the next morning feeling somewhat better. Team doctors thought it made sense to try to get me to Denver for the game. It was not one of their better ideas; the change in pressure on the plane wreaked havoc with my inner ear problem. By the time I got to Denver, I was feeling terrible again. When I got to the locker room I threw up again. I lay down on one of the training room tables and I ended up staying there the entire game. The flight home was as pleasant as the trip in. The doctors apologized to me when we got back, but I knew it hadn't been their sole decision to send me. I'm sure they got pressure from the coaches. The conflict between what's best for the player and what's best for the team is as old as football itself. Unfortunately, the players' best interests usually lose out.

I practiced that week, but the team decided not to fly me to Tampa the following weekend. A week later, however, I was feeling strong again and was ready to make my first start, against the New Orleans Saints. After everything I had been through the previous weeks, I felt I could handle anything. I had the confidence of the coaches and I was ready to take the next big step as an NFL player. I was comfortable in my new role as the number one guy now. I did get a bit rattled at one point when Ty came up to me and said, "Robert, you're on punt return. A.P.'s down!" Anthony Parker, our regular punt returner, had just been injured while playing defensive back. Our normal second returner didn't dress that week, so I was left as the only returner. I hadn't done that since the preseason.

There's a huge difference between returning kickoffs and returning punts. You've got much more time and much more distance between yourself and the coverage teams on a kickoff than you do on a punt. This is especially true in the NFL. Many kickers are capable of kicking the ball high enough that their own players would be able to run downfield and catch it. They must allow you a three-yard cushion to enable you to catch the ball, but it still can be pretty intimidating—especially when you've never done it in a regular-season game. I had already proven how difficult it could be to try to return a ball for the first time! The first couple of times I was kicked to, the ball was kicked too high to try to get a return so I ended up calling for a fair catch. The last time I got kicked to, I figured I'd just try to return one. It was another high kick and I could see the coverage team was right on top of me. I caught the ball, made one guy miss, and then got buried. I think I got three yards on the return.

I ended up rushing for 94 yards in a losing effort. More than at any other time that season, I felt as if I belonged. I was a starter and I was playing well. I felt as if I was finally justifying my draft position. It was going to be a tight race for us to make it to the playoffs, but I felt that we would make it and that I would be a major contributor. We traveled to Detroit that following week to play the Lions. It was clear from the start of the game that Denny wanted to feature me on offense. I was the go-to guy on our first couple of series. I was taking handoffs and catching balls out of the backfield. I was showing that I could be a complete featured back. Everything seemed to be falling in place nicely for us as a team and for me personally. And then it happened.

CHAPTER FIVE

SISYPHUS

Oh Fortuna   Oh Fate,
Velut Luna   Like the Moon,
Semper Variabilis! You are ever changing!
                  – Opening line from the opera,
                        Carmina Burana, Carl Orff

It was a routine play…the kind you see at least 10 times in every game. I was lined up by myself in the backfield and I swung out toward the sideline at the snap. Jim McMahon threw the ball to me. I caught it and started running up the right sideline. One of the linebackers was running towards me and I leaned into him as I planted my right leg (on replay, I saw that I actually was out of bounds). The force of the linebacker's hit rotated my upper body over my right leg. The torque was more than my body could handle. You hear players talk about the pop they feel when they tear ligaments in their body, but you don't realize what it feels like until you experience it. Let me tell you: It's a horrible sound. And it's a horrible feeling to instantly know what the sound means. I went flying out of bounds and dropped the ball, immediately grabbing for my right knee. The pain of realizing what had happened was far worse than the physical pain that shot through my right leg like a bolt of lightning. I lay on the ground, holding my knee and rocking back and forth in agony.

"No! No!...Not this! Not now! Goddamit! It's gone!" Cris Carter came over to me and said, "Stay down, stay down." His instructions weren't difficult to follow. I lay there until the trainers arrived and I told them what I felt. "All right, let's get you up," Fred Zamberletti said. Zamberletti and Chuck Barta were the trainers and they each leaned down putting an arm under each of my underarms to help me up. The cheer from the crowd actually made me feel a little better. Let's face it, many people love the violence of football, but most fans don't want to see players get hurt. And most players don't like to see it, either. I hobbled across the field with the trainers. Chris Spielman, a former Buckeye who played linebacker for Detroit, came over and said, "You'll be all right, man." It sure as hell didn't feel like I would at that point, but I appreciated his concern. When we got to the sideline, the players moved away from us as if my injury were somehow contagious. There's nothing worse than watching helplessly as one of your teammates is being helped off of the field. It's a cruel reminder of the capricious nature of the game.

On the bench, the team orthopedist did some preliminary tests. He was very careful not to further damage my already swollen and disfigured knee. "Let's get him into the locker room," he said. His tone seemed to confirm my worst fears. Scotty Graham, another Vikings running back I had played with at Ohio State, came over and offered me some encouragement. "You're gonna be all right, Juice," he said. (Scotty had nicknamed me Juice my freshman year in college because I wore the same number, 32, that O.J. Simpson had worn and because I ran with a long striding gait similar to the former NFL great). I was in a daze. I'd never had an injury this serious. I was just getting into my groove as a player and now my season would be over. Not only that, but I knew I'd have to have surgery and go through a lengthy rehabilitation process to get back on the field.

They put me on a Detroit Lions' helmet cart and we drove towards the locker room, passing the area of the stadium where they seated visiting family members. Some of my friends who were at the game later told me that they had never seen such a sad look on somebody's face. When we got to the locker room, one of the players who wasn't dressed for the game helped me to my locker. I felt like a feeble old man. I gingerly took off my uniform and hobbled into the shower. As I showered I looked down at my grotesquely swollen knee. I walked slowly back to my locker and put on some shorts and a T-shirt. I waited on a training table in a small room until the doctor got back for the halftime break. The doctor put both hands on my lower right leg, just below the knee. He pushed gently. The laxity in the joint was the final confirmation. "You've got a torn ACL," he said. I lay back on the table and cried.

I had torn my ACL and cracked the bottom of my thighbone. I had some experience with anatomy and orthopedics, so I knew the injury would not threaten my career. As a matter of fact, players who have the operation performed by a good surgeon often can come back as strong as ever; a strong rehab commitment also is vital. Leroy Burrell, a United States sprint and jump Olympian, tore his ACL and later went on to set the world record in the 100 meter-dash. My agent, Neil Cornrich, fixed me up with Dr. Richard Steadman in Vail, Colorado. "He's the best in the world," Neil said. "Cheer up! Life is good! [Neil's favorite phrase] You've got some money, you've got some time off and you'll be ready for next season!" My attitude instantly changed. I was actually more excited about returning than I was concerned about the injury or the surgery.

The ACL, or anterior cruciate ligament, is one of two ligaments that "cross" (hence the term cruciate, derived from the Latin word crux which means cross) inside of the knee. The other ligament is called the posterior cruciate. Together, these ligaments help to stabilize the knee joint. The anterior and posterior ligaments keep the knee from hyperextending and hyper-flexing. The reason that the ACL tears more frequently is that the knee has less mobility in extending than in flexing (it's like bending your knee the wrong way). Knees were definitely not intended to withstand the pounding of pro football. The problem is exacerbated by artificial turf surfaces, which do not allow the foot to give way and take some of the pressure off of the knee. I really can't say that I'm against artificial surfaces. They do provide a consistent playing surface week in and week out when they're properly maintained. For a guy who relied on speed and maneuverability more than sheer strength, it was worth the extra cuts and bruises. Some of those fields were pretty hard. It would be like playing on your living room carpet, placed over concrete. Technologies are being developed that will allow artificial surface to have both the consistency and speed of a classic turf field, combined with the softness and give of a grass field.

I went in that night for an MRI (magnetic resonance image) to determine the exact extent of the injury. When I got to the facility the next day, I informed the team orthopedic doctor (David Fischer) that I wanted the films sent for Dr. Steadman to review. There can be some hard feelings when players decide to go see a doctor outside of the organization, but it is usually in the player's best interests. You have a right to see your doctor of choice (thanks to some negotiating by the players' association) and have the team pay for it. It ends up being like a workman's comp claim. Most teams have competent doctors on staff, and Minnesota is one of those teams. But why not go for the best? This decision impacts your career in a very real sense. The problem here is that many of the players don't understand their rights and sometimes feel pressured by the team to use the organization's medical staff. The union and its representatives have made a concerted effort to focus on player safety issues and to ensure that players' know their rights when it comes to a choice of doctors.

You rely on your body to function at its peak when you're a professional athlete. Thus, it's vital to seek the very best treatment. After all, you don't take a Ferrari to a Jiffy Lube.

I was amazed at how much better my knee felt already. It really wasn't very swollen in appearance, but it did have some swelling on the inside of the joint. I could tell this immediately when I tried to do some range-of-motion drills. Dr. Steadman prefers to wait at least a couple of weeks following an injury to allow the swelling to go down inside of the joint. This allows the joint to settle down and gives him the best chance to have a successful result. I would be nearly fully recovered by the time camp started, so it didn't make any sense to rush things along. I was more concerned about my long-term health, so I knew that this was the best approach. I would go into the training room and work to get as much flexibility in the joint as I could.

When you have an injury like that, it changes your life. An athlete depends on his body for his livelihood and when you become seriously injured, your body just isn't the same. You can't do things you want to do. You are truly less than your full self. I knew that I was more than "just" a football player, but it was obviously a huge part of who I was. I couldn't run. I couldn't jump. I wasn't the me that I once was…and it bothered me. I knew that I'd work hard and make it back, but for the time being I had to walk around very gingerly with a body that couldn't function the way I wanted it to. The physical aspect of being injured is difficult, but the psychological battle can be just as daunting.

You're not really even a part of the team at that point. You go over to the facility and sit in on some of the meetings, but you know that you won't have any real part in wins or losses. You go in and out of the training room for treatment and then you go home while the team is still practicing. You feel a sense of isolation that is heightened by your inability to perform your job. Your physical ability is intimately tied to your profession. It's somewhat akin to a singer losing his voice. The other players try to keep your spirits up, but at that point in the process there's not much they can say to make you feel better. You're in a holding pattern, and until you land on that operating table, you're no closer to getting back to where you want to be.

There were some moments of amusement from the injury, though. You sometimes forget that you're injured and move in a way that your body doesn't care for—and you find out real fast. I was walking around my apartment one day and got my right foot caught up in a phone cord. My cat-like reflexes worked faster than my dog-like mind and I jerked my leg up quickly. The pain was excruciating. I must have sworn loud enough for everyone in Bloomington to hear me! There was another very painful reminder of my infirmity when I received a visit from my girlfriend around Christmas. We were putting up a Christmas tree and I wanted to get a shot of it with my camcorder. I leaned down onto my right knee and bent it past the point it could handle. I instantly shot up in pain and went into another round of loud expletives. The great part about this incident is that I have it on tape. Every time I see it I feel like

I'm watching a horror film: "Don't do it! Don't bend down! Awww—you idiot!"

Three weeks passed and it was time for me to head to Vail. I had intended to go alone, but my mother would have none of that. She was concerned for her little boy. We arrived in Vail the day before I was scheduled to have surgery.

I was amazed at what a nice person Dr. Steadman was. This guy is "the man" when it comes to knee surgery. Universities and hospitals from all over the world invite him to speak and perform surgeries. He is the Olympic ski team surgeon, the team arthropod for the Denver Broncos, and he's operated on everyone from Dan Marino to Terrell Davis. His list of achievements could fill a book by themselves, but you'd never know it to meet him. He's my favorite kind of person: truly humble, truly successful.

Dr. Steadman knew I had an interest in medicine so he went into quite a bit of detail about the procedure. He also gave me the option for anesthetics. Of course, I wanted to be awake to watch the carnage, so he recommended an epidural. He prefers that people be awake so they're lucid after surgery. Dr. Steadman is very aggressive when it comes to rehab so he likes his patients to be ready to move around the same day. I went back to the condo with my mom and tried to get some sleep. I really didn't sleep well that night—partly from anxiety and partly because I still had a little trouble breathing in the 8,000-foot altitude. It absolutely amazes me that Sherpas can climb Mt. Everest past 29,000 feet without the aid of supplemental oxygen.

The next morning, I was excited to see what it was going to be like. They brought me a shaving kit and told me to shave from the middle of my thigh to the middle of my shin. The anesthesiologist came in the room and prepared me for my epidural. I've never had too much trouble with needles, but when he had me curl up on my side and prepared to stab that thing into my back, I got a little apprehensive, even after being slightly sedated. Once the medication started to kick in, I could feel my legs getting very "heavy." In a matter of minutes I couldn't even raise them a couple of inches. It's a very bizarre feeling to lose control of your body like that.

They wheeled me into the operating room and hoisted my left leg up into the air. They put a screen in place to keep me from looking directly at the knee. I could watch some of the operation on a TV screen on the wall. I could feel the pressure of their movements and feel my leg moving around, but I didn't feel any pain—thankfully! Dr. Steadman was performing a patellar tendon graft. In this procedure, he cuts a sliver from the patellar tendon (the large tendon that you can feel just below your knee cap) and he uses this as a replacement ligament. He attaches the new "ligament" to the tibia and femur with screws. The entire procedure only took about 2½ hours. Immediately after surgery, my repaired leg was placed into a "constant passive motion" machine, or CPM. These devices automatically bend and straighten your leg to preset values. This quickens the healing process by keeping the knee joint from stiffening.

I was in the rehab room six hours after being out of surgery. They want you to gain confidence in the knee as quickly as possible. On the first night, they just had me bend and straighten the knee with the aid of my healthy leg. You sit on the edge of a table and pull your repaired leg back with your healthy leg. You're still heavily bandaged and have a number of tubes sticking out of your knee to drain extraneous blood and other fluids. You feel a little hesitant to bend the knee too far. The pressure makes it feel as if your knee is going to pop. It was scary at first. That night was the last time I used my crutches. I had to wear a bulky brace, but I was allowed to bear as much weight as I could tolerate.

I flew to Cleveland with my mother a couple of days later. The Vikings had advanced to the playoffs, and were to play the New York Giants in New York. I couldn't travel to the game, but I ended up listening to most of it on the radio as I drove from Cleveland to Columbus. It was strange to listen to my own team on the radio. It had been nearly a month since I had played, and there I was, with a repaired knee, driving my Jeep some 500 miles away from teammates who were struggling to win a playoff game in the freezing New York winter air. If you've never had the displeasure of being in the Meadowlands on a blustery winter day, do your very best to continue avoiding it. To make matters worse, they ended up losing the game. I talked to Scotty Graham after the game and he told me that it was the coldest game he had ever played in. Now I had at least one thing in common with the rest of the team: We would all have to wait until the next season to get back on the field. Of course, I would have to go through months of rehab to get back out there again.

I decided to do my rehab in Columbus. I went over to the Ohio State football facility and started working with head trainer Billy Hill. Those first few weeks were still the basic range-of-motion exercises, but Billy got cranking on my knee pretty good. I'd be up on one of the training tables with Billy bending and flexing my knee to the point that I broke out in a sweat. That was the most painful part of the recovery process. I knew that regaining range-of-motion was the most important part about getting better, so I accepted the pain with an almost masochistic fervor. It felt so good to be done with those sessions and get some ice onto the knee. Progress comes slowly at that stage of the game, though, so you have to be patient. You have to follow all of the rules if you want to get better, no matter how difficult it may seem. It was the little things that bothered you the most. Like having to wear a huge rubber cover on your leg to keep your wound from getting wet. I also had to sleep with a cumbersome brace, so I didn't sleep well for the first few weeks.

The rehab was tough, but I enjoyed my time back in Ohio. You're basically six months on and six months off when you play professional football. The six months on are pretty intense, though. You're in the "office" most of the time and you're constantly reminded of the office when you're away. Everyone wants to talk football with you when you're off the field. You can't even watch TV without being constantly reminded of your job. I would do my best just to avoid watching the local stations and ESPN so I didn't have to hear about football all the time.

It was also nice to have some free time to do some traveling. Not many of your friends have the freedom and resources to travel the way you want to when you reach the off season. I ended up doing a lot of traveling with other football players. I could pass for a "normal" citizen because I wasn't so conspicuously large. The guys I was traveling with were another story altogether. We tended to stand out. Anytime white people see a group of large black men, they think it's a sports team anyway. People would come up to us at a pool and ask in pure amazed excitement, "Are you guys football players?"

I had time to travel, but I had to spend most of that off season rehabbing my knee. And as the months went on, I could feel my body returning to normal. I was regaining strength in my right leg and was nearing the point at which I could start jogging again. Before I could do that on my own, though, I had to go out and see Dr. Steadman again to get his approval. I met with Topper and John Atkins, his head trainers at the time, and told them that I was ready to try jogging. They grabbed Dr. Steadman and we all went out into one of the hallways in the medical center. "All right, walk down to the end of the hallway and then jog back towards us," Dr. Steadman said. I walked down the hallway. I knew it was ready. As I started down the hallway, I felt the exhilaration of move- ment that I hadn't felt since I was a little boy. I got moving at a good steady pace and felt like I was I gliding. I could feel the interruption of air as I flew past them standing in the hallway. I was so excited I wanted to jump. As I turned and walked back towards them, I saw them all smiling. They looked on like proud parents. "That's beautiful," Dr. Steadman said. I was taking deep breaths, partly due to the thin air and partly due to my excitement. I couldn't stop smiling.

I felt like myself again. I wasn't healthy enough to run safely at full speed yet. And I also wasn't ready to do a whole lot of changing of direction, but I could sense that my body had turned the corner towards a full return to health. I had become accustomed to reading my body from years of competing. When I got back to Columbus, I started doing some light sprints and some change-of-direction drills. I wore a brace during these drills, so I was very confident that my knee would with- stand the increase in activity. I got a little more swelling with the increase in activity, but nothing unusual.

I went back to Minnesota for our May mini-camp. I was amazed at how much more comfortable I felt there. The place had seemed so for- eign just a year earlier. I remembered how strange it felt to sit in that locker room for the first time. Things were different now; I was a veteran.

I could see the look of confusion and apprehension in the eyes of the new class of rookies. I never got involved in any of the rookie hazing stuff. I figured they'd get plenty of it from the other players. I really couldn't do much in practice, but I did have the chance to show them how well I was doing. They were impressed with my progress, but they cautioned me to take my time towards a complete recovery. There was really no hurry for me to return. Scotty Graham had proven himself to be a reliable back and Terry Allen also would be available again. Terry was also recovering from ACL surgery, but he had about a five-month head start on me. I headed back to Columbus to finish up the quarter at school and continue my rehab.

Billy really started to pick things up in my rehab sessions. He was working with me one-on-one and definitely wasn't taking it easy on me or my knee. You really have to push yourself to get over the final hump in the rehab process. Your body changes slightly when you have this type of surgery and it takes time for it to adjust to the difference. You get scared sometimes that you're reaching a point where you'll re-injure the joint, but you have to force yourself to believe that it is actually stronger in many ways. It's somewhat like breaking a bone and having it stronger when it heals.

I entered camp feeling as if I was capable of performing at 100 percent. The team had a different idea. They decided to place me on the physically unable to perform list, or PUP squad. This meant that I wouldn't be able to join in on the regular practices. It was a bit disappointing to not be able to participate in drills after all I had been through, but I understood their desire to err on the side of caution. The team had added another back, Amp Lee, in the off season, so we had plenty of runners to pick up the slack. Fred Zamberletti was known for the torture sessions that he put injured players through. He truly was "old school" in his rehabilitation philosophy. He had been the team's head trainer since the team's inception in 1961 (Freddy handed over those duties to Chuck Barta in 1999). Freddy was convinced that a player was best served by attempting to heal "on the run." And he definitely believed in the adage that "more is better." Being able to practice and not having to run with Freddy was added incentive to stay healthy. For most of the practice, the injured players just stood around watching. But then Freddy started gathering his injured troops. You could see grown men trying to hide behind their teammates so Freddy wouldn't see them. It just delayed the inevitable. He gathered us together on one of the fields and got started. The activities themselves weren't particularly difficult, but Freddy wore you down with sheer volume. Groups of fans at practice would take the time just to watch these injured guys suffer. The players got a kick of it, too: "Get 'em Freddy! Don't let 'em slack!" You'd get so tired that you could barely think straight. Your only clear thoughts were the fantasies you had of ripping Freddy's head off. In one drill, he'd have us push him as he sat on one of the golf carts. He swears he never uses the brake, but anyone who had to go through it knows differently. I was always in pretty good shape, but these sessions even drove me to the point of spewing streams of profanity.

I got into normal practices a couple of weeks later. The knee was tested immediately. We got into a pass blocking drill against the linebackers early in my first practice. I was a bit apprehensive about the knee. Running around in drills was one thing. Having it hold up against a charging linebacker was another thing altogether. I was wearing a knee brace that provided some protection, but the scary thoughts were inescapable. I set up in low blocking position with my legs firmly planted in a wide stance. The linebacker came right for me. The violence of the impact caused my right leg to slip underneath me. I lay there on the ground with my leg bent behind me. But I was all right! I had survived the play without a problem. I never doubted the knee again.

I got into my first action a week later in a pre-season game at the University of Washington. The Kingdome was going through some repairs, so we had to play the Seahawks at Huskie Stadium. I remember my first carry. It was the first time that I had been in on live play since I injured the knee eight months earlier. It was an off-tackle run to the right. I got the ball and quickly got to the corner for a seven-yard gain. I was knocked out of bounds pretty hard, but I felt great. I still had it! All those months of rehab had paid off. I was back. Now it was time to prove that I could do it in a regular-season game.

Our first game of the year was in Lambeau Field against the Packers. I had missed the game against them in Green Bay the previous year. That game was played in December, and I was glad that our schedule this year had us playing there when the temperature was still in positive numbers. Lambeau Field always was my favorite stadium in which to play because the atmosphere has a college football feeling to it.

After I got to the stadium, I dressed in my shorts and T-shirt and headed out to the field to warm up. It was a beautiful day –a perfect day. I headed back to the locker room after working up a good sweat. As I sat there getting ready to put the rest of my gear on, Ty came over and sat down next to me. "Hey, Robert, we've got a change of plans for today," he said. "Cool," I thought, "I'm gonna get the start!" "We're not gonna dress you today," he added. I was devastated. All those months hadn't paid off the way I thought. I was going to be one of the six inactive players for the day. The team carries 53 men on the regular roster, but only 47, including one emergency quarterback, dress on game day. I don't remember if I said anything to him. I was so shocked and disappointed that I probably just sat there in stunned silence. I could understand caution, but this seemed extreme. I jumped in the shower and put my street clothes back on as my teammates continued preparing for the game. I had to just stand and watch on the sideline for the entire game. It was a long day. We lost the game and I have to admit that I felt a guilty satisfaction.

They dressed me the next week against Chicago and I responded well. I scored what ended up being my only touchdown of the season in relief of Terry and we won the game. I felt like I was back on track. My success was short-lived, however. The next week against Miami I took a shot to the hip that kept me out of practice all week. College players are required to wear hip pads, but in the NFL it's up to the individual. Most people didn't wear them. It offers you more of a feeling of freedom, but it also exposes your hips to some pretty mean shots, especially at running back. Anyone who has ever taken a shot to the hip knows how vulnerable this area can be. The dreaded "hip pointer" is one of the most painful injuries you can receive. I felt I was healthy enough to play on the weekend, but coaches rarely allow back-ups to miss practice time and play. If they feel your presence on the field is vital to the team's performance, then they'll let you miss all the time you want and still play. They don't make such accommodations for players who were in my situation. I was back at full speed the following week, but it didn't seem to matter to the coaching staff. They seemed intent on *not* getting me into the game. To this day, I've never discussed their reasoning behind holding me back that year with Denny or Ty. I'm sure part of it was that they felt I should take more time to let the knee completely heal. And part of it was that they felt Terry was a better back for the time being. Whatever their reasoning, it was an extremely frustrating year for me because I never really got the chance to show that I could be a consistent performer. I felt that I had shown that the year before, but apparently they still had lingering doubts about my ability to stay healthy. It seemed like it was all people talked about when they referenced me. "That guy's injury-prone."

Once you get labeled there's no going back. I did have a pretty nasty string of incidents, but calling a football player injury-prone is like calling a race car driver accident-prone. Sure, they may get in more accidents than the general public, but you have to remember that is a part of their job. It's dangerous driving a race car for a living, and it's dangerous playing football for a living. Chances are you're going to get hurt if you do either one long enough. A player such as Emmitt Smith is an exception to the rule. I'm sure he'd tell you that he considers himself fortunate to have remained so healthy through the years. But I don't believe in luck. Which is to say that I don't believe that some people are more or less "lucky" than others.

On the field, things could have been better, but I was starting to feel even more at ease with my teammates. I think they could sense my frustration and they sympathized with my position. Flying back from one of the games, one of the players even invited me over to his place to smoke some weed. This was before I smoked (during the season that is- I had tried it before), so I refused, but it did make me feel accepted. It may sound funny, but that invitation meant a lot to me. I've always been seen as different, but these guys knew me now; I wasn't putting on an act. I was just being me, and I wanted the same things they did: to contribute and to be appreciated.

It was hard for me to question Denny's judgment, though. He was right to bring me in there, and maybe he was right to limit my playing time that year. I may have felt as if I was fully recovered, but there was probably something he noticed that kept him from pushing it with me. The man has won a lot of games and he's made the right call on a lot of players, so he must have known what he was doing. That still didn't make things easy for me. I only ended up carrying the ball 31 times in 14 games. I felt like a scrub; I felt like I had to start all over again. We ended up making it to the playoffs again, and lost in the first round to Chicago. I was glad to have that year done with.

My contract was up, but because of the free agency rules, I wasn't free to move to another team. You have to complete four seasons before you're free to negotiate with any other team. I would have to re-sign with Minnesota. Neil and I had planned on my first two years going much better than they did, of course. I still think we made the right decision. The up-side of being able to re-negotiate was worth the risk. The Vikings played their hand very early. They decided to release Terry Allen in the off-season. You would have thought that this would have made contract negotiations go a bit more smoothly. Not so.

Jeff Diamond was the general manager at the time, so he handled negotiations with Neil. It really is a good thing to have an agent negotiating for you because the talks can become very emotional. Players would want to jump through the phone and rip the GM's throat out if they heard some of the things that were being said about them. You have to realize that it's just business, and attorneys are very good at leaving their emotions at the door. It's good to have a buffer between you and management. It went something like this—Diamond: "Robert will never stay healthy; we need to keep other backs on the roster in case he gets hurts, so we can't pay him starter money." Neil: "Well, you obviously thought enough of him to get rid of Terry." Diamond: "We were going to do that anyway." They'll say anything, and try to get away with everything. We didn't have much leverage in the negotiations. And they were right: I hadn't stayed healthy and that was obviously a concern. But from our point of view, I should have been paid something at least approaching starter's money, with performance incentives to bridge the gap.

We were nowhere close to an agreement when camp opened. I wasn't concerned. It's not like I really wanted to be in camp anyway. I know this issue has been covered before, but there really is very little reason for veterans to expose themselves to the dangers of training camp. It's important for the coaches to get a look at the rookies and it's important for the rookies to acclimate themselves to the NFL environment, but veterans have more to lose than something to gain by being in camp. In the past, veterans often used this time to get themselves back into shape. However, NFL players stay in much better shape in the off-season now, and most of them show up ready to play. The league likes to have players in early these days so it can collect full gate receipts for preseason games and only pay the players a small fraction of what they make during the regular season. Players don't start receiving their salary until the regular season, so teams really rake in the dough for these boring, meaningless contests. So players end up risking their health and livelihood in weeks in which they make only about $1,000.

This is all about perspective again. This may sound like more whining from spoiled professional athletes, but you have to put yourself in the same position. Imagine if your boss asked you to come in a few hours early every day and said he was going to pay you 1 percent of your normal salary. Would you be excited to get to work on time? Would you show up early at all? Would you be so insulted that you'd seek employment somewhere else? Well, I didn't have the option of going anywhere else. The only option I had was to withhold my services, a one-man strike, of sorts. Denny Green would often refer to players as one-man corporations, and he's right. You want to be with your teammates and you don't want to seem greedy, but there are times when you have to do what you think is best for you.

It was painfully obvious to me how vital it is to maximize dollars when you're healthy. Who knows how long you'll be able to play. You have to get what you can when you can get it. The Minnesota media was all over me and so were the fans. But you can't make decisions based on the opinions of people who aren't affected by them. People may complain and they may act like they understand the situation, but they lack the perspective needed to make a good evaluation. To them, it's about greed; to you, it's about fairness. Once again, they get caught up in the numbers and try to make purely monetary comparisons without thinking of the market values involved in contact negotiations.

I was still unsigned when camp ended. I never thought I would be in this situation, but I still felt I was doing the right thing. The regular season was quickly approaching. Whenever I decided to report, I would have to do so without the weeks of practice. I had been training on my own in Columbus, so I wasn't concerned about being in shape. But I still wanted to get in to start working with the offense to get a sense of timing. I hadn't played much with the first unit the previous season, so it was important to get a feel for the flow of things.

A running back performs at a much higher level after he gets a feel for the flow of games. You accustom yourself to the movements of your blockers and you can react much faster to the action on the field. Speed, vision, and maneuverability are all vital aspects to being a good runner in the NFL. I think that the best runners develop a sixth sense that allows them to anticipate movement and feel their way through traffic. In *The User Illusion: Cutting Human Consciousness Down to Size*, probably my favorite book, author Tor Noretranders discusses the lag time between the perception of an event and the time the event actually reaches your conscious mind. It's an amazing .4 seconds on average. The upshot of this is that you end up reacting to stimuli before you even become conscious of the event itself! Who's really in control of your actions, then? Without going too deep into the question, it's clear that a runner on the field must be reacting at some sub-conscious level in order to effectively negotiate the hazards he encounters. You improve your reaction time by conditioning yourself to anticipate certain events on the field. This is why it's so important to get repetitions in practice. The more times your body has performed a particular task, the easier it is to adapt to variations it may encounter on future attempts.

Both sides of the negotiations wanted me on the team for the first game. We were going into this season with little experience at running back. None of the runners on the roster had a career total of 1,000 yards rushing. I signed on the night before the final preseason game, which gave me only one week to prepare for the regular-season opener in Chicago.

I walked into the locker room for the first time that year as the team was preparing for the last pre-season game. "Way to get 'em, Smitty!" "I see ya' Juice! Don't take that shit!" I'm sure there were players who weren't happy I had missed so much time, but I think most of the guys understood what I was trying to do. It felt great to be back, but I knew I was going to have a rough time ahead of me trying to get into game shape. I was returning in great shape, but there was really no way for me to simulate the type of running I would need to do in a live game. There's also the issue of getting your body used to the contact of the game. Denny Green didn't like to run completely live drills during the course of the week. We only wore pads one day a week and even then we would only hit live for a few periods during practice. I was going to have to go into the first game fairly raw.

I didn't start that first week in Chicago, but I had a chance to prove my readiness early in the game. We advanced the ball to the 1-yard line and had a first-and-goal. On first down, Warren Moon handed the ball off to one of our running backs, who was stopped cold. Second down brought the same play call with the same result. I stood there next to Carl Hargrave (Carl had replaced Ty Willingham, who had taken the head coaching job at Stanford) hoping anxiously that I'd get the chance to go in. "Get in there, Robert!" Carl said. It felt like I was flying as I ran out to the huddle. The play came in from the sideline. Another run. My heart was racing.

It takes a special mentality to run the ball on the goal line. Many people think you need to just stick your biggest player in there and have him lower his head and bowl his way into the end zone. It just doesn't work that way most of the time, though. Oftentimes, on the goal-line, the defensive players use a technique they call "submarining," which is just what you would guess it to be. They get into a four-point stance and immediately dive low into the gaps. The resulting jumble of bodies can make an almost impenetrable wall. This is where you see players attempt to jump over the pile. The problem with jumping is that you lose your ability to generate power. The momentum you have when you leave the ground is all you'll have to make it into the end zone. To make matters worse, the linebackers usually jump, too. The problem is that you don't have very much time to make this decision; it takes split-second reactions. It's what made Marcus Allen such a great goal line runner. He wasn't the biggest guy (about 200-210) but he had a knack for finding pay dirt in goal line situations.

At the snap of the ball, my eyes immediately shifted to the line of scrimmage. The coaches always tell you, "It's the quarterback's job to get you the ball, so get your eyes upfield right away. I could see that there was a gap that was quickly filled by one of the linebackers. It seemed as if he knew we'd be running to that side. He came towards me and went for one of my legs. He caught a piece of one my legs and the force of the hit sent my leg flying backwards; it stopped me dead in my tracks. I was able to keep my balance. I got both legs onto the ground and continued towards the goal line. One of the other linebackers was closing in on me. He was far enough from the goal line that I thought I'd have a chance to extend the ball over and in for the score. You have to be careful about extending the ball away from your body; it's easy to get it knocked out, especially near the goal line. I leaned forward, ran as fast as I could, and briefly extended the ball, pulling it back towards me as I made crushing contact with the linebacker. I looked to the side and saw the signal. I was in! I got up and ran to the sideline as fast as I could. I could barely contain my excitement. I got to the sideline and was greeted with enthusiastic high-fives and slaps to the shoulder pads. I was back again. Unfortunately, the rest of the game didn't go as well for us. I did well on a limited number of runs, but we lost 31-14.

We won two of the next three games, and I posted 100 yards rushing in each of them. In the loss, I actually had a moment when I thought I would lose my life. We were playing Dallas in the Metrodome in a Sunday night game. I broke into the secondary and could see one of our receivers closing in on the safety, Darren Woodson, who was bearing down on me. From the angle I could perceive, it appeared as though the receiver would block him and keep him from getting a hit on me. I was wrong. Darren caught me with his helmet in my gut! I dropped to the ground and jumped up quickly, unable to catch my breath. I literally could not breathe. I was trying to draw in air, but nothing happened. As the trainers got out to me, all I could think of was how embarrassing it was going to be to die on a football field on national television. Anyone who has had the breath knocked out of them knows how disturbing the feeling can be. As I caught my breath, I started laughing, partly because I had been caught so cleanly, and partly because I was so convinced that my life had reached its end.

One of those three games was played in Three Rivers Stadium against the Pittsburgh Steelers. It was the first time that I played in the stadium of my favorite boyhood team. It was a great day for us as a team and for me personally. Things didn't start off that great, though. After breaking into the clear on a 20-yard run, I had the ball stripped away for my first NFL fumble. There's nowhere to hide when you fumble the ball. When you make that long walk back to the sideline, it feels as if you have the entire world on your back. It's a lonely feeling. Your position coach comes over and tries to get you to settle down. The only remedy is to get back out there and start over. That's exactly what I did, getting a 58-yard touchdown. To make things really interesting, I ran the last 30 yards with only one shoe on. It was pulled off as I cut back against the grain and headed up the sideline. It was the first time in my career that I would score one of the long touchdown runs for which I became known. We dominated the rest of the game and won 44-24.

We had a bye week after this game and I had the chance to get back to Columbus to watch the Buckeyes beat Notre Dame. Before that season, people would ask me if I still played for the Vikings; now there was no doubt. I was starting to be considered one of the best backs in the league. We got back from the bye and faced the Houston Oilers. It was a tough day for running the ball. We fought hard to gain anything on the ground. The game went into overtime and on our first possession in overtime we quickly advanced the ball to the Houston 20-yard line. The play came in as a run. I took the ball and ran into a pile of players near the line of scrimmage. I was able to keep my feet moving and ended up breaking free. I crossed the goal line, checked for flags, and then jumped excitedly into the arms of one of the lineman. It's the great part about scoring in sudden-death overtime: The game is over!

We lost the next week in Tampa and headed into Green Bay with a 3-3 record. We got off to a strong start against the Packers, relying heavily on our running game. I scored a touchdown early and was finding a lot of running room. We had the ball on their 4-yard line when the call came to me again. I started inside, and then broke for the pylon. It was going to be tight. As I neared the sideline, I prepared to extend the ball inside the plane of the goal line. I dived for the pylon and stuck the ball out, clearly (at least in my mind) getting the ball over the line before going out of bounds. There was no instant replay at the time, so all we could do was complain. We got back to the huddle and the call came for another run. This time I got caught in the middle of the field and was stopped near the line of scrimmage. As I hit the ground, Gilbert Brown fell on the back of my foot and severely twisted my ankle (Gilbert was pushing 400 pounds at the time, so I'm lucky he didn't break every bone in my foot). The pain was instant. I knew that something was seriously wrong, but I was in denial. I went back to the huddle and didn't say a thing. The next play was a pass, and I had barely moved when the pain shot up through my leg. I don't know what I would have done if it had been a run. I don't think I would have even made it to the handoff spot. I got back to the sideline and called Fred Zamberletti over. I told him what had happened. They put enough tape to wrap a mummy on my ankle, but nothing would have allowed me to run. I had no power in the ankle with which to push with. They cut the tape off and put some ice on the ankle. I sat on the sideline and cursed my fate.

On the replay, it was obvious that I had put the ball inside the pylon on the play from the 4. I don't know what the ref was looking at. Fate doesn't play favorites, and it certainly doesn't care who you are, but I couldn't believe it was happening to me again. My development had been coming along so well. To have the injury occur on a play that never should have happened made it seem even crueler. I couldn't worry about why it happened though; I had to concern myself with getting back on the field. We went on to lose that game against Green Bay and would face Chicago at home the following Monday night.

I was in the training room all week trying to heal the ankle. It was another "high" ankle sprain— I was embarrassed to be hurt again. The reporters had a field day. ("I guess that's what you get for holding out of camp..." "This guy will never be healthy an entire season..." "The Vikings need to cut their losses with this guy..." I had heard bad things said about me before—much more personal things—so their comments really didn't bother me. It was rare that I caught a glimpse of the sports section, anyway. What really bothered me is that I felt I was letting the team down. I was a much more integral part of the offense than I had been in the past, so not having me in there was more detrimental to the team's plans. I also felt like I was embarrassing Denny Green. He was the one who had brought me there; I was his guy. He had cleared the way for me to be the starter and now I was in danger of being out again.

I didn't progress much during the week, and I was nowhere near being able to run effectively by the time the weekend rolled around. I hoped that the extra day would somehow bring sufficient strength to the ankle to enable me to play. It would to be a game day decision. The night of the game, Fred Zamberletti had me go out into the tunnel to show him how well I could run. I was terrible. I had no strength in the ankle; I couldn't raise up on to my toes to get into proper running form. I would have to sit the game out. We went on to lose our third straight game, which just added more salt to my wound. I became so frustrated during the following week, that I asked the team to put something else into my personal wound—a needle.

You hear stories about players' bodies and careers being ruined by over-zealous team doctors' use of injections. Cortisone is the usual culprit. Cortisone is a synthetic steroid that is used for its anti-inflammatory properties. It usually is injected directly into the affected area. I went to the trainers and team doctor and asked them if they thought it would help. They cautioned me about using an injection to play, because the effects of the drug often can mask problems and can cause injuries to worsen. I was willing to take that risk. Forget what you've heard about players being forced into using injections. Some team doctors may be less scrupulous than others, but they're not stupid. It's the players who agree, and often ask, to be injected. The desire to play overrules the knowledge of the possible dangers. I saw a poll that asked Olympic-caliber athletes if they would use a performance-enhancing drug if they knew they wouldn't be caught and they were guaranteed a gold medal by using it. The caveat was that they were also told that the drug would cause long-term health problems. A full 50 percent of the respondents said yes. Anyone intimately involved in sports wouldn't be too surprised by this. Most players are willing to risk their health to perform.

The needle went a good two to three inches inside my ankle. It made me a little woozy. There was only one other time in my life in which I had a similar reaction to something I saw. It was the first time that I watched a surgery. They were literally sawing off the top of this woman's skull as I walked into the room. I stood there for a few minutes and felt fine, but one of the doctors looked over at me and suggested I step out into the hall. He said I looked a bit flushed. I got a soda and went back in for the remainder of the procedure, but I'm sure he saw something that made him want to get me out of there. This needle in the ankle wasn't nearly as dramatic a scene, but it still stunned me. I had never seen a needle go that far into my body. The effect was almost immediate. I couldn't believe how much better my ankle felt. The next day at practice I jogged through some plays for the first time since injuring the ankle.

I got to the stadium the next day and started preparing as I normally would. This time, Freddy took me out to the field to watch me do some cutting and accelerating. The ankle didn't feel like I was 100 percent, but it did feel strong enough to play on. Whatever it was he saw, Freddy wasn't convinced. They told me I'd be sitting out again. This time I was absolutely floored. I couldn't believe that they weren't going to let me play. I went back towards the showers with my pants and shoes still on and just sank down against one of the walls. I sat there with my head in my hands, barely able to believe what was happening.

I did play sparingly in two more games that year, but my season was basically through. I spent time trying to rehab the ankle during the week, but it never healed to the point where I was able to perform at peak level. It was an extremely frustrating time for me because I spent the last half of the season "almost" healthy enough to play. I would go into the training room and receive treatment every day. I would ride the bike and run in the pool to try to stay in shape, but I just never got over the hump. I wanted to be out there so bad, but my body just wouldn't cooperate. We ended up missing the playoffs for the first time in Denny Green's tenure and the only time during my career.

I had only signed a one-year deal, so I would have to go through the whole negotiation process again. The Vikings were committed to re-signing me, but they still didn't want to pay me anything near what other starters in the league were making. I could understand their reluctance to put the money in salary; I was very aware of my medical past. We just wanted them to allow me the opportunity to make up the difference with incentives. If I got hurt and couldn't play the whole season, they wouldn't have to pay me starter money. If I played the entire season and performed the way we all knew I could, I'd be compensated appropriately. Sounded simple enough, but when you have no real leverage (meaning the ability to threaten your departure), they've got you—or so they think. You can always refuse to sign. It truly becomes a matter of principle. People laugh when they hear a professional athlete talk about principles in contract negotiations, but they once again fail to understand the relative scale involved.

So I ended up sitting out again. The start of camp came and went without old number 26. By the way, it was sometime during the previous season that I stopped signing autographs with the number 26 on them. I began to consider my labeling as a number an insult. People would ask: "Why don't you sign your number?" I would respond, "I don't have one, I only wear one." Only prisoners and slaves have numbers. I knew the Vikings had no real alternative to me. It's not like they could go out and sign someone else at that point. A trade was possible, but they knew that having me was preferable to not having me at all. They didn't make what we saw as an acceptable offer until the final week of training camp. Teams always try to say that their offers haven't changed "significantly" in negotiations like this, but this is just damage control. If players have the mental endurance to wait, they often can maximize their contracts.

Obviously, teams don't want this information to get out, so they say what they need to say to the media to make it seem as if the hold-out were meaningless.

I reported to camp in great shape, ready to show that I was capable of being among the league's elite backs. Our early schedule would give me plenty of opportunities to prove it. In the first four games, I rushed 106 times for 372 yards, and we started 4-0. The team was treating me as a featured back, and I was responding well once again. The following week, we traveled to New York to play the Giants. We never got our running game started and I ended up carrying the ball only 17 times, my low total for the year. We suffered our first loss. We came back strong with our running game the following week and won over the Carolina Panthers to go 5-1, then lost the next week in Tampa. We had a 5-2 record heading into a Monday night home game against Chicago.

My first few runs of the night against the Bears brought little move-ment of the chains—at least in the positive direction. My fourth carry of the night brought an even worse result. I headed toward the left side-line and as I was running out of bounds, a Chicago player pulled me down from behind. My left leg buckled under my body and went into a severe hyper-flex position. I knew something had gone terribly wrong. I walked gingerly back to the huddle and I could feel instability in my left knee. I motioned to the sideline and walked out of the huddle. I was scared to try to jog on the knee. I went straight to our bench and sat down. Dr. Fischer came over and asked me what had happened. After I told him, he had me straighten my left leg. He gently picked up my left foot with his left hand, placing his other hand on the outside of my left thigh. He pushed out on my lower leg and the joint opened up into a grotesque angle. Clearly, there had been some severe damage. I had torn the medial collateral ligament (MCL), which runs along the inside of the knee. I had also torn my posterior cruciate ligament (PCL), which crosses with the anterior cruciate (ACL) inside of the knee joint. I couldn't be-lieve it had happened again.

I got up from the bench and headed towards the locker room. To make matters worse, my mother was at the game. I was glad that she didn't have to see me writhing in pain on the turf. The family section in

125

the Metrodome is right above the tunnel that leads to the Vikings' locker room. Before I went into the tunnel, I motioned to her to meet me by the locker room. We drove over to the MRI facility to see my old friends. I had been to that place three out of my first four seasons. The tests confirmed my worst fears, and the thought of retirement crossed my mind. The thoughts didn't last long. I couldn't leave like this. I had to come back.

I ended up going back to see Dr. Steadman in Colorado. The procedure went well again, and I prepared myself for another off-season of rehab. I headed back to Ohio State to work with the training staff there again. Billy Hill, who had played such an integral role in my rehab the first time around, had passed away the previous year. It was tough to be around the Ohio State training room without seeing him. Billy was only 53 when he died of a heart attack. Everyone at Ohio State loved him and missed him. It was a cruel reminder that there were more important things in the world than football. But football was still my chosen profession. Some people questioned my commitment to the game when I played because I was so well known for my off-field interests. I always took my job seriously, though. I was never late—not one second—during my entire career. When I showed up to play, I played with fire. And when I was injured, I worked hard to get back. No one can question that.

This injury was particularly bothersome because it came right before my first chance at free agency. I had played the required four years and now was free to sign with any team I wanted. But no teams were willing to take the chance on a player who was rehabbing and who had such a poor health record. I sat by and watched as other free-agent running backs signed lucrative deals. We would have to negotiate with Minnesota again.

We hoped that things would go differently this time… in more ways than one.

CHAPTER SIX

SERENDIPITY

Fortudinae Vincimus   By endurance we conquer

—Unknown

Our doubts are traitors, and make us lose the good we might oft win, by fearing to attempt.

——William Shakespeare

I have my fears, but they do not have me.

——Peter Gabriel

We had minimal leverage in these negotiations. My history of injuries had become the most well-known aspect of my career. I was just glad the team—Denny Green in particular—believed in me enough to give me another chance. I ended up re-signing before mini-camp even started. I hoped that everything else would go that smoothly for the rest of the year. The contract was basically the same as the one I had signed the previous year. I wouldn't have a salary as high as the other starting running backs in the league, but I would have the chance to make up some of the difference with incentives. I just wanted to get out there and show what I could do. Nobody questioned my talent, but they had doubts about my ability to sustain my health.

Rehab went smoothly and I was ready to perform when camp rolled around again. For only the second time in five years, I reported to camp on time. But like the last time, I wouldn't practice with the team immediately. The team wanted to make sure my knee could withstand the pounding again. Still, I only spent a couple of days running with Fred Zamberletti. I wanted to get back to regular work and I sure as hell didn't want to spend any more days pushing him around on that damn cart. Every day I got the same question: "How's the knee?" "Robert, how's the knee?" "Robert, will you sign this? By the way, how's the knee?" Unfortunately, people ask me that to this day. "How's retirement? Oh yeah, how are your knees?" They're very good, by the way, considering everything I've put them through.

Our first game was in Buffalo against the Bills. The schedulers had done us a favor by having us play up there before the brutally cold winter days arrived. I was as excited as I had ever been to start a season. I kept telling myself that this had to be my year. It was a great day for us. We put on a strong performance and I clearly proved that my knee was healed. In the fourth quarter, I broke off a 78-yard touchdown run to seal our victory and cap a fantastic personal day. I carried the ball 16 times for 169 yards. It felt great to be back on the field, and my performance made it that much more special. I was given the offensive game ball the next day and I have it on display in my office at home—the only ball I've ever displayed.

Everything just had a different feel for me that year. I could sense that I was being seen in a different light. Everyone, from fans to reporters, treated me with more respect. Which is saying quite a bit for reporters. Up to that point, they had had field days tearing into me for my infirmities. Some reporters just love to go after you, especially guys like me. Some of them saw me as a disruption to the football player/reporter balance; they had trouble dealing with articulate, intelligent players. It was funny how some of them would tip-toe through interviews with me, being careful not to make mistakes in grammar or pronunciation.

Speaking of funny, it was always amusing to watch female reporters as they pretended *not* to watch. It truly never bothered me to have them around (I'm not shy), but everyone knows that they look. I don't care what they say about being professionals, they still do. How many guys would change their major to journalism if they thought they'd get a chance to go in a locker room when Anna Kournikova was changing?

Normally, they put a notice in your locker on Wednesday mornings if there's someone in the media who wants to talk to you. The reporter then waits near your locker until you get back from lunch and conducts the interview. When you really get popular, though, they put you in front of "the group," which is a collection of all of the local news stations, as well as any other reporters who want to ask questions of you. They were mini-press conferences. "Robert, what do you think of the Green Bay defense?" "How do you think the running game will work this week?" The questions were pretty mundane. After the group session, you'd usually have reporters who wanted to ask more specific questions. You would have spent your whole lunch break doing interviews if they had their way. Sometimes you'd just have to say no. Then they'd look at you as if you thought you were too good for them. But you need some time for yourself and your time is very limited during the season.

People forget that athletes have normal lives outside of their jobs and that they have to deal with real issues like bills and families. You don't have "personal" days in the NFL. You may hear about players missing games for the births of their children, but this is rare. If a player becomes distracted by a problem at home, he still has to show up to perform. You can't just say: "Sorry guys, I really need to take care of this, have a good game!" There are extreme cases where this does happen, but for the most part, you're expected to show up and play.

Anytime I went out somewhere in Minneapolis, people began to take more notice of me. I was used to people recognizing me, but now it became different. People began treating me with a deference that made me uncomfortable. When you're aware of all of your faults, it becomes almost amusing to hear people refer to you highly. I was the same person I had always been, but these people began to look up to me as if I was truly a heroic figure. "Hello, Mr. Smith, it's a pleasure to meet you, sir." "Thanks, but you can call me Robert." It's an amazing feeling to have the respect of so many people; in fact, it's truly humbling. But it does give you the satisfaction of knowing that you must be doing a pretty good job.

But sometimes rudeness entered the equation. I'd be out to dinner with my girlfriend or my family and someone would come up to our table. "Hey, I don't mean to be rude, but do you think I could get your autograph?" "You may not mean to be rude, but you're doing a pretty good job of it," I would say. "I'll be glad to sign it after dinner." They'd walk away in a funk. Well, learn some manners. Everyone deserves the right to some privacy.

Or, they'd send their kid up to the table. "Excuse me, Mr. Smith, could you sign this for me?" I've got a weak spot for kids, so I would always sign for them, but I blame their parents for sending them in the first place. Much of the time, kids are too shy to ask for autographs. They could be standing right next to you but it's their parents who prod them by saying, "Go ahead—ask him!" Parents should know better than to have kids interrupt someone's meal. I understand that people get excited, but they should stop to think about it from the player's perspective. It's flattering to have people respect what you do, but that doesn't give people a license to act any way they want. You hear the stories about people asking athletes for autographs and being turned down. They act as if the player owes them something.

When we would leave the stadium after home games, the fans would surround us trying to get autographs as we walked to our cars. You actually would see grown men pushing kids out of the way to get signatures. You try to sign some, but inevitably someone would be left out and yell, "Don't forget the fans! We're the ones who pay your salary!" It sounds like the things that people say to cops, "Hey, my taxes pay your salary!" Does that mean the cop's not supposed to give you a ticket? I got paid to play football, not to sign every autograph. Don't I have a right to leave the game with my family and get home? Do I have to spend every minute off the field doing what fans want because they supposedly contribute to my salary?

People ask me: "What's it like to be a celebrity?" Well, first of all, "celebrity" is a relative term. I was a well known athlete, but I wasn't like Michael Jordan or Tiger Woods. As hard as it is for some people to imagine how difficult it was for me to handle, I can't imagine how those guys deal with it. They can't go anywhere in the world without being mobbed. I remember talking to Warren Moon about this issue. I asked him how he dealt with all of the attention he received in public. He said that you just have to prepare yourself mentally and only put yourself in environments in which you feel comfortable. You just don't go certain places if you're not ready for the attention. You don't go to a sports bar in Minneapolis and expect people not to recognize you. Of course, sometimes we'd use it in our favor. It definitely made it easy to find women to talk to—or, better yet, have them find us. We had the routine down: First, you enter the bar and do a lap to do some scoping of your own and create a buzz in the crowd. Then just find a seat with a good view of the bar... and wait for the action.

We traveled to Green Bay the fourth week of the season. As we came out for the game, I could see something that let me know just how much people around the league were starting to respect me. It was a little #26 doll being hung down from the stands by its neck. I was being hung in effigy. You know you've made it when the other team's fans start to show a personal hatred for you. I was a primary target for the other team now. They knew they had to respect our running game. We had been known primarily as a passing team, but we now had a powerful and well-balanced offense. We fought hard, but ended up losing a close game, leaving us with a 2-2 record. It was a good day for me personally, though, with 160 yards of total offense (132 on the ground) and a touchdown. The game had begun to slow down for me; I was starting to see things more clearly and easily on the field. I was starting to find my groove.

We won our next three games and headed into the bye week with a 5-2 record. I had two more 100-yard rushing days in those three games, giving me 745 rushing yards after the first seven games. A 1,000-yard season is a benchmark for a running back. In a 16-game season, it's an average of 62.5 yards per game. It sounds easy enough but it's never easy to run in the NFL. Teams know the danger of allowing the opposition to establish a running game. It allows a team to control the tempo of a game and it also opens up passing lanes, because teams must commit extra players near the line of scrimmage. So defenses tend to focus on stopping the run. It's also not easy for a running back to make it through an entire season healthy (as I had proven quite effectively). The number carried extra significance for me that season because I had a clause that paid me a significant bonus for reaching it. I couldn't help but think about all the things that had gone wrong in the previous seasons. I kept telling myself that it had just been a bad run of chance, but bad thoughts are inevitable. My two previous injuries had come at about the same time of year. In 1995, I was injured in game 7. In 1996, I was injured in game 8, one week after the bye. Now, in 1997, I would be heading into game 8 one week after a bye. I'm not a superstitious person, but I couldn't stop thinking about the eerie similarities. We would also be playing in Tampa Bay, a place where we had had some difficulties in the past.

Tampa Bay had always presented problems for us. This was their second season under Coach Tony Dungy, who had served as defensive coordinator under Coach Denny Green in Minnesota. Tony's teams were always tough against the run, and this year was no exception. They had beaten us in our first meeting in Minnesota earlier that year. I only carried the ball 10 times in that game, finishing with 54 yards. You don't want to get caught up in the past, though. I got into the flow of the game in Tampa and completely forgot about my "jinx." On a passing play in the second quarter, a player fell on the back of my right ankle. The pain instantly shot through my leg. I was able to jog on it, but it didn't have a lot of strength. I went to the sideline and had them tape it up for me. I tried running, but I could only manage a quick, flat-footed hobble. My game day had ended. I knew that the injury wasn't as serious as the ones I had suffered in the past, but I was still amazed that anything like this could happen again.

At the Vikings' facility the next day, I was feeling better already. I was confident that the injury wouldn't keep me out long. I hadn't completely dodged the bullet, but it had only grazed me. The team had no interest in pushing the return schedule with the ankle. I had a good back-up in Leroy Hoard, and they knew the risks of trying to get me to play too soon. We had defeated Tampa Bay and were in good shape with a 6-2 record, so there wasn't a sense of urgency. They decided to rest me the next two weeks. We won both of those games and were in great shape to make the playoffs with an 8-2 record heading into Detroit.

My ankle was healed and I looked forward to getting back and continuing what was already my best statistical season. We never had a chance to get our running game going that day, and we fell behind early. We ended up losing, 38-15, and had to go on the road again the following week to play the Jets in New York. Once again, we had trouble getting the running game started and we struggled to stay in the game. To make matters much worse, we ended up losing one of our most important players late in the game. Jeff Christy, our center, broke his leg with less than two minutes to go as we were trying to go in for a touchdown. Because we had no time-outs left, Jeff had to get off the field without the help of the trainers to avoid a penalty. All of our linemen were tough, but that was one of the most impressive displays I saw in all my playing days.

We lined up with our new center, Scott Dill, and scored a touchdown to bring us within two points. The offense stayed on the field to attempt a two-point play. The huddle call was a run/pass option. On these plays, the quarterback lined up under center and evaluated the defense. If he liked the pass, he went through his normal cadence and threw the pass. If he wanted to change to a run, he signals to everyone on the offense and we knew to switch to a pre-determined running play. The sound in the stadium was absolutely deafening. Brad Johnson got to the line and switched to the run. At the snap of the ball, I could see one of the Jets' defensive linemen break free. I tried in vain to elude him but ended up buried under a mountain of players. The crowd went crazy. This happened near the end zone on the opposite side of the stadium from the locker room. It was a long walk back. You want to have the opportunity to make big plays. Situations like that one are when the team relies on its star players to make the difference. I didn't get it done, and the sound of the Jets' wildly cheering fans pierced through me like daggers. Things didn't get much better for us in the following weeks.

In the next game, Brad broke a leg and was lost for the season (Brad and Jeff Christy went on to win a Super Bowl ring with Tampa

Bay in 2003; I can't think of two guys who deserved it more). We went on to lose that game, as well, and our season was in jeopardy. We ended up losing the next two games, leaving us with a five-game losing streak heading into our final game at home. I did hit one milestone during that stretch that gave me some consolation: I went over the 1,000-yard rushing mark in our game against San Francisco. I was upset that we hadn't won the game, but it was a relief to reach that magic number. Incentive money aside, it represented a break from my struggles of the previous seasons. I remember going online the next day and looking at the updated stats for the season. There it was: Robert Smith, Minnesota Vikings, 1,005 yards. It was incredible to actually see the number on the screen. Things had gone so wrong for so long that I had wondered if they'd ever turn around. They had, but I needed to focus on the team and trying to help get us into the playoffs. We needed to win our final regular-season game, against Indianapolis at home, to clinch a Wild Card playoff spot.

We had a great day offensively, both running and passing the ball. Randall Cunningham had replaced Brad at quarterback and been giving some dazzling performances. I had heard a lot of bad things about Randall's attitude before he joined us in Minnesota. People called him a prima donna and accused him of being a selfish player. I don't know what he was like in Philadelphia, but he never showed anything but competitiveness and professionalism in Minnesota. Randall and I would always sit next to each other on the team plane and have great conversations about life and football. You hear a lot about players claiming to be Christians and how good they are as people. Randall is a man who truly lives his life as a good Christian. He practices what he preaches, and he isn't the type to push his religion on you. It was a pleasure to play with him, but it wasn't just because he was a nice guy. He came in and made some great plays for us. The Colts' game was no exception.

We won the game and made it to the playoffs. I rushed for 160 yards in that game, giving me 1,266 for the season, a team record. But I couldn't celebrate for long because we had to head back to the Meadowlands to face the Giants in the first round of the playoffs. It was my first playoff start. New York is a tough town in which to play, both for the New York players and those on the visiting teams. Say what you will about New Yorkers, but you have to admire their consistency: They don't like anybody. They're as hard on their own players as they are on the out-of-towners. Make no mistake about it, if they don't like what you're doing, you'll hear it.

Things didn't go our way most of the day. We were trailing 22-13 with less than two minutes remaining. The Vikings had not won a play-off game during Coach Green's tenure, and it appeared as though we would extend that streak. Appearances can be deceptive. We got the ball in Giants territory and Randall led us on a drive that culminated with a 30-yard touchdown pass to Jake Reed. Trailing 22-20, we then lined up for an onside kick. We all held our breaths as our kicker, Eddie Murray, approached the ball. It took a couple of bounces, then deflected off of one of their players...and we recovered it.

I took the field with our offense. Randall managed the huddle masterfully. We marched from our own 39 to the Giants 22. The call came into me, and I took the handoff and shot into the Giants' secondary. I eluded a player in the secondary and headed for the goal line. I was stopped at the 4. We lined up quickly and Randall spiked the ball to stop the clock with 10 seconds remaining. Eddie Murray came out to line up for the kick. We were in position to win the game, something that seemed impossible a short time before. Clean snap, clean hold...and the ball sailed through the uprights...23-22 Vikings. Our sideline exploded in celebration. It was the fifth largest comeback in playoff history and the biggest on the road since the year I was born (1972).

We ended up losing the following week in San Francisco. Our season ended, but we had proven ourselves to be a rising force in the NFL. I had also proven myself to be among the top backs in the league. Most importantly, I had earned the respect of my teammates for overcoming adversity. Every year, NFL teams give out an award for courage to one player; it's called the Ed Block Award. It's a great honor to win this award because it's voted on by your teammates. They're the ones who work with you every day and who get to see your level of commitment to your job. They know your struggles and they know the pain that you must endure. You can't fake things with teammates. I hoped that I would have the chance to play with those guys again, and prove to them that they had chosen the right player for this prestigious award.

I had only signed a one-year deal before the season, so we would be making yet another trip to the negotiating table. This trip was going to be a luxury cruise compared to the 11-hour drive with screaming children that we had in the past. All of the leverage was on our side; until I got a call from Denny Green. Denny: "Hey, Robert, how ya' doin' today?" Me: "Good coach, how are you?" Denny: "Not bad… well, we've decided that we're going to franchise you." He was referring to the "franchise tag," which a team can place on one player to restrict his movement as a free agent. In order to do this, a team must offer a contract that pays the player at least as much as the average of the top five players at his position. The problem with this is that the player who's been designated with this tag doesn't get the opportunity to shop around and possibly move to another team. We did have an ace up our sleeve though. Neil Cornrich, my agent, argued that the tag had already been used the year before on Randall McDaniel and that the team shouldn't be allowed to use it again until his contract expired. Randall had initially accepted the team's tender offer for the average of the top five at his position. He then signed a new longer-term contract before the start of training camp. Our position was that Randall had accepted the offer knowing that he would re-negotiate soon thereafter. The team was trying to get the franchise tag back unfairly. The case went in front of an arbitrator, and we won. I would be free to negotiate with other teams, further increasing my leverage.

I was in New York visiting some friends and competing in a celebrity slam-dunk competition at the NBA all-star game, when the Vikings made their first offer. When I got back to my friends' place that night, I saw that Neil had faxed me the Vikings' proposal—a four-year deal at almost $4 million a season. Those kinds of numbers had seemed inconceivable to me when I first started my career. Now I was going to become one of the league's highest paid runners. But Neil said, "Don't even think about it. They'll go much higher." Neil had always been right before, so I had no reason to doubt him. The numbers they offered were in line with running back contracts from the previous season. But a new, lucrative TV contract was in place this year, so there would likely be a corresponding leap in salaries.

I wanted to be back in Minnesota, but it wouldn't be at any price. I decided to make a couple of trips to other teams to put some pressure on them. My first trip was to Kansas City. I really didn't think much of Marty Schottenheimer, so they would have to say some pretty incredible things to get me there (partial team ownership probably would have gotten it done). I remember asking Marty what his off-season policy was like. He said that they liked to have all of their players up there for off-season workouts. That was it for me; not a chance. "I think a veteran player should be able to decide that for himself," I said. I'm sure he wanted to throw me out of his office right then.

I went from Kansas City directly to Seattle to visit the Seahawks. This was a place that felt good. I had met their head coach, Dennis Ericcson, when I visited the University of Miami in my high school days. I liked coach Ericcson and his coaching staff. The team had been struggling, but that's why they needed me. The Seahawks also had plenty of cash, and they were ready to spend it. I extended my stay up there, to give them a chance to make a contract offer. The deal they offered was higher than Minnesota's. Imagine, another team placed more value on me than the one I had played with for five years. I was very close to signing, but I wanted to give Minnesota more time. I flew to Baltimore for the Ed Block awards, knowing that I would have to make a decision soon.

The award ceremony was a beautiful event, but it was the trip we took earlier in the day that truly impacted all of the Award winners. The Ed Block Award Courage Foundation raises money to assist abused children in different communities. The Foundation sets up "Courage Houses" in cities around the country that cater to the special needs of these children. To hear some of the stories of abuse made us all realize what it means to be courageous. I had always known that football wasn't the most important thing in the world, but the visit to this facility really touched me. It was proof once again that life is not about what you get, it's about what you give. (You can find information on the Ed Block Foundation at www.edblock.com.)

While I was still in Baltimore, Neil called me with good news. The Vikings had agreed to our terms. Neil had done it again. He's a very intelligent and thorough individual. He got them to accept clauses that would ensure my ability to maximize dollars throughout the rest of my career. The Vikings were offering less money for a signing bonus, but they were a bit higher in overall dollars. All things being even close to equal, I wanted to be back in Minnesota. My contract was for five years, but there was a clause that would void the last two if I reached certain performance incentives. The next morning, which happened to be my birthday, I looked at the *USA Today* sports section and could hardly believe the headline for the article about my signing: "Smith Re-Signs with Vikings for $25 million."

It was the kind of money that quarterbacks were getting when I first got into the league. I never dared dream that I ever would sign a deal that big. In retrospect, it was a good thing that I had been injured the first time I became a free agent. The difference in money would have been staggering. I had been making great money before, but now I was going to be making as much in one year as I had in the previous five years of my career combined.

I flew to Minnesota that day to sign the contract. I felt an amazing sense of satisfaction and serenity. It wasn't just about the money; I didn't have to worry about getting hurt and not finishing the season. Now I could just concentrate on playing football and helping us win games. Not that the money wasn't a factor in the way I felt. Money isn't every-thing, but it sure can make some things a lot easier. If I took care of my finances, my family and I would be set for the rest of our lives. "I could even retire in a few years," I thought.

When I went into Jeff Diamond's office to sign the contract, it felt like a dream. I called Neil to go over the contract, which was long and complicated. But there's really only one paragraph that matters: para-graph 5. That is the one that gives your salary for any given year. Forget all the legalese; this paragraph simply states how much you're going to get paid. I received a $5 million signing bonus that was going to be paid in installments over the next couple of years. My first installment was for more than $2 million. When I left the office that day, I walked out with a check for more than $1 million.

The one certainty was that I wasn't going to just relax and get lazy. More than ever, I wanted to win and show that I belonged among the league's elite players. It's not that I felt I had anything to prove; it's just my personality. I like to feel that I'm always getting better at everything I do. This was my job, and I wanted to be as good at it as anyone. I also wanted to help the Vikings win a championship. As you progress in your football career, this becomes your primary focus. I've never been driven by personal accolades. Sure, I set goals for myself, but they were always based on what we achieved as a team. I still had not been part of a championship team, and I wanted that badly. I knew that I would play an integral part in any championship run, so I needed to work as hard as possible to get myself ready. We added more firepower to our already potent offense in that year's draft.

With the twenty-first overall pick, we drafted wide receiver Randy Moss of Marshall University. I remember seeing some of the highlights from his games as I sat in the players' lounge between meetings. Like everyone else, I was impressed with his speed and athleticism. It looked as if he was playing against children. It seemed so easy for him that I had to think it was because he wasn't playing at the highest level of Division I football. Randy had transferred from Florida State University after his freshman year. He never played there and he had only played two seasons at Marshall. The knock on Randy was that he had a bad attitude as well as some legal troubles. He had been arrested for fighting and for marijuana possession. He was also known to have a tendency to get mouthy with coaches and other players. Denny Green prides himself on his ability to bring the best out of all his players, regardless of their personalities. He believes that people are worth taking chances on, and that reputations don't always translate into reality. We couldn't believe that Randy had slipped down so far in the draft, but NFL personnel are like most people in that they oftentimes get caught in a particular mode of thinking. If they hear something bad about somebody enough times, they'll start to believe it. Most teams were afraid to take a chance on Randy. Denny wasn't.

When we got into camp that summer, it was an absolute zoo. People flocked by the thousands to see their beloved Vikings and rookie sensation Randy Moss. He was swamped by autograph seekers and media. People back home were constantly asking me how he looked in practice. I told them that I was stunned by the way Randy performed. I had seen plenty of great athletes perform in my day, but I had never seen anyone like him. He accelerated so smoothly and effortlessly that I could see how he could run right past embarrassed defensive backs so frequently. The most impressive part to me was that he had such "soft" hands, which means that he absorbed catches without struggling or using his body.

But you also got the sense that Randy's mouth had the potential to get him into trouble. I never had any problems with him that year, but I did have a couple of run-ins with him before I retired. It sounds funny for a man of 32 to say, but Randy's just part of a different generation. He walks around with a chip on his shoulder and oftentimes doesn't respect authority. It's one of the unfortunate possible side effects of hip-hop culture. The music talks with a lot of bravado and attitude towards the world, and many young people don't realize how to fit this into their own view of the world. Most of the music has become much less politically driven than the stuff I used to listen to. Public Enemy was always my favorite. They would talk about issues that really affected peoples' lives, not just about how much money they made or how many "bitches" they slept with. Artists like KRS-1 (knowledge reigns supreme over nearly everyone) used to rap about the need to educate yourself and improve your life; I don't hear much of that type of rap anymore.

I do believe that Randy is a good person. He's just had some trouble adjusting to his superstar status. He went through a media circus that's hard for me to imagine anyone enduring. I think the mask he sometimes wears shields him from a spotlight that burns on him with extraordinarily intense brightness.

The year had an amazingly different feel about it from the very beginning of camp. Everyone—players, coaches, and fans—had an infectious enthusiasm from the start. Part of that enthusiasm could be attributed to our new and extremely lively owner, Red McCombs. The first day he came storming in the locker room during camp, we all thought he was nuts (or drunk!).

Imagine this scene: a 70-something man with a bright purple shirt comes bounding into the locker room barking and shaking his fist in the air. Then he yells out cheerfully: "Purple pride! Purple pride!" (Korey Stringer later did the best imitation of Red.) Then he went into an enthusiastic speech about how proud he was to be the owner of such a great team and how he promised to do everything he could to help us win a championship. Red is in the used car business, and from the way he sold himself to us that day, I can see why the man's a billionaire. Red and his wife Charlene are truly nice people, and you can tell that they genuinely enjoy their relationship with the organization and the players. On one of our many trips to Manny's restaurant (which has the best Oysters Rockefeller on the planet), a group of us saw Red and Charlene having dinner. We said hello and went to have our meal. When we were finished and asked for the check, the waiter informed us that Red and Charlene had picked up our tab (it's funny, but when you finally make it and have your own money, you often find people picking up your tab; I wish I had had that luxury in college when I really needed it).

We breezed through the pre-season undefeated. This isn't usually very impressive by itself; the final outcome of these games is generally meaningless. Some teams that go winless in the pre-season will be quick to remind you of this. And when a team goes undefeated in the preseason, the media quickly will remind the world that the games don't count. But it wasn't the fact that we won all these games that was impressive; it was the way our first team performed in those wins that turned so many heads. Our offense seemed to be an unstoppable force. We didn't play the entire games, of course, but our efficiency and potency surprised even us. Clearly, we were no normal offensive power; it was something the league had never seen.

It was time to show what we could do in real game conditions. Our offense was going to be tested immediately by one of the strongest defensive teams in the league, Tampa Bay. The Bucs never had a chance that day. Although a very strong team defensively, Tampa didn't have much to offer on the offensive side of the ball. The Bucs relied on their stingy defense and a time-consuming, running game. If they fell behind, they were incapable of using their passing game to catch up. This was the situation they faced against us. Our defense held their running game at bay while our offense put on a well-balanced assault that left their defense reeling. We ran away with the game 31-7, an unusually large margin of victory for us over any division opponent, let alone Tampa Bay. The preseason had been no fluke; we were the real thing.

I'm glad I didn't have the job of trying to stop our offense that year. Put simply, we were loaded. We had so many weapons it seemed unfair. The running game's not working? No problem, throw to one of the receivers downfield. They're tightening down on the passing game? No problem, go back to the run. They've shut the run and the downfield passing game? No problem, throw it to the tight end underneath. We were a finely tuned and efficient offensive juggernaut. Brian Billick, our offensive coordinator, masterfully orchestrated us in dazzling performances. He was skilled at exploiting defenses' weaknesses and utilizing the full potential of his offensive arsenal. It didn't take long for the league to take notice.

The thing that made us most dangerous was the fact that we could score from anywhere on the field at any time. I had already shown my capabilities for the long run, but the addition of Randy Moss gave us an equally potent ability to strike with the long pass. In week four against Chicago, I caught a screen pass and sprinted up the left sideline for a 76-yard touchdown. Along the way, Randy ran next to me and we high-fived as we ran down the field. He was the only guy on the field capable of catching me.

I had made it down the field untouched (apart from the high five), but when I turned around to greet my teammates, I received a permanent reminder of the dangers of end zone celebrations. I had undone my chinstrap after I reached the end-zone and one of the linemen, Dave Dixon, came up and gave me a head butt. The force of the blow sent my helmet crashing down in the front and rammed my facemask into my mouth, knocking out a good portion of my two front teeth. I hadn't worn a mouthpiece since my rookie season because of the problems I had with my gag reflex. I had never experienced any troubles with my teeth through all those years of pounding, despite the fact that I had no mouth protection. Now I found myself spitting out pieces of my own teeth because of a friendly fire incident. I guess it was worth it, though; we won the game and improved our record to 4-0. It was time for a trip across the border for another match-up with Green Bay. They were also 4-0, and had not lost at home in their last 26 games at Lambeau.

When Green Bay visited us, it was sometimes hard to tell who was the home team. Green Bay has had an NFL franchise much longer than Minnesota, and it has built up quite a large fan base over that time. I'm not sure if it was Minnesota fans selling their seats or some other factor, but there were always an awful lot of Wisconsin Cheeseheads in the stands when the Packers played in the Metrodome. By contrast, there weren't a lot of purple jerseys in the seats at Lambeau Field. It was an atmosphere Denny loved—us against the world. Green Bay had been beating up on us up there for a few years, but this was a completely different Vikings team. To add to the excitement, the game was to be played on Monday Night Football.

A light drizzle that evening left tiny drops of water on everything in Lambeau. The glistening drops looked like stars illuminating a distant galaxy, and added a mesmerizing, dream-like atmosphere to the evening. It seemed like the perfect stage to perform magic. To those who witnessed the game, that's exactly what we did. It was an impressive show. Randall Cunningham had taken over for Brad Johnson at quarterback in week two after Brad had begun to lose feeling in his throwing hand. Randall got right back to his spectacular athletic displays. The constant threat of him running kept defenses honest every time he rolled out of the pocket. Combined with the threat of our strong running attack, it made for a long evening for the Pack. They just couldn't figure out what to focus on defensively. Even when they did guess right, it was no guarantee of success. They wanted to shut down Randy and the long passing game, and they often double-covered him—but not enough to stop him.

Randy caught five passes that night for 190 yards. Among those five catches were two long touchdowns in which Randy appeared to be well covered. The defensive backs must have wondered what they did to deserve the duty of defending against such an athlete. I also had the chance to get involved in the action of the passing game that night. I caught a screen on the left side and weaved my way through some defenders on the way to a 24-yard touchdown. When I turned around I saw Dave Dixon heading for me to celebrate again. The previous weekend's head-butt debacle with Dave was still fresh in my mind. I pointed at him and gave the signal for him to stop and get away from me. We laughed about it. We had a lot to be happy about that night. We went on to win 37-24, but the game was nowhere near that close. Doubters across the country began jumping on our bandwagon.

The locker room is always a fun place to be after a win. Everybody's just so happy, laughing and telling jokes. It gets pretty lively. They can even laugh about plays from the previous day that made them look stupid: "Alstott, trucked [ran over] your ass yesterday!" "I know man, I was just trying to get out of the way!" Even the coaches get in on the action. We would be watching film and someone would get leveled and Denny would say, "Way to give your body up for the team!" One of the players would yell out, "Hey, Denny, we better get him a CAT scan!"

It's hard to make anyone mad the day after a win. This season was going so well that the locker room rarely even had the blow-ups that inevitably occur between co-workers. There's always someone at your job that you just don't like. I don't care what your job is, it's pretty rare, if not impossible, to get along with everyone. And a football locker room is a less homogenous group than most offices. The personalities are just far more diverse. The physical nature of the game lends itself to conflict between employees. This is especially true with the offensive and defensive linemen. They get pretty riled up during their live one-on-one drills during the week. Normally, there would be some sort of altercation every week. Not that year. Everyone was so focused on getting better and winning that they didn't have time to start fights with one of their teammates. Like any office, the locker room divides itself into certain groups.

Normally these groups would be based on positions. Offensive linemen hung out with other offensive linemen, running backs with other running backs, offensive players hung out with other offensive players, etc. Of course this was partly due to the fact that you had most of your meeting time with players at your position or on your side of the ball. There just seemed to be less of a divide that year.

Since 1994 I had been sitting next to strong safety Robert Griffith. He and I made perfect neighbors in the locker room. It's a popular myth that players are just dumb jocks, but it is just that—a myth. Griff had been an electrical engineering major at San Diego State, and we always had some interesting things to talk about. Our topics ranged from religion to theoretical physics. People walking by would catch a few words and then hurry by. "Juice and Griff are gettin' deep again!" I remember the first year that Griff came into the league. He was under-sized for his position, but he played with such ferocity that he often knocked players many times his size flat on their backs. He had a great rookie training camp and seemed to be a lock to make the squad. The other defensive backs decided to play a joke on him on the final cut-down day. When players get cut, they have a letter in their locker that tells them to go see their position coach. They took one of those letters and put it in Griff's locker before he got in that morning. We all sat there with long faces looking dejected as Griff walked in. He looked into his locker and dropped his head. "Damn, man!" he said. One of the other defensive backs chimed in: "Man they're making some fucked up cuts this year!" Griff ripped the paper from his locker and started walking down the hall to go up and see his coach. One of the players finally ran down the hall and jumped on his back. "We were just messing with you, man!" They stared wrestling around and laughing. It was a cruel but funny joke.

We entered week nine of the season with a 7-0 record heading into Tampa Bay. We had trouble playing down there in the past, but this season was different—or so we thought. The day had a bad feel to it before we even took the field. The running back group would always go out before the pre-game practice to catch some passes from our position coach. When the time arrived that morning, our coach was nowhere to be found. He had stayed out a little late the night before and missed his wake up call—and multiple knocks on his door. They ended up having security open the door to get him up. He finally arrived about 45 minutes before kickoff. The rest of our day didn't get much better. Tampa controlled the clock with its best ever rushing performance (246 yards) and never gave us a chance to get things going with our running game. Randall threw the ball well to keep things close, but we ended up losing 27-24. It was a tough loss to take, but we were still in better shape than we thought we'd be at that point in the season. Even though 7-1 is a great record, "it depends on when you get the seven and when you get the one," as Denny said after the game.

No team was able to withstand our offensive onslaught the rest of the season. We finished with a 15-1 record, matching the second-best record in NFL history. We set a league record for most points scored in a season with 556. Randy Moss scored 17 touchdowns, the most ever by a rookie, and the list of Viking records for our team went on and on. I rushed for 1,187 yards despite missing two games with a knee injury. The season had made us the talk of the nation; our offense had reached almost mythical status.

They even used some of us in a commercial to hype the playoffs. The commercial was called "The Body." It talked about the way a team was similar to a body in that all of the parts played a role and needed each other to function properly. It showed some game clips and added some shots of us in various poses with our shirts off. I'm sure women loved this commercial! (I became something of a sex symbol in my last few years in the league. In my final season, there was a list on AOL that named me one of the world's 15 sexiest male athletes.) By the way, the narration for "The Body" commercial was:

Like the body, the eye cannot smell and the nose cannot hear
Running backs cannot run, unless linemen interfere.
Like the body, the mouth cannot see and the ear cannot speak.
Quarterbacks cannot survive without receivers' lightning feet.
We are a body—no jealousy, as a team we can get home.
Believe me, the I can't do it alone.

We also got a bye week to open the playoffs, so we'd have a chance to take a little time off. I decided to go to New Orleans to see the Buckeyes in the Sugar Bowl. In my hotel down there, one of the bellmen recognized me. "Hey, Robert Smith, right?" he said. "Hey, I really enjoy watching you play. Man, your first few years in the league you didn't go to camp, you got hurt all the time. You didn't do shit! But hey, man, you really turned out to be pretty damn good!" I laughed and thanked him. I had to appreciate his honesty; he had my career pretty well pegged. Things were drastically different for me now. Everywhere I went people were asking me for autographs and to have their picture taken with me.

If we had elevated status throughout the rest of the country, we were absolute giants in Minnesota. We were all people talked about. They even took one of those songs in which they changed the lyrics of a popular hit to add team names and player references. The song was originally called "Welcome to Miami" by Will Smith. They altered it to "We're Going to Miami" (the Super Bowl was in Miami that year). Almost everyone thought we were a lock to make it. Minnesotans started booking flights before the regular season was even over (you have to do something like this if you want to get a flight). Our dominating performance during the regular season was behind us now, though. If we wanted to win the ultimate prize, we were going to have to win three more games. Our first test was against the Arizona Cardinals. This game ended up looking like a carbon copy of one our regular-season games. They couldn't handle us. We won 41-21 to advance to the championship game. One more win and we were in the Super Bowl. Our final hurdle to clear was the Atlanta Falcons.

Throughout the week leading up to the game, I kept trying to tell myself that this was just a game. I was wrong. I had always tried not to get myself too worked up for games but I just couldn't help myself this time. It was all I could think about. If we won that Sunday, we'd be advancing to one of the biggest sporting events in the world. It's the day when nearly everyone in this nation becomes a spectator. And for the players, it's a chance to become the very best at what they do. It's about winning that ring. It's about being crowned world champions. Just get by this last team and you're in. Minneapolis had worked itself into an absolute frenzy. I remember driving to the hotel the night before the game and seeing buildings lit up with Vikings logos on them. We knew we were the better team. We just had to perform.

When I got up the morning of the game, I was struck with the finality of the day. At one of the meetings earlier in the week, Denny had asked all the players who had played in a championship game to raise their hands. Only three hands went up. "You see men," he said, "This is the opportunity of a lifetime. This chance may never come for you again."

I got to the Metrodome and took the stairs to the locker room. We had to walk through the press level to get to our locker room. The media had already arrived in large numbers, preparing to cover the game. You could see the field from the press level. The NFL logo was painted on the field with the words "NFC Championship Game" around it. There was no question that the time had arrived.

The locker room looked the same as it did on any game day, but it felt completely different. There was a palpable atmosphere of intensity I had never experienced. You could sense the desire and focus in the players. We went through our normal pre-game activities, but with a purpose of action appropriate for the task at hand.

They were going to announce the offensive unit, so we hung back in the crowd of players walking down the tunnel. We slapped each other on the helmets and offered last words of encouragement. "Let's go, Juice!" "Let's go, Big K!" "Let's go, Moss!" "Let's get it done, Randall!" The sound of the crowd thundered through the opening of the tunnel. They had erected an inflatable Viking ship at the entrance to the field, and the offensive players stayed in the tunnel as the other players stormed through the ship. They announced the starters on offense. As usual, I was last. "At running back, number 26, Robert Smith!" I slowly jogged out through the tunnel and slapped low fives with the other players lined up in a gauntlet. The stadium was an absolute blaze of raging fervor. It was hard to contain my emotions. I wondered how the fans in the stands could handle this level of stimulation without the release that playing would bring us as athletes.

The high intensity of play was apparent immediately. The Falcons didn't care that they weren't favored. To them, the game represented the same thing it did to us—an opportunity to advance to the biggest game. They weren't going to give up that chance without a struggle. We started the same way we had all year—we were dominant. We moved the ball at will. Atlanta had the top-rated defense in the league that year, but it just couldn't contain us. We built a 20-7 lead with less than a minute to go in the first half. We had the ball deep in our own territory when chance took a turn against us. Randall dropped back to pass and had the ball knocked from his hand. Atlanta recovered the ball and scored a quick touchdown. We went into the half with a 20-14 lead.

We came out for the second half determined not to let this be our last game of the year. We scored a touchdown early in the second half, but we couldn't muster much offensive production as we entered the fourth quarter. The Falcons had kicked two field goals to make the score 27-20 with just over six minutes to go in the game.

As we stood on the sideline ready to take the field, we all understood the importance of the upcoming drive: If we went down the field and scored, the game was all but over and we were on our way to Miami. We spontaneously held hands in the huddle, something we had never done. Randall spoke: "All right men, it's on us. Let's do it!" The call came to me. I ran for about 8 yards. They came back to me. I took the ball and headed up the right sideline into Atlanta territory, a 20-yard gain. I needed a little break. I jogged to the sideline and Leroy Hoard took the field. He gained five yards on the play and I returned to the huddle. They came back to me again…another good gain. *They want you to do it man. Stay on the field… This is your time!...Come back to me!...Give it to me!"*

We were all breathing heavily in the huddle. "We're coming back to you, Juice!" Randall said, "Let's get it done!" I broke through the line and took the ball down inside the Atlanta 30. I was gassed. I could barely stand up. Luckily for me, one of their players was shaken up on the play, so I got a rest. We were nearing field goal range.

"All right men, let's finish the job," Randall said. He completed a pass to Randy Moss for a first down on the 25. I took the ball down to the 20, then was stopped for no gain on second down. On third down, I went out for a pass over the middle. Randall dropped back and threw the ball out of bounds. On the play, the linebacker came up to engage me and his knee ran into my thigh. I instantly dropped to the turf in pain. *"Get up!...We've got it!...Get your ass to the sideline and get ready to heal-up for the Super Bowl!"*

Gary Anderson and the field goal unit took the field. Gary had not missed a kick all year. This kick seemed to be guaranteed. But he pulled towards the left upright...and missed the kick. It seemed impossible. The man who was perfect all year had missed the kick that would have clinched the Super Bowl.

It's all right, we can hold them... but it wasn't to be. They marched down the field and scored a touchdown to tie the game and send it to overtime. On the play before their touchdown, one of our defensive backs dropped a potential interception in the end zone. We seemed destined to lose at that point. The Falcons lined the ball up in overtime to kick the game-winning field goal. The entire stadium held its collective breath as the ball sailed through the uprights...and with it our chance at a Super Bowl championship.

We walked to the locker room in a daze. As we entered, we saw the banners that had been set up to celebrate our victory. Some yelled, some cried. Some, like me, just sat stunned in front of our lockers. We had come so close. We had it in our grasp. We had let it slip away. I felt so empty, so helpless. When my team needed me most, I was there—but it didn't matter. Our season was over. Our chance to be the best was shattered. Not many players wanted to speak to the media after the game, but I felt I had a responsibility to talk. A reporter asked me how it felt to lose in such a heart-breaking way. I sat silently for a second, then answered with choked back tears: "It's an awfully miserable feeling, but if this is the worst thing that ever happens to me, then I'm a pretty lucky person."

It's been more than four years since that game—and it still stings. In order to get the details of the last drive, I had to go watch a tape of it. The general details and the emotions involved were easy to recall, but I had forgotten the exact numbers. Up to that last drive, I had carried the ball 15 times for 27 yards. On the last drive, I ran 6 times for 45. As always, it took great line play and persistent downfield effort from the wide-outs to be successful in the run. We committed ourselves to the run on that drive and that took a special kind of attitude considering the way they had defended the run earlier. Looking back on my career, I can say that I stepped up when my team needed me most—and I'm proud of that.

On the game tape, John Madden is the commentator. He referred to me as a warrior for my performance on that drive. He mentioned Michael Jordan and Larry Bird as he described my obvious desire to rise to the occasion. It's flattering to have been mentioned with such great athletes but there's a big difference between me and those two giants of their sport: They won championships, and that's a void that I'll never be able to fill.

Brian Billick, our offensive coordinator, took the vacant Baltimore Ravens' job not long after the game. He was instrumental in designing and implementing the offensive scheme that had so dominated teams that year. It's hard to hold on to assistant coaches who are that talented. When teams perform as well as we did that year, it gives opportunities to all members of an organization. That's why it's so difficult to keep teams together now.

I had been voted an alternate for the Pro Bowl during the season. The league told me that it was having difficulty contacting Barry Sanders, so I would need to be available to fly to Hawaii to take his place. As it turns out, Barry had played his final NFL game and, apparently, didn't want to make one last trip to the Pro Bowl. So I ended up going out there and playing in the game. Football is a sport that doesn't need an all-star contest; it's just too dangerous. Football is not the type of sport that lends itself to easy-going games; you have to go full speed if you want to protect yourself (unlike baseball or basketball.) It was fun to be in Hawaii and be recognized as one of the best in the NFL, even if it was only because Barry had decided to hang up his cleats earlier than everyone expected. Maybe he was on to something, I thought.

We opened the next season by avenging our loss to the Falcons. We posted a 17-14 victory in Atlanta, and it felt good. But it did little to erase the memory of the painful NFC Championship Game loss.

We returned most of our players from the previous year's team, so our prospects were good for this season, too; however, things didn't go well for us early in the year. We just couldn't get things going offensively. We had a new offensive coordinator, but we hadn't changed much dramatically from last season. The way of the league goes like this: If you have the talent and you have the system, then somebody isn't running things the right way. The first finger usually gets pointed directly at the quarterback. They are undoubtedly the most important players on the field. When things are going well, they usually get too much of the credit, and when things are going poorly, they get too much of the blame. When things aren't running smoothly offensively, the back-up quarterback is the most popular guy in town. Things were no different for us. Denny Green felt that we needed a spark offensively, so he turned the quarterback position over to Jeff George (from Randall Cunningham).

Denny made the change in the middle of the game in Detroit. I had been struggling with a groin problem in the early part of the season and the truth is that I needed to come out of this game before the quarterback change was made. As it turned out, I had a double inguinal hernia. This is truly a condition I wouldn't wish on anyone. The abdominal wall develops a weak spot, and a portion of the intestines begins to protrude in that area; it's extremely uncomfortable. I'm still amazed by the litany of injuries I suffered through during my career. I was a veritable case study on the various physical problems that a player could develop during a career. It was just another thing I had to work through; there was no sense in complaining about it.

We ended up with a 2-4 record after six weeks—quite a departure from our previous run, and Minnesota was looking for answers anywhere and everywhere. After one of the losses, a fan sent an e-mail to one of the assistant offensive coaches complaining about the behavior of some Vikings players after a game. He talked about me and a couple of other players getting a little wild at one of the local establishments despite the fact that we had just lost. The fan said that our lack of concern must be a contributing factor in our sub-par start. He said we were carrying on with a bunch of women,(he said that I had two—I sometimes wish that my life was as wild as some people thought it was!) smoking weed, and acting in a way that wasn't appropriate for guys who had just been defeated on the field. What did this guy want us to be doing? Are athletes supposed to climb into a hole to hide themselves from the world because they've lost a game? If you have a bad day at work, do you walk around with your head hung in shame? The fact is that we hated losing but we weren't going to act as if losses depressed us. Being a professional athlete is stressful work, and when games were over we let off steam. The celebrations and lamentations looked pretty much the same. We smoked weed occasionally, but we were never so bold or stupid to do it in a bar. A lot of people don't feel that athletes deserve the attention they get, and the guy who sent the e-mail was probably just jealous because of the women who were with us. This isn't to say that we were angels though—who is? Sunday nights after games and Monday nights were our big nights out, and it wasn't hard for us to find some action in town.

Up to that point in my career, I had been dating the same woman from back home. But I had broken up with her after the previous season, so this was the first time that I had a taste of the true single life of an NFL player. It's funny, but, until then, I was the guy whom players would use as an alibi and a reason to trust that an evening out wouldn't get out of control. "Yeah, I was out with Robert," they would say. I was seen by many people as somewhat of a saint. I never got in trouble, and when I did go out I was pretty reserved. It didn't take me long to establish a very different sort of reputation. Every game day, I'd sit next to my partner in crime, Mitch Berger, and we'd discuss the evening's plans. "What's goin' on tonight, Mitch?" "My parents are in town," he'd say, "so I'll meet them for dinner, but then we'll hit it." Mitch was a famously single guy as well, and we quickly became known as two of the team's most prominent party fixtures. It's an absolute miracle that we didn't get arrested; we came close a few times.

One night after the bars closed we took a couple of girls to one of the grocery stores to grab some food before going back to Mitch's place. Of course, we had to get in a little shopping cart bobsledding first. The game is simple enough: one person gets in the cart and the other person does a full sprint down one of the aisles while pushing their bobsled teammate. It's a pretty amusing game, at least for the inebriated participants. The grocery store workers weren't nearly as amused. We could sense that they weren't real pleased with our antics, so we decided to make an early exit without picking up any food. It was a good thing we did, because the cruisers were rolling into the parking lot just as we were rolling out. It was announced on the radio the next morning that I had been arrested the previous evening. The report was incorrect, of course, but it wasn't for lack of trying.

We became fodder for the local gossip columnists and talk radio shows. Some girl went on the air and said she had an affair with me and then found out I was married. This was untrue, but that doesn't matter when you reach a certain level of celebrity. People basically can say whatever they want about you. Of course, sometimes the media gets out of hand and reports rumors that have no truth to them. The things that people were saying about me were pretty harmless. I didn't care if some people thought I had kids or that I was gay or that I was married. But I could see how someone such as Tom Cruise would go through so much effort to pursue someone making remarks about his sexuality. How would you like to be in the grocery store checkout line with your kids and have them read something like that about you?

It's ridiculous how obsessed America is with celebrity and it's even more absurd the things that they'll believe. And just because something is said certainly doesn't make it true. Like Jim Rome calling me the smartest man in the NFL. Was I? I doubt it. I didn't even have the highest score on the team on the Wunderlick test. I guess if someone's going to say something about you that might not be true, it might as well be a compliment. Rome's show is very popular, so what he said just kind of stuck. Everywhere I went people would say, "Hey, it's the smartest man in the NFL." They automatically assume that you're smarter than the average player if you're the least bit articulate. It goes with the myth that players aren't as smart as the rest of our society. Of course, the truth is that "most" people in our society aren't that bright.

I couldn't believe how my popularity had grown. It amazed me how they could even recognize me with my helmet off. Everywhere I traveled around the nation, someone would recognize me. "Hello, Mr. Smith, welcome to the Plaza Hotel." "Hello, Mr. Smith, welcome to L.A." I was making appearances on national television shows and I started appearing in national commercials. All this from a guy who could barely finish half a season only a few years earlier. I was on *The Wheel of Fortune*, *Jeopardy* (only to give video answers, not as a contestant.) I also had a spot on the *Late, Late Show, With Craig Kilborn*.

Jeff George (we called him "Trigger" because of his quick release) came in and gave us the needed spark. Randall Cunningham said that he wasn't used to the drop-back style offensive coordinator Ray Sherman had implemented that year and that that was the reason he struggled early on. I don't know the quarterback position well enough to know if that held any truth, but I still felt bad for Randall. The guy had done a great job for us the previous year, and now was relegated to the back-up position on a team that was improving all of the time. That's the way things go in the league, though: One minute you're on top of the world, the next minute it seems like the same world is against you.

We turned things around with Jeff and finished the season with a 10-6 record. We played Dallas at home in a Wild Card playoff game. We dominated them with a well-balanced offensive attack and I had a huge day rushing for 147 yards and scoring two touchdowns. I was really starting to come into my own as a player. It wasn't that the game was easy for me, it just felt more natural. Confidence played a major role in my new-found comfort. I had always believed that I could play with the league's elite, and now I was proving it to everyone else. I was happy we were winning games, but I still had a burning desire to play for the championship. The thought consumed me. Our hopes for a title were once again dashed as we lost in the next round to eventual champion, St. Louis.

It was clear that we were among the league's top teams but we just didn't seem to be able to make it over the last hurdle. Denny Green had taken over as general manager of the team and was feeling increased pressure to at least make it to the big one. He made some personnel changes after the season that seemed to reflect this stress. He fired our offensive coordinator and made the controversial decision to let both Randall Cunningham and Jeff George go. He had drafted Daunte Culpepper in the first round the previous year but Daunte had looked shaky and unprepared for a starting role in practice. It seemed as if Denny was ignoring everyone else's advice, and even scaring some people within the organization. One of the reporters asked me to confidentially remark on Denny's attitude and I told him that it reminded me of Saddam Hussein's method of imposing his will. Of course, I didn't think that he was that bad, but it did seem that he was a bit paranoid and unwilling to listen to anyone's input. I don't think Denny had much trouble figuring out who had made a reference like that. I always have been, and will be, an ardent supporter of Denny, but we all need to be willing to listen to the advice of those working alongside us.

Denny was dead set on making Daunte the starter. Most of us thought it was a questionable idea. Some of the players joked while they watched him in practice the previous season that their kids would be playing professionally by the time Daunte was ready to start. He really just didn't look very good in practice. He would run the two-minute drill against our defense and oftentimes look mechanical or confused. He definitely had the physical tools. I remember seeing him in his first mini-camp meeting and thinking that he was a defensive player. He also had a strong arm but that doesn't mean a thing if you can't play the position. He was pretty defensive about his play and seemed unwilling to listen to constructive criticism. I didn't think he'd make it as a starter. I thought he had a bad attitude. I thought he'd be replaced as the starter very early in the year. I couldn't have been more wrong, but I wasn't the only one who questioned the wisdom of using Daunte as a first-time starter. Most of the "experts" around the country felt the same way. There was only one person that needed to believe in Daunte and that was Daunte himself.

Daunte showed how dangerous he could be in our regular-season opener at home against Chicago. He accounted for 260 yards of offense (190 through the air) and ran for three touchdowns. He had all the weight of the world on his shoulders heading into that game and he responded exquisitely. Daunte weighed about 260 then and the sight of him breaking into the secondary must have been truly frightening to anyone charged with the task of bringing him down. Daunte played like a younger and much bigger version of Randall Cunningham. Daunte also led with a fiery competitiveness while exhibiting cool generalship of the huddle. I'm not sure of his exact story, but Daunte's grandmother took care of most of the responsibilities of raising him. She did a great job; he is one of the most humble and polite superstars you'll ever meet. He came in and proved everyone wrong about him. But he didn't gloat. Daunte just wants to win...and be a good person at the same time. It was a pleasure playing with him and more of a pleasure to know him.

Behind Daunte's running and throwing and my running we roared out of the gates to another 5-0 start. The team had decided to use me in all offensive situations. Previously, I had come out on goal-line and third-down plays. I also was approaching Chuck Foreman's Vikings' career rushing record. I had never been caught up in records, but this one was important for me. After all the problems I had experienced early in my career, this record seemed like a vindication of sorts. I ended up passing Foreman in the sixth game, against Chicago. Most importantly to me, though, is the fact that I was awarded the game ball for my performance in that game. The record was important, but it was still more important that I help us win games. We had been down 9-0 early in the Bears' game and I broke off a 72-yard run to change the game's momentum. We went on to win 28-16. I rushed for 170 yards and became the team's all-time leading rusher that night. More importantly, we moved to 6-0 for the season. We won our next game, making us 7-0 heading into a game at Tampa Bay.

That place just had us. Some teams just don't play well in certain venues, but I recently read a study that tried to elicit reasons for the so-called "home field advantage." It mentioned a few factors like crowd noise and fatigue from traveling but the most interesting possible explanation was that home teams, on average, have higher levels of testosterone in their systems. It's the theory that males prepare themselves mentally to defend their home territory. It makes some sense. Whatever the reason, we just couldn't put it together down there. We lost 41-13 and headed to Green Bay the following week for a Monday night match-up against the Packers. It ended up being a painfully similar experience to the one we had in the championship game against Atlanta. We fought closely for most of the game and lined up for a field goal in the fourth quarter that would have all but sealed the victory for us. It seemed like a good hold but Gary Anderson didn't feel he should kick, for some reason. Mitch Berger was the holder on field goals and did his best to salvage the play, but ended up throwing the ball to one of their players. The game went into overtime and we lost 26-20. It was an extremely frustrating loss for all of us. We had decided to concentrate on running the ball late to put us into position for a field goal attempt. I had a big night—my best ever on Monday night. I ran for 122 yards, had 67 additional receiving yards, and scored a touchdown. Before the field goal attempt, Bob Hagen, our media director, told me that the sideline crew for *Monday Night Football* wanted to talk to me after what had appeared to be a game-winning performance. So much for that interview. As it turned out, winning that game would have given us home field advantage in the playoffs.

It didn't take us long to get back on track after those setbacks. We won four straight games, including a big prime-time performance over Dallas on Thanksgiving. Daunte threw for 200 yards and two touchdowns, and I added 148 yards on the ground and scored a touchdown. Daunte, Randy, Cris, and I were chosen as recipients of John Madden's six-legged turkey award. We were winning games and looking good doing it. We won the following Thursday night against Detroit to extend our new win streak to four games. We seemed primed to roll into the playoffs and make a run at the championship. But things didn't go well in the last few weeks. We just couldn't get into rhythm offensively. I carried the ball 15 times or less in each contest. Our defense also gave up 104 points in those three games. It wasn't the ideal way to head into the post-season. We finished with an 11-5 record but, once again, it depends on when you get the 11 and when you get the 5.

The season marked the first time in my career that I had played in all 16 regular-season games. I ended with 1,521 yards to break my own team record. I also led the NFC and was second in the league in rushing.

I was named to the Pro Bowl, named an all-pro, and even made the all-Madden team. The award that meant the most to me, though, was the NFL Alumni naming me Running Back of the Year. I thought to myself, "What could make this season better?" And the clear answer was to finish it with a championship. We had a bye the first round of the play-offs and then faced New Orleans in a Divisional game. It was a good confidence re-builder for us. We got things in order again and walked away with a 34-16 win. Once again we found ourselves one win away from the Super Bowl. If we had had one more regular-season win, the championship game would have been a home game, but as it was, we would have to travel to New York to play the Giants.

I don't know how many times road teams have been favored in championship games, but I'm sure it hasn't happened too often. We were favored to win. The week of preparation left me convinced that the odds-makers were right. We seemed to be over the troubles that plagued us in the final three regular-season games. We seemed poised to advance to the Super Bowl.

I had been considering making this my last season since I signed my last contract. I knew that I would be able to void the final two years of my deal, making myself a free-agent after the season. The year had gone so well and so many things had gone right that I thought the scenario pointed to only one conclusion: I would be able to retire as the team's leading rusher following my best year and with at least a Super Bowl appearance and very likely a ring. I ran onto the field that cold day in New York with an excitement and sense of purpose that I had never felt throughout my career. It seemed like this would be the day I would get one step closer to completing the most important achievement in my career. I felt like there was no way we could lose.

But something went terribly wrong. We were down two touchdowns before we even had a chance to realize what had happened. And we never recovered. People ask me to this day what happened to us in that game. I honestly don't know. It was as if the team that had prepared all week failed to even make an appearance on that frozen field. 41-0. Yes, 41-0! We had never been shut out my entire time in Minnesota. We had one of the most potent offenses the league had ever seen. And, yet, when it came time to play, we lost our composure. We were embarrassed in one of the greatest upsets in championship history—again. At least the last time we put up a great fight. This was a trouncing, an ass-kicking. And this was the end of my career.

?

I'm the one that's got to die when it's time for me to die, so let me live my
life the way I want to.

—Jimi Hendrix

I know why the caged bird sings.

—Maya Angelou

I announced my retirement from professional football on February 6, 2001. The announcement was simple: I thanked my teammates, my coaches, the Vikings organization, and my family and friends for their support throughout my career.

The thought process that led to the decision was much more complicated. And like all important decisions in life, it was a difficult one. The choice came as a shock to many people, based on its timing, because I was only 28 and coming off an all-pro season. Why would someone do something like this?

I recently looked at some articles that discussed my retirement and saw some of the reasons that people considered for my "surprise" move. The first and most obvious was that the pounding had become too much for me to take, that my knees had given out. This is simply not true. Granted, my knees had taken their share of pounding and I had gone under the knife four different times, but they were strong enough to continue. After the 2000 season I went back to Dr. Steadman to have a procedure called micro-fracture performed on my right knee. I also had some loose pieces of cartilage removed from the joint. Dr. Steadman uses the micro-fracture technique to help stimulate the growth of cartilage in the articular surfaces of the knees. These are the areas that line the ball segment of the knee joint. When holes or large areas of these surfaces are damaged, it can cause a great deal of discomfort because the bone becomes exposed and comes into contact with other bone within the knee. The knee is an amazing joint. These surfaces, along with the joint lubricant (synovial fluid), ensure that the knee operates smoothly and pain free. I did have small holes in places in this cartilage on my right knee but nothing that would have prevented me from playing in the years ahead.

When I went to see Dr. Steadman the week before I retired I told him that I was considering leaving the game. I guess a part of me wanted to hear from him that he thought it was a good idea because of the condition of my right knee. It seemed as if his support would have made the decision less difficult. But he actually told me that he wanted to see me play more. I was shocked. Here was a guy who had worked on my knees on four separate occasions telling me he thought it would be a better idea to go back to continue the abuse. I think he just enjoyed watching me play and overcoming all of the problems that I had had early in my playing days. Dr. Steadman is very proud of the work he does—and he should be. He's an unbelievably talented surgeon. It must make him feel good to see the players he's worked on go back to regain their former level of proficiency. (Dr. Steadman did tell me later that year that he thought my decision was the right one; he came to understand the reasons behind it.)

Then there were those who thought I retired because I couldn't stand being on the same team as Randy Moss. This argument didn't make sense because I wouldn't have had to stay with Minnesota. I was a free agent and I could have gone to any team I wanted because my agent had put the clause in my previous contract that did not allow the Vikings to place any restrictions (franchise or transition tag) on my movement.

That is not to say that I always enjoyed being around Randy. I had had a couple of run-ins with his mouth that left me less than impressed with his attitude. In his second training camp I had approached him to get some jerseys signed for the charity I started (see Chapter 8). I had told him earlier that morning that I had six or seven for him to sign (those were the numbers that my foundation director had given me over the phone). When the director gave me the box of jerseys, it contained 12. I took them to Randy as we waited to go up into the lunch room between practices. He was sitting in front of a TV playing a Playstation game. He stopped signing after about half were signed and said that I had told him that there would only be 6 or 7. "That's what he told me, Randy—is it gonna kill you to sign a few more?" "Well you said there'd only be 6 or 7." "Man, just forget it!" All of the jerseys were for charity and he couldn't even take a few extra seconds away from a video game to sign them for one of his teammates? I knew that he was bothered all the time for autographs, but this was ridiculous.

Then there was the time in the locker room before a Tampa Bay game when Randy put his laptop on a table right behind where I was sitting and started blasting his music. Everyone on the team knew that you were supposed to wear headphones in the locker room so you don't bother other players. Everyone prepares for games a different way, and I liked to listen to fairly quiet music to calm myself before the storm (I got on an Aretha Franklin kick my last couple of years in the league). I got up and told him to turn it off or put on headphones. "You know what Denny says about that shit," I said. "Fuck Denny," Randy said. "He ain't here." "Look, Randy, you either turn it off, or I'll turn it off for you!" "All right, fuck it, man!" This incident made it into the newspapers and they said that we had to be separated. It never got to that point, but I assure you that if it had come to that, they wouldn't have been separating us, they would have been pulling me off him!

In all seriousness, Randy and I didn't have a bad relationship. We weren't "boys," but we got along. And I was glad to have him as a teammate. He's taken quite a bit of heat for some of his comments and for taking plays off, but I have to say I think Randy is an unbelievable player who did a great job most of the time blocking down field. Did he take some plays off? Yes, but you can't go full speed every play after running down field five times in a row. There were some runs in which his guy got me downfield, but there were more times when his block sprung me on one of those 50-yard runs. When Randy had his incident with the "super" fake traffic cop in downtown Minneapolis a couple of years ago, I came out in his defense. I basically said that the guy's not perfect but he isn't a murderer or a rapist. The guy tries and you could see from his emotional apology that his hard exterior hides a sensitive, sometimes overwhelmed superstar. I think Randy's a good man and that people are just waiting to pounce on him for any infraction. I wanted to hit him in the mouth a few times, yes, but that doesn't mean I think he's a bad guy. And I certainly wouldn't have retired just to get away from him.

There were some who suggested that my embarrassment over the 41-0 Championship Game loss to New York forced me into retirement. I like to think of myself as a pretty reasonable person. I certainly have a greater sense of perspective than to become so upset with losing a game that I would retire. I hated losing, no question about that, but that was a stretch. If anything, losing that game made me want to stick around.

An even greater stretch was the theory that I feigned retirement in a negotiation ploy. This was ridiculous. I had all the leverage I needed from the season I had just played. I was completely free to sign with another team and was positioned to sign one of the highest running back contracts of all time. People were surprised and confused by my decision. They couldn't understand how I could walk away from so much money. But money wasn't the only reason I had for staying.

The failure to win a championship was at the top of the list. I knew that retiring would leave me with no way to alleviate the pain of those two championship losses. Football isn't war, but it isn't "just" a game, either. We failed in the opportunity to reach the pinnacle of our profession. Winning a Super Bowl championship can be the defining moment in a player's career. It's not that players can't be considered great without a championship, but I'm sure Dan Marino would trade all of those records he has for a Super Bowl ring. I've never worn jewelry—and I wouldn't wear something as gaudy as a Super Bowl ring—but that ring was something I had a burning desire to get. If I retired, that desire was going to remain unfulfilled.

Most jobs do not have such a clearly defined event that marks the ultimate level of achievement in their field. To people outside of football, Super Bowl Sunday is a day of parties, gambling, and a few memorable commercials. But for people inside the game, it stands as the only chance to end a grueling season's work victoriously. People on the outside don't see the work that goes into preparing for an NFL season. They also don't realize the number of things that must go right for a team during the course of a season in order for them to be successful. There must be supreme coordination between all phases of the game and all the players on the field if a team is to triumph on game day. This says nothing of the luck a team needs to stay healthy enough to qualify for the playoffs. And then the playoffs are sudden-death elimination: You lose, you're out. In the playoffs, you can't say, "Oh well, we'll get 'em tomorrow." If you don't win every game, you go home unfulfilled for at least another year. Regret for the things you do is tempered with time, regret for the things you fail to do is inconsolable. I don't know who said that, but it's certainly true.

I also felt that by quitting I'd be letting Denny Green down. Denny was always willing to be my corner man—and it wasn't always an easy thing to do. I sustained a few minor injuries in my last season at Ohio State and many people felt that I would be unable to stay healthy during an NFL season. This, combined with the fact that I had challenged the coaching staff by sitting out a season, made some teams shy away from me. Not Denny. He used the first first-round pick the Vikings had in 5 years to take me. I remember the phone call as if it was yesterday. "I'm not going to let you get away again," he said to me.

There's a special bond that develops between a great coach and his players. There's a mutual respect that you feel because you can sense that you're both after the same thing: winning. From a coach such as Denny, you get the feeling that he would gladly suit up and join you on the battlefield. You can feel it in the way he talks inside the locker room. You can see it in the intensity of his stare on the sideline.

And with me, Denny had to be patient. I sustained injuries in my first four seasons that caused me to miss 23 games. The media and fans were trying to convince Denny that I was a hopeless cause, that I would never be able to contribute to the team the way I should. I remember sitting in Denny's office on the verge of tears because I needed to have another surgery. In my mind, I was letting him down. I wasn't able to prove that he was right, that I was capable of being one of the best in the game. Many corner men would have thrown in the towel, but Denny stuck with me. In my final four seasons, I was finally able to live up to the expectations that Denny had for me. More than anything else, that is what made my last four years as enjoyable as they were. I was one of "Denny's guys," and after all the years of me being able to call on him, he could rely on me to do the things he knew I could do. I wanted to win a ring for him as much as I did for myself. Then why walk away? For one thing, I knew it made more sense to walk away early than to limp away late.

I had always known that football takes a tremendous toll on the body, which simply was not made to withstand the pounding that it takes in football. You are one play away from your career ending whenever you play football. It is not so much a contact sport as it is a collision sport. Every year people sustain injuries while playing that affect them the rest of their lives. I didn't want to be one of those people. I considered myself fortunate to still be at the top of my game after the multiple surgeries I had had. But I also knew that I couldn't go on without risking further damage to my knees. It's not that I couldn't continue, but I felt it made more sense to leave. I could have come back and signed a blockbuster contract, but you can't make decisions based solely on anticipated rewards. You also must acknowledge and evaluate risk. I had to ask myself if the money I would earn by continuing to play was worth the possible damage to my body that could result. Think about it: If you'd give any amount of money to regain your health if you lost it, is there any amount of money you'd accept to have it taken away?

The fact that I played running back meant that my chances for injury were even greater. Running backs take a tremendous pounding in football and have the shortest average careers. Every player on the defense is attempting to come at you when you carry the ball. Quarterbacks are pursued, but they are often only hit by one or two players at a time. Receivers, as well, usually only get hit by one or two players. But running backs are attempting to carry the ball through the congestion in the middle of the field. You often get hit by three or four players moving at you from different directions. It actually amazes me that running backs don't get hurt more often. I was greatly impressed by players such as Emmitt Smith and Barry Sanders, who seemed to defy logic with their ability to stay healthy.

But there was more to it than simply being concerned about future injuries. You have to retire from pro football at some time. It's simply not the kind of game you can play indefinitely. I had been playing for eight years, and that was longer than I ever thought I'd play. I had always envisioned football as a means to an end and when I felt that it had done enough for me, I would move on. I truly enjoyed the level of competition and being considered one of the best in the world in my profession. But I knew I wasn't one of the players that would have to be dragged kicking and screaming away from the sport. I would have been crazy not to take advantage of the opportunity to play professional football. It provided a life of comfort for me and my family. It also gave me enough money to pay for my education many times over. However, I was different than most players: I loved playing, but I was never in love with the game.

NFL football is a business, and players spend many hours each week preparing for games. Players eat, sleep, and drink football for six months a year. Meetings, films, chalkboards, practice—it all became very tedious for me. I had never been a big fan of football and to have to spend all that time preparing to play a game really started to wear on me. It was like being caught in a remedial math class each week. The game was not intellectually challenging for me. Once again, playing games is not like being at war, but football training has a structure similar to the military. Management feels that you perform better as a unit if you spend time together constantly. You eat together; sit through meetings together, shower together. And it becomes very difficult to handle season after season. Players would oftentimes fly out the day after the season ended just to get away from each other.

It's not that I had an immediate plan for what career I wanted to move into, but I also knew that my desire to leave the game was stronger than my desire to stay in it. Some players only know football. It is all they are. I never let football define me as a person. Football was what I did, not who I was. I had gone over the scenarios in my mind enough times. I had thought about all the positive things I could achieve if I stayed in the game. I had thought about all the people I would make happy if I continued to play. But it boiled down to the most important person in the process—me. I was the one who would have to live with the consequences of my decision. I gave a great deal to football, and I received a great deal in return. I had made more money than I ever thought possible. I wasn't going to be going out and buying a private jet, but I had done pretty well for myself. I had played eight seasons and would be able to walk away healthy and on my own terms, something few players get the opportunity to do. My mind was made up; it was time to move on.

I decided to make the announcement through one of the reporters who had covered me in high school. Bob Fortuna had worked for the *Euclid Sun Journal* when I attended Euclid High School. He had since moved to the *Cleveland Plain Dealer* and I thought it seemed appropriate that a guy who had covered me since the beginning of my career should be the one to break the story about the end of it. When the story came out the next day, the response was quick and dramatic. Even CNN thought it was big enough news to use it as a tease: "A surprise retirement from the NFL, coming up next on Headline News!" I had calls coming in from everywhere. Every major news station and paper in the country called me to do interviews. I needed to get away and fortunately I didn't have to wait long. I had planned a trip to Australia with a couple of Viking teammates, so I'd be able to escape the questions for a while. I knew I wanted to make my decision quickly after the season. I didn't want to have to deal with the free-agency process if I ended up not retiring and I also wanted to give Denny and the Vikings plenty of time to come up with an idea for a replacement if I did. I was a free man. It was kind of ironic that a free man then took his first trip to a former prison colony. Australia was amazing (I made a return trip in December, 2002 to see a total solar eclipse). This was a new life for me and I was spending some of my first days of it in a totally different world. Australia is a "western" country, but its mentality is completely different. Everywhere you go it's "cheers, mate!" It was very refreshing. And the women were unbelievable. Beautiful women with great attitudes—what a concept. I even had a chance to see my first Formula One race (now I'm hooked). I felt as if I was catching up with life. I also knew I wouldn't be happy doing nothing for the rest of my life. But what to do?

I had thought about life after football well before it came, of course. I had started a construction company with my friend Bill Laurenson in 1996. He had been working with another company in Marysville, Ohio and had approached me with the opportunity to form a separate company. We started by buying older, beat-up houses and rehabbing them. It's not a bad business if you find the right opportunity, but it can get tricky. It's easy to put too much in and not get enough out. We have since moved into building spec and custom homes. This is a very rewarding industry. You literally get the chance to see a patch of dirt turn into a home for somebody. It's the American dream in action.

Also, now that I was out of football, people were constantly coming up to me and asking, "Are you going to be a doctor now?" Not quite, but I did find a way to make it into a different aspect of healthcare.

Before I retired, former Buckeye and Browns linebacker Tom Cousineau approached me about a software company that helps to manage healthcare needs. Tom knew of my interests in both medicine and technology and he thought this would be a perfect fit. He was right. We've been working with doctors' offices, hospitals, and governments to help them streamline their service to bring down costs. It's been enlightening for me to see where so much waste and inefficiencies lie in our healthcare system. So much of the high cost of health care stems from the problems of using paper and telephones to carry out transactions that can be executed far more efficiently and securely electronically. The federal government realizes this and has enacted legislation that will require healthcare transactions to move to an electronic format. There's no doubt that this will lower costs as well as save lives.

Neil Cornrich, my agent, was approached by some of the networks that wanted me to do some work commentating. We set up a couple of interviews but then I began to think that it wouldn't be the right thing for me. The last thing I wanted was to have to go to a football game every week. The sport just doesn't hold that level of interest for me. I watched football because I had to, not because I loved it. I'll sit and watch parts of big games or games in which my friends are playing, but that's pretty much it. My football life is pretty much over. I can see myself working some camps for kids and possibly even college or pro, but nothing permanent.

This has been a fun transition for me. I'm in the "real" world now and I like it. I feel like I can have an impact on lives with the things I'm doing. But it's never enough for me. I feel like that life-long desire of mine to make a difference has yet to be fulfilled. You get a very strong voice as a celebrity. People will automatically listen to what you have to say, even if you don't know what you're talking about. It was easier for me to be heard when I played, but hopefully I'll find a way to get my views out there and make a difference. Do I miss playing? Of course. But I don't miss it enough to go back. Since I decided to retire, there was only one instance in which I even seriously considered coming back.

I was walking in the grocery store with my girlfriend, laughing and carrying on, when I got the call. It was Pete Bercich, one of the Vikings' linebackers. He told me that Korey Stringer, the team's right tackle, had passed out from heat exhaustion and needed to be taken to the hospital. He added that Dave Dixon (he played next to Korey on the line) had just left Korey's room sobbing and that things didn't look good for Korey. I hoped that Pete was exaggerating; he wasn't. The phone rang again at about 5 in the morning. It was Mitch Berger. "Korey died, man." "What?" "He died, his organs started failing. He's gone." Already fighting back tears, I told Mitch to call me back and let me know what they were going to do about services.

I got up from bed and walked down to my basement in a daze. Big K's gone…he's gone. I tried to stay composed as I called my mother and brother to break the news. I had played with Korey in my last year at Ohio State and then for six years in Minnesota, so my family knew him well. When I got off the phone I began sobbing uncontrollably. I sat there on the stairs crying for 20 minutes. I didn't know what to do next. My girlfriend came and put her arms around me, calming me down a bit. It seemed impossible. I had seen Korey a couple of weeks earlier at a golf outing in Minnesota. He talked about how excited he was to come back after his first Pro Bowl and show how good a leader he could be. I called him later that night to meet us. He got my message late and didn't get the chance to join us. He left a message on my cell phone: "Hey, Juice, sorry I missed you man. I'll see you up here during the season." It was the last time I heard his voice.

Reporters started calling that morning to get quotes and reactions. My emotions were fragile. The thing I remembered most vividly about Korey that I wanted to get across was the way the man was truly loved by everyone who had the pleasure to know him. I never walked into a room where Korey was without smiling. The man had a presence that infected everyone around him with joy. He was a natural comedian. Apart from calling me Juice (he never once called me Robert), he would call me Rupert. He did this as a joke that referred to the way fans would sometimes call him by the wrong name when they wanted an autograph. Of course in response to this, I'd call him Kordell. And my favorite, and probably most appropriate, for the man: Special K, or Special for short. The man touched lives in a way that anyone would envy. I say that if everyone likes you then you're probably lying to someone, but it didn't apply in Korey's case. You've seen the interviews after people die where everyone talks about how great the person was. They didn't have to exaggerate for Korey Stringer.

Korey was always one of the first people to get downfield to help me up after a run. Korey was a very big man—upwards of 380 at one point. But no matter how big he got, he always felt it was important to try to get to where I was to help me up. Linemen and running backs have a special relationship. After all, they are the ones who make our job possible. They don't receive the accolades from the fans and media, but I always knew they were the ones responsible for my success. The scene was always the same: I'd get tackled downfield and when I went to get up, there'd be one of Korey's big paws waiting to help me to my feet.

Korey was always Korey, a real person. It was evident from the turnout at the funeral that I wasn't the only one who felt this way about Korey.

The entire town of Warren was in mourning over the loss of Korey. There were signs on businesses that read: "We're Going to Miss You #77" or "We'll Always Love You, Big K." It was an extremely difficult day but seeing signs like that helped ease the pain somewhat. When I saw my former teammates at the funeral it occurred to me that I had been dealing with this ordeal on my own. I didn't have the people around me that could truly understand what I was going through. I almost broke down when I saw Korey in his casket. I said, "I'm going to miss you, big man" and I started sobbing. I had to sit down quickly. And there was Denny coming up to put an arm around me. He was there for me again. As I sat there I started thinking that maybe I should return for one more season as a tribute to Korey. It was the first time that I thought about coming out of retirement. But the more I thought about it, the less sense it made. Korey knew why I retired and he was happy for me. I'm sure he would have wanted me to do what I had always done: Be true to myself.

Losing Big K had a profound affect on my life. I have always known that life rarely goes according to plan, but something about this just seemed so wrong. How could it happen? Truth is, it can happen to any of us at any time. I know that's a bit morbid, but it's true. Tomorrow isn't promised to any of us. You have to try to make a difference with whatever time you have on this planet. A couple of weeks after Korey died, I took a trip that let me see how important using your time effectively can be.

A friend of mine from New Jersey told me about a camp for kids with cancer. Some of the kids are still receiving treatment and some are in remission. The camp is held annually near Scranton, Pennsylvania. They bring together young people ranging in age from 5 to 18. The camp is sponsored by the Valerie Fund (thevaleriefund.org), a non-profit organization that provides support for medical care for children with cancer and blood disorders. They usually bring in about 150 children, who are divided by age groups and put into cabins for the week. Volunteers serve as counselors and are divided among the cabins. The children go to scheduled events such as arts and crafts, tennis, water skiing, fishing, and golf.

I wasn't able to stay for the entire week, but the time I did spend there gave me a renewed sense of vigor. This was tough for me. After losing Korey, I was still pretty shaken up. Being around these young people was extremely refreshing. Some of these kids have been battling cancer for most of their lives. To see them running around and enjoying this camp really puts life into perspective. We look at our lives sometimes and complain because we're not making enough money or because we think we could be happier and we forget that there are people who struggle just to stay alive. These children know what it really means to persevere. But to them, it's just normal. It's what their lives are. Thanks to the Valerie Fund, these kids get the chance once a year to escape from the reality of their world and spend time with other people who truly understand what they have to endure. Many of them are inner-city kids who don't get the chance to enjoy such beautiful surroundings. It's an honor for me to get the chance to work with such brave people. They look at me and see a hero; I look at them and see young people whose bravery surpasses anything that I've ever achieved.

CHAPTER EIGHT

KING CORNELL

The one-eyed are kings in the land of the blind.

—French proverb

If I meet a 95-year-old with something to learn, I'll teach. If I meet a 5-year-old with something to teach, I'll learn.

—Confucius

I was a senior in high school the first time someone I knew got cancer. It was my best friend Bill's uncle, Greg Legan. Greg and Bill were very close and Greg would take us down to Ohio State to see football games once I started to get recruited. When I heard he had cancer and was getting treatment, it never even occurred to me that he might die. Maybe it was the way in which I was told, but I just thought: Hey, he's getting treatment, he'll be fine. Then things started to get worse. He couldn't leave the house and he didn't want me and Bill's other friends to even see him. When he died, it shocked me. Bill and his family were devastated. Greg was just one of those truly likable people that everyone enjoyed being around. He was only 32.

When I saw his body at the review, I was shocked at how emaciated and drawn he looked. How could this disease have done this to him? I wished there was something I could have said to help ease my friend's pain, but I came to realize that sometimes the best thing you can do for people is just be there.

174

A couple of years later, we heard that our high school principal was losing his struggle with skin cancer. Mr. McGinnis had always been friendly to us and gone out of his way to help me with the pressure I was receiving as a heavily recruited high school athlete. I remember visiting my high school the year after I left and seeing Mr. McGinnis. He had a bandage on his arm that covered an area that had been cleared of some cancerous tissue. Once again, it just didn't seem like a big deal at the time. He was a large man and looked as healthy as ever. Bill and I made a trip to Euclid to see him when we heard about his deteriorating health. The memory of Greg was still fresh in both of our minds. Mrs. McGinnis warned us when we arrived that her husband wasn't looking very good and that he was a bit confused from his medication. Bill decided not to go in the room; it was too harsh a reminder for him. I went in and stood next to Mr. McGinnis' bed. He was a pale and thin shell of the man he once was. He did his best to muster a smile and then he reached for my hand. He told me that I meant more to him than any student he ever had. I didn't know what to say. Choking back tears, I said something along the lines of "you just have to keep believing and have faith" (I wasn't an atheist at that time). I said goodbye to him and left. He died two days later. I was stunned at how devastating this disease was. At Ohio State, I began to learn why.

I had the opportunity to work in the Hematology/Oncology lab at the Arthur G. James Cancer Research Center at Ohio State. Dr. David Schuler taught me about the way cancer takes over a body. The most insidious aspect of the disease is that it is our body's own mechanisms that allow the disease to start and to proliferate. The malfunctioning of our genes is the root cause of cancer. It's ironic that the very mechanism that allows for adaptation and evolution is the same one that gives rise to this deadly disease. Cancer cells are basically cells that multiply uncontrollably. Without getting too technical, there are a myriad of reasons that can cause this malfunction, ranging from exposure to radiation to smoking. The cells' genes that regulate growth become compromised and allow the cells to divide continuously. Normally the body can stop this type of uncontrolled growth, but sometimes the brakes fail. This is when cancer develops. When these cancers metastasize, or migrate through the body, more and more organs become affected and the person's life is in jeopardy. We have various treatments that attempt to control these cancerous growths, but they are not always able to completely rid the body of the illness. Now that we have solved the human genome we may be able to come up with better treatments, but it's going to take time and, more importantly, money.

Denny Green liked to call Tuesdays during the season "Community Day." It was the one day off a week that we had. He encouraged the players to go out into the community and do whatever they could to impact lives. Some visited schools, some went to nursing homes, some visited hospitals. The team would actually organize groups to visit hospitals. We would meet at a hospital and have a representative take us around to see different kids. We were usually accompanied by a film crew and other hospital workers. It really was a bit of a circus. You'd go into a kid's room, take a few photos, say a few things for the camera, and then move on. You didn't really get the chance to talk to the kid or their family.

Before the 1997 season, I approached Brad Madson, our Community Relations Director, and told him that I wanted to start my own program with Children's Hospital. I wanted to be able to go in without cameras and spend more time with the kids and their families. Some of these children are in the hospital for months at a time and they benefit from having visitors come in and break up the monotony. So, a couple of Tuesdays each month, I would go to the hospital and a hospital representative would meet me and take me to children that they thought would enjoy a visit. I would go into the room, sit down, and just start talking with the kids and their family. Of course, the football season was the usual subject, but I would let them decide what they wanted to discuss.

This was extremely rewarding for me. The kids knew you cared about them. After leaving the room, the nurses would come up to me and say, "I haven't seen him smile like that in weeks." I felt as if I was really making a difference. It felt great to just sit in there and really get to know some of these courageous young people. They wasted no time in berating me if we had lost the previous weekend: "You guys looked awful!" The parents were very appreciative and gracious. It's hard for me to imagine how difficult it must be for them to see their children like that. I'm thankful that I was in any way able to make their ordeal easier for them.

As I started to visit the hospital more often, I really began to get attached to some of the kids; it's not hard to do. I decided to continue the program when I returned to Columbus that off-season. One day they told me that a young man was extremely excited to meet me. His name was Cornell and he was 18 at the time, a recent high school graduate. Cornell had spent most of his time in the hospital but he had built up enough strength to make it to his graduation ceremony. He was in an isolation room, which meant that I had to go through a series of doors to keep unsanitary air from his room. He had a smile from ear to ear when I walked in. His head was clean-shaven and he wore a pair of gold-rimmed glasses. He looked thin, but not in a sickly way. He immediately took the opportunity to show me his senior picture. He was wearing a Cris Carter jersey in the photo. I told him that I would get Cris to sign a card for him when I went to camp the following month. He seemed surprisingly unmoved by my comment. We took a photo together and I signed a few cards for him. After leaving the room, the nurse told me why he hadn't seemed very excited about the prospect of waiting a month to get an autograph from Cris. She told me that he probably didn't have that long to live. I had never asked about the state a child was in before entering the room. It made me feel stupid that I was asking him about all of these future events when he probably wouldn't even be around to see them. I felt sick to my stomach.

I called Cris as soon as I got out of the hospital and left a message describing the situation. I started going in to see Cornell at least once a week. I brought him one of my jerseys and he was so excited I thought he might jump out of bed. We had some great conversations. He talked about future plans and he never complained about his plight. He had been fighting cancer since he was nine years old—a full half of his life. I thought about my own life and what I had been through and was

ashamed for ever thinking that life was treating me unfairly. We too often forget that some people must fight for their lives every day. I still
hadn't heard anything from Cris and was starting to get upset. After a
couple of weeks, Cris called me and apologized for not returning my
calls. He had been in Europe doing some commentating work and hadn't
received the messages. He overnighted an autographed jersey and some
of his trading cards.

I went to Canada to play in a golf tournament and received a message that Cris had stopped in to see Cornell. He really went out of his
way to try to comfort that young man. I've had my run-ins with Cris, but
this was the defining moment for my view on Cris. Whenever I think
about who Cris really is, I think about what he did for Cornell. I called
the hospital to check on Cornell when I returned from Canada. They
told me that he had passed away. I was floored. I knew deep down that
it was coming, but it didn't matter. I had learned so much from this
brave young man in such a short amount of time. He changed my life in
a very real sense.

I went to the hospital to make a visit that week and the nurses told
me how careful Cornell had been with my jersey and how he would only
let certain people touch it. They told me that his funeral services would
be held later that week. My mother called and asked me if I wanted her
to go with me to the services. I told her that I didn't want to go because
I didn't want to see the body that had betrayed Cornell the person. I lied.
The truth of the matter is that I was scared to break down in front of
people that I didn't know. I knew that my jersey would be displayed at
the services and it was more than I thought I could handle. It's the tough
part about working with sick children and cancer patients in general. I
was touched to have cards and letters thanking me for my visits, but
every so often, I received notice that the young person had died. We
can't save them all, but we try to make their remaining days as comfortable as possible. Since that time with Cornell, I've been to a service
where a young man was buried in my jersey. It was tough to see. But it
was even tougher for his family, and that's why I knew I needed to be
there. Cancer affects entire families, not just the people who are afflicted

with it. We've got to do what we can to help find a cure. I've been in the lab and I know how difficult that work can be. I also know that those research facilities need financial support to help them in their search for a cure. While having some drinks in a Vegas casino, a friend of mine came up with an idea to help in this search.

He suggested that I form a foundation to help raise money instead of just making the visits. "That's a great idea! You run it, and let's see what we can do." This was how the Robert Smith Foundation was formed. Originally, we wanted to focus on children's hospitals and cancer research. After a couple of years, we decided that we should branch out into other children's charities and events. The biggest thing that I've learned is that it's very difficult to raise money. You go in with the idea of being able to raise all of this cash and disperse it to charities, but the reality is that things aren't that simple. You really have to work hard to get people involved. It takes corporate involvement as well as individual participation. You hear a lot of bad things about athletes' foundations spending money on lavish events and then not paying any money out to the charities. Well, it's not that simple. It takes a great deal of coordination and there is a learning curve that you have to fight through. In our first few years, we operated in the red and I put up most of the money myself. As we move forward we hope to be able to create excitement about our events and get people to support our efforts throughout the community.

Lately, I've been working with some schools in Columbus to try to emphasize the importance of education. Young people need to know that education is the most important aspect of their lives. Young people look up to athletes, actors, and singers and aspire to be in those fields. What some of them fail to realize is that they need to have back-up plans. There's nothing wrong with dreaming of being in the NFL or becoming a famous singer. But I think too many of these kids lose focus on their education, fall behind, and never catch up. It takes an entire community to raise children though, and I think we all can do more to support our schools and improve our educational system. There is no easy answer to the problems. It's hard to draw in good teachers when they know that they won't be rewarded financially. I've heard about initiatives that reward our best teachers financially, but there's only so much that can be done with the tax revenues. The bottom line is that we are not doing enough to properly educate our children. I saw a statistic recently that said that less than 50 percent of Americans can read at a tenth-grade level. This is inexcusable. We may be the greatest country in the world right now, but we can't stay that way if we continue to fail in our attempts to completely educate our population. We waste our time trying to introduce ridiculous concepts like "intelligent design" into school curriculums when most of our kids can't even spell the phrase.

I think we need to completely overhaul the way in which we teach our kids. The current curriculums lock them into a type of "linear" thinking that doesn't help them in their ability to improvise and be independent thinkers. I don't know exactly how we could accomplish this, but it at least needs to be discussed. We could start by trying to get our children to be better world citizens. They're always told how great America is. They don't get the opportunity to truly learn about other cultures and other ways of thinking. This is the information age, but we need to be careful what information our children are exposed to. Information is only as good as its source. Our society has become confused in the age of information. We simply rely too heavily on what we're told. If you want to learn about the world, you need to be diligent in your search for knowledge. People fall into the traps of misinformation too easily. When you only attempt to see the tip of the iceberg, you're bound to be deceived.

For more information on the Robert Smith Foundation, go to rskids.org

PART TWO

SERAPHIM

Power tends to corrupt; absolute power corrupts absolutely.
— Lord Acton

If I was a holy man and you were the devil's song, and if I liked what you played, does that mean you're right and I'm wrong?
—Seal

CHAPTER NINE

THE "GIANT" MYTH

There is nothing in the world more dangerous than sincere ignorance or conscientious stupidity.

—Dr. Martin Luther King Jr.

Truth is in the mind of the believer.

—Robert Smith

We can deal with rockets and dreams, but reality, what does it mean?

—Curtis Mayfield

The world has always loved a hero. But what is a hero? The dictionary's first definition defines a hero as "a figure in mythology and legend renowned for great strength, courage, and daring." That is how heroes were introduced to the world-as myths. The great epic poems, such as Homer's *Odyssey,* may or may not have referred to actual events, but it's the morals of their stories that counted. The ancients didn't have paper or books, so they memorized these myths and perpetuated the stories as oral histories. They told the stories of heroes—such as the brave warrior, Achilles, to inspire both young and old. Naturally, there was a great deal of improvisation and exaggeration in the re-telling of these tales, but the details weren't what really mattered. They were outlining the morals that were most cherished by their society. So to be a called a hero in those times you had to have something to distinguish yourself from those around you. This usually meant that you achieved something in war. But what if there was no war to fight? How could someone distinguish themselves in peacetime?

Sports offered an answer. You could show your strength and agility by besting your opponents on the fields of sport as opposed to the fields of war. People have always been fascinated and impressed by feats of physical performance. We've always placed a high priority on physical prowess—especially by males. Olympic athletes achieved status formerly reserved for war heroes. It's the same sort of phenomenon you see today as cities root for their home team and its players.

The Romans took the spectacle of sport to an extreme level. The Coliseum in Rome was home to some of the most brutal displays of violence in history. It started with gladiators fighting to honor emperors. These fights to the death became so popular that they became regular events to entertain the blood-thirsty fans. The gladiators usually were slaves or imprisoned individuals who were forced to fight. But the gladiators achieved such high levels of respect and notoriety that free citizens began to volunteer just so they could elevate their status in society. The emperor Commodus even participated in gladiator events to prove his worthiness as a leader. These were amazingly gruesome events, driven by the desire of the population to see live carnage. The fans would cheer gladiators on to kill their opponents.

The next type of hero defined in the dictionary is the man who is celebrated for certain achievements or attributes. Jesus is an example. Historians and theologians disagree on the exact year (most figure about 4 BCE), but Jesus was born somewhere around the start of the Millennium. His message of peace and understanding sharply contrasted with that of the Romans. I think the cruel environment of the Roman Empire provided a perfect background for his message to flourish. People throughout the empire (particularly Jews) were persecuted and ridiculed by the polytheistic Romans. Even the Jewish faith, which tends to be exclusive as opposed to inclusive, gave Jesus' message added strength. In a time of oppression he told the world that the "meek shall inherit the Earth" and to "turn the other cheek," a sharp contrast to the Bible's earlier message of "an eye for an eye." You can believe or disbelieve in Christianity, but no one can question that Jesus was a role model and hero.

The story of Jesus helps to illustrate a defining characteristic of heroes and myths. The further one is separated by time and distance from these events, the more likely they are to believe the exaggerations and additions to the "real" person or story. In the environment of the ancients, it wasn't difficult to believe that Achilles had been dipped in the river Styx and, therefore, was nearly invincible (legend has it that he was held by the tendons that bear his name, hence his vulnerability in that area—and the phrase that bears his name). There may or may not have been an Achilles, but I guarantee you he wasn't invincible. He may have fought bravely in battle and distinguished himself as a leader, but this doesn't make him supernatural. Those supernatural powers were no doubt created to give the man a more heroic appearance in the minds of the people who heard about his deeds.

The same can be said of Jesus. Early writings about him don't make mention of his divinity. They talk about him as a great leader and a prophet, but don't mention him as being the Son of God. Jesus was arrested for vandalizing a temple and because the Jewish leaders feared his power as a challenge to their own. It wasn't because he claimed to be a divine being, but people believe what they want about legends and legendary figures. Author Robert Park refers to it as "the belief engine." You are simply more likely to believe the things you want to believe. We want to believe in heroes. We want to believe in the goodness of mankind. We want to believe that we can overcome any opposition if we just try hard enough. This makes us willing to believe that some people are truly different and are capable of feats that the rest of us would find impossible. It is how legends are born and how heroes and myths get created.

Our founding fathers are a perfect example. It's easy to look back nostalgically and idealize the men who helped give birth to our nation. George Washington and Thomas Jefferson were giants among men. These were men who founded our country under the auspices of a document that claimed that "all men are created equal....they are endowed with certain inalienable rights...life, liberty and the pursuit of happiness."

These men did some great things, and we wouldn't have the freedom we enjoy if it weren't for them, but there is also no denying that they were racist and sexist hypocrites. Slavery ownership is morally indefensible, regardless of the cultural norm.

There were Nazis in Germany who refused to kill innocent Jewish women and children at the possible risk of their own lives. It could be argued, without much stretch of the imagination, that these Nazis displayed more moral courage than our founding fathers. But this is the problem with all the people we define as heroes. When is the spotlight shining? Heroic acts are individual events; they do not define entire lives. Lives take many twists and turns. There are moments when we shine at our brightest and perform acts that truly could be defined as heroic. This doesn't mean that we're perfect. It doesn't even mean that we would automatically be defined as "good" people. But who is a "good" person. It's human nature to try to define the world around us. The problem is that we tend to make those definitions too quickly and based on incomplete or even incorrect information. The world is not black and white, but many people try to see and define it that way.

The late 1800s brought professional sports and, with it, a new type of hero figure. The Cincinnati Red Stockings became the first completely professional team in 1869 (www.baseball1.com). Until then, teams were comprised of players who were, for the most part, unpaid. The Cincinnati team learned that you could attract the best players if you paid them. Why do something for free if you could be getting paid to do the same thing? Cincinnati went 65-0 that season. The timing here is not coincidental. America had just come through the Civil War and the nation was healing itself by turning to athletic pastimes.

In 1920, professional football joined pro baseball. Pro sports offered America a new type of entertainment and a new type of hero to worship. Babe Ruth was the first mega-hero. I've never been much of a sports fan in general, but even I knew about Babe Ruth when I was young. It had been some 50 years since he had played when I was growing up and yet people still talked about him as if he had just left the game. It must have been an incredible sight for a young child to go to a game and see this player in person who they had only heard about on the radio or read about in the newspapers. Ruth must have seemed like Superman or Flash Gordon. Having never even seen images of him play on TV must have added even more suspense to the spectacle.

Radio had a huge impact on sports and our society in general, but television brought nothing less than a cultural revolution in the early '50s. It's impossible to exaggerate the impact that television has had on every aspect of our society. It hasn't just changed the way we view sports and movies, it has literally transformed the way in which we perceive the world. Many of us base our views on the world solely on the images and messages we see on TV. It becomes the filter on our window of the world. But this leaves people at the mercy of the accuracy of the media images they witness. Someone is deciding which images and sounds to show us. Thus, it is up to us to be sure that we don't just accept them as absolute truth. Just think of the way it has influenced our view of war.

Vietnam gave America a view of war that it had never experienced. Television covered the brutality and gruesome nature of the battlefield for the first time, exposing the American public to the harshest realities of war. Up until this time, we were sheltered from these types of scenes and we tended to see our troops in a more heroic light. There was no heroes' welcome for the troops who fought in Vietnam. This was partially due to the unpopularity of the war, but I think for the most part it could be attributed to the scenes of carnage that were transmitted by our television sets. I believe this is why the military makes so much of its operations public. They want us to know what's going on out there in the field and reinsure the public that they are trying their best to avoid the inevitable "collateral damage" that occurs in war.

A new class of television stars also began to emerge. People became enthralled with these new celebrities. The lines between hero, star, and role model began to blur. Anyone on TV was considered a star. Our culture became increasingly fascinated, even obsessed, with celebrity.

This rise of television has been a windfall for professional sports, transforming athletes from sports heroes to cultural icons. Sports are everywhere you look. There are all-sports networks, many devoted only to your favorite sport. You can't see a news broadcast without seeing sports stories. You can't pick up a newspaper without reading about sports. Sports have become an integral part of who we are as a society. People feel as intimately tied to their sports teams and heroes as they are to their nation.

We live in an age of information that demands transparency. We want to know everything about everyone, especially celebrities. The arrival of the Internet on a large scale has increased this demand exponentially. People want instant information and you better believe the media is going to deliver it, accurate or not. This has exposed today's athlete, celebrity, and politician to an unprecedented level of scrutiny. If you get a DUI and you play for a professional team, it will make the paper—guaranteed. If you star on a sitcom and get into an argument with your wife and she calls the police, you will be on the news—guaranteed. If you're running for office and they find out you cheated on your wife 20 years ago, it will make the headlines—guaranteed. America has soured on what used to be its most cherished citizens. This is especially true with athletes. Athletes are at times the most exalted and vilified people in this nation. One minute we talk as if they were gods; the next we curse them as demons polluting our youth.

What's really going on? Have athletes and other public figures changed significantly? Are they just following the apparent downward spiral of American morals? Many Americans decry our athletes and public figures, and long for the heroes of old—the "pure" heroes of the past. Or is America deceiving itself? Are we just waking up to a reality that has always been the same? We need to be critical thinkers who are diligent in the search for "complete" truth. It's similar to a criminal trial. The jury doesn't come to a verdict based on the testimony of one witness, and people shouldn't determine opinions based on one source of information.

Today's heroes are investigated and reported on in an unprecedented way. This has resulted in a "fall from grace" of today's public figures and celebrities, particularly athletes. What people need to remember is that like the heroes of antiquity, the new "giants" are the concoctions of willing and eager minds searching for ideal role models. But these role models never asked to be placed on a pedestal. It is society that elevates them; and now it is the same society that tries to cause their descent. The

188

truth is that there are no ideal people, and they, like John Milton said of the angels, were made "sufficient to stand, yet free to fall." You can't blame people for being people. Athletes and other public figures have a responsibility to act like good citizens, but so does everyone else. Many are accusing these people of the very same acts they commit themselves. You can't expect a person to have higher morals just because he carries a football and kids look up to him. It's not the athletes' fault that this society chooses to place them in such high regard. It's not like becoming a priest or teacher; those jobs carry a much greater burden for higher standards of behavior. And yet, it is the public figure that gets singled out for improprieties because of his or her high visibility.

This is not all bad. It is important for our young people to know that no one is perfect. It's similar to the realization we all make at one time or another about our parents. When we're very young, it seems as if these people are larger than life figures who can do no wrong. As we get older, we come to the somewhat sobering realization that parents aren't the superheroes we once imagined. It's especially important for young people to know that the celebrities and athletes they look up to aren't perfect, either. I actually think it's good for them to see these people get in trouble. Apart from teaching them the fact that celebrities are fallible, it also teaches them that no one is above the law.

Most people consider Babe Ruth to be the greatest baseball player of all time, but no one claims the man was the ideal role model. His womanizing and drinking are almost as legendary as his hitting and athletic skills. The fans of the time really didn't care that much. Maybe they realized something that fans today don't: Who cares if he's out there having fun? He's a grown man; he can do what he wants in his free time. Somehow I doubt that Babe's lifestyle would have gone over as smoothly with today's media and society. Athletes aren't the only ones who have been excused some moments of indiscretion. Many highly praised politicians were anything but the picture of perfection.

Winston Churchill is recognized as one of the most well respected leaders of the 20th century. People see him as a pillar of strength and moral courage that stood up to the evil ideas of Adolf Hitler. However, Churchill himself was a proponent of eugenics before he took the office of Prime Minister: "The unnatural and increasingly rapid growth of the feeble-minded and insane classes…constitutes a national and race danger…the source from which should be cut off and sealed." Now, Churchill wasn't proposing that they be killed; he thought the solution was sterilization, but it still contrasts sharply with the stance he took against the 20th Century's most notorious villain.

The United States has had its share of politicians with questionable moral character. John F. Kennedy is one of our greatest presidents and yet his illicit affairs in the 1960s never made it into the media while he was alive. It just wasn't talked about in those times. Fast-forward 30-some years and Bill Clinton got impeached after it was revealed he had had an affair. He wasn't impeached for the affair, it was for perjuring himself about the affair in a civil trial—but I'm sure the media would have caught wind of the affair eventually and made more of it than they should have.

Do we want saints, or do we want real people who are capable of running our country? Why should we expect our leaders to be any different than the rest of the population? Of course you want politicians to have a certain level of morals, but we all make mistakes.

The problem, once again, is perception. People forget that public figures are a part of this society and any evaluations of them need to take the entire society into consideration. Our society has a tendency to take partial truths and make them their reality. They have forgotten that they are the ones that created the celebrity "monster" (it's funny how we always refer to Mary Shelly's monster as Frankenstein. The doctor who created him was named Victor Frankenstein, but the monster had no name), and they now see it as a hideous beast to be condemned. But everyone has his or her right to an opinion. There are reasons that people believe the things they believe. In the next three chapters, I'll go over some of the specific reasons I think that people have misperceived and misjudged today's athlete and public figures and how this speaks of problems in our society as a whole.

CHAPTER TEN

THE HAVE$ V$ THE HAVE NOT$

I don't know what they want from me, it's like the more money we come around, the more problems we see.

——Notorious B.I.G.

Athletes are overpaid!" "He got *how* much? That's ridiculous!" "Nobody should get paid that much to play a sport!" "Why don't we give that money for important jobs like teaching?" "I'm tired of hearing about those spoiled overpaid, overrated jerks getting all of that money!" "I work my butt off and those guys get paid millions to play a game!" "Who the hell do these prima donnas think they are going on strike?"

If you haven't said one of these things yourself, you've probably heard someone else say them. High salaries and labor troubles cause the most discontent among fans when they talk about players. Here's what people think: Why do I have to pay high ticket prices in order to see a bunch of guys with no education running around on a field or arena? Of course, I heard all of these things when I played and, it didn't stop after I retired.

When baseball players were heading towards a strike in 2002, the venomous statements in the newspapers reached a feverish pitch. Everyday I picked up the paper, I read about fans cursing the players as crybabies and talking about how athletes didn't deserve what they already made. They talked about research scientists and teachers while questioning our society's willingness to pay these high salaries to athletes. I figured that being a common citizen myself at the time, I should chime in as well. I wrote an editorial for *USA Today* to help speak for the other side:

> *As a former professional athlete and team representative of a player union, I am tired of hearing the complaints about "overpaid athletes." People are paid on what they collectively produce. No salary is based on a job's intrinsic value. Is an ad executive really "worth" $100,000 a year? What is a CEO of a company who goes bankrupt and loses thousands of peoples' retirement money "worth?" I am only familiar with the NFL Collective Bargaining Agreement, but I know that NFL salaries are based on what the league brings in from revenues, which is predominantly TV revenue. If Americans didn't spend so much time watching and reading about sports, then athletes wouldn't be paid as much as they are. It's a shame, but I'm sure more Americans know who the center for the L.A. Lakers is than those who know who the Senate majority leader is.*
>
> *As far as teachers and research scientists, I agree they should be paid more. But many of these individuals are paid by taxes, and who pays most of those?—high income individuals like professional athletes. People say they want teachers to get better pay and then they complain when taxes are raised or they vote down school levies. Their ridiculously myopic view is that any high-paid individual should accept any working terms that management implements. Get real, people! I don't think anyone should shed tears for athletes who face labor problems. Most workers face those problems at one time or another. But try to understand the real issues at hand before you start whining about athletes' salaries. Maybe these people should put down their sports page and pick up an economics book—or any book for that matter.*

I'm sure that last sentence brought more than a few curse words directed towards me. This involves the same problem of perspective. People making $40,000 a year find it hard to rationalize million dollar salaries. The thing that they most fail to realize is that it's their own behavior that gives rise to the salaries. People spend hours in front of their TVs watching sports each week. And if they're not at home watching them on TV, they're at a bar watching them there. And what do they do during the day? They read their sports section or listen to sports radio. I'm still amazed at how much emphasis this society places on sports. Don't get me wrong, I'm glad it does. It made a very comfortable life for me and my family. But why is it that salaries are so high today compared to 20 years ago? And how could athletes ever have the nerve to go on strike when they already make so much money? It's time for a history lesson.

Baseball's Cincinnati Red Stockings became our nation's first professional sports team in 1869 and it didn't take long for labor troubles to develop. The owners quickly realized that their costs would skyrocket if they had to compete for players in an open market. They got together and decided to honor each other's contracts and added a "reserve" clause that allowed them to automatically renew a player's contract at the end of the season. This basically meant that that the owner controlled their players for life. They were allowed to trade players to other teams, but a player could not switch to any team he chose. They also instituted the first salary cap, claiming that it was for "the good of the game." A man named John Ward decided to organize the players, forming the first union called the Brotherhood of Professional Baseball Players. His rhetoric sounded as if it came straight from the abolitionists: "Players had been bought, sold and traded as though they were sheep instead of American citizens…Like a fugitive slave law, the reserve clause denies him a harbor and a livelihood, and carries him back, bound and shackled, to the club from which he attempted to escape." His word choice may have been a bit dramatic, but his point was correct.

Can you imagine any other industry controlling the movement of its employees in this way? Imagine working for a company that operated under these circumstances. These are the rules you'd have to live with: Number one, you don't get to decide what company you work for. Number two, you can't go to another company even if you want to. Number three, if the company for whom you work wants to transfer you to a different company, you have to go. The argument the owners always used is that the players are compensated at a level that makes up for this seemingly unfair practice. Sound fair? Or does it sound like unfair collusion? Shouldn't people be able to work for anyone they want, anywhere they want? Well, in a suit filed against the league in an attempt to get them in line with fair business practices, the Supreme Court sided with the owners. They claimed that baseball wasn't interstate commerce, so anti-trust laws wouldn't apply.

Despite the restrictions, professional sports still provided a pretty good living financially. In 1930, Babe Ruth was paid $80,000, $5,000 more than President Hoover. When asked about it, Ruth replied, "I know, but I had a better year than Hoover." Professional sports were becoming a huge industry and the owners wanted to keep as much of this money for themselves as they could. By keeping players off the open market, teams didn't have to compete with each other for the top players, so salaries were kept artificially low. You can't blame owners for wanting to make money, but they should have had to abide by the same labor rules as any other company. Despite what most people think, from the players' perspective, this is not just a monetary issue. There are a lot of reasons a player may want to move to another team. Maybe he wants to be closer to his family. Maybe he doesn't like the coach. Maybe he thinks he has a better chance to win a championship on a different team. Whatever the reason, to be a free agent, to be able to choose which team they played for, was the ultimate goal of professional athletes in this era. But there were more important issues on the minds of players—especially players in the newly formed professional football leagues.

The game's attrition rate was of most concern to football players. Football is an extremely violent game and players often received disabling injuries that kept them from playing. In the 1950s, football players began to organize themselves in an attempt to negotiate for better working conditions and especially for pay after a player was injured. It's hard to believe now, but the players at that time even had to pay for their own equipment. The owners scoffed at the players' requests, assuming that they had the same legal protection from anti-trust litigation as the baseball leagues. They were wrong. The Supreme Court sided with a group of players who had filed an anti-trust suit against the league. Then, surprise, the owners came around. Emboldened by this success, the players began to make progress in their demands for benefits. The threat of further legal action meant a quick response from the owners' side. The players were able to secure health benefits as well as a retirement plan.

People mistakenly believe that the labor troubles that arise in professional sports are always about money. This couldn't be further from the truth. The owners usually push this idea to try to win the propaganda war in times of trouble. But the owners of professional football teams are like the owners of any other company; they want to improve their bottom line, and they'll resort to some pretty ruthless tactics in order to do so. Professional football players aren't the type of people that garner much sympathy from the public. Fans tend to see them as big, strong, rich individuals who should be able to take care of themselves. But they fail to realize the power that the owners are capable of exerting. The owners have deep pockets and, despite the fact that they know of their vulnerability in anti-trust court, they have always tried to push the envelope as far as possible. When the players approached them with a plan that would pay players based on a percentage of gross league revenues, the owners rejected it. The players went on strike and two months of the season were lost.

The owners finally conceded in this matter and settled on a new Collective Bargaining Agreement or CBA. It seems unfathomable, but before this strike in 1982, a team owned a player's medical record and the player could not see it or take it to another doctor without team permission. If that doesn't convince you of the lengths that teams will go to control players, I don't know what will. The players also were able to secure better benefits, including a severance program. And, for the first time, players secured salaries that exceeded 50 percent of league revenues. Now that they had positioned themselves more strongly with the owners, the union and players turned their efforts towards the greatest prize: free-agency. A limited free-agency system had been implemented after the strike in 1987 (the year of the "scabs"), but this was merely an attempt by the owners to give an appearance of fairness. "Real" free-agency was going to take the "real" determination of the players and their union. The players had a favorable decision reversed because the judge ruled that they could not seek individual damages so long as they were represented by a union. The union decided to decertify and both sides ended up back in court. This battle came to a head in late 1992, and, in early 1993, a settlement was reached. The players had won their cherished free-agency, but it came with a price that many felt would minimize its effect: the salary cap.

I was drafted three months after this agreement was reached. We would be the first rookie class to have to deal with a rookie pool, which amounted to a separate salary cap on rookies. This meant that we would be the first class that got paid less money than the previous year. Normally, a player could figure to make about 15 percent more than the player picked at his draft position the previous year. Not only did we not have that increase, we actually ended up making less than the class from the previous year. To make matters worse, we would take less of it home because of the new tax law that was passed by congress that year. That really changed the way I looked at taxes.

I had never really paid much attention to politics. The 1992 election was the first in which I voted (I was 20 at the time). It's a shame, but most of us don't take an interest in politics until they affect us directly. I voted for Bill Clinton in 1992 and I didn't regret it, even after the tax hike. I must say, though, that my political ideology has shifted in a more conservative direction. I wouldn't consider myself a Democrat or a Republican, though. I'm more concerned with candidates and issues as opposed to political sentiment. Partisan politics stall our efforts at improvement, but I don't think there's any end in sight. This tax/money issue directly applies to the way in which athletes are viewed. It's almost like a class war. It's the haves vs. the have nots; rich vs. poor; Republican vs. Democrat. It's embarrassing how simplistic these arguments become. These groups disagree with each other just to disagree—and it's almost as if real issues don't even matter anymore. The latest round of tax cuts by George W. Bush is a great example. It's needlessly divisive to go back to the old cliché "it's just a tax cut for the wealthy." The top 5 percent of money earners pay about 70 percent of the taxes in this country, so it makes sense that they would get the most relief when a tax cut is proposed. Democrats just know that this is a good line to use to turn public sentiment against the other side. It's funny, but I didn't hear anybody saying "it's only a tax hike for the wealthy" when the highest brackets saw the largest increase in the 1993 tax law revision.

At the time, I fell victim to a similarly skewed line of thinking by some players in the NFL and turned my anger towards the union and, more specifically, its executive director, Gene Upshaw. I was upset that we were the first class to have to deal with these new rules, and I felt that it was Upshaw's leadership that must be responsible. I had not dealt much with the union at that point and I readily bought into the theory, espoused by some players, that Gene was "on the take" and only had his best interests in mind. But I was making judgments based on my situation alone; I wasn't seeing the big picture. I was guilty of the crime that I had accused Gene of—I only had my interests in mind. It wasn't until I became a team representative my second year in the league that I really began to understand the operations of the union, and everything that Gene had done in order to ensure that *all* of the players would benefit from the new system.

Every team in the league selects a player, or players, to represent it in the union. The representatives then help disseminate union information and organize team meetings. The union holds meetings once a year and gives the representatives the opportunity to hear reports from its various departments. I went to my first meeting honestly expecting to expose the union for the fraud that it had committed against its constituency. I was stunned at how wrong I was. The meetings are run in a "Robert's Rules" environment and all present are free to speak and voice their opinions. It was the transparency of the system that impressed me most. Every dollar was accounted for and no decision was made without a supporting vote. I was surprised to see just how heated some of the discussions became. A lot of new players are at the meetings each year, and some of them feel that their voices aren't properly heard. On the other side, you have players who have been reps for 10 years and get frustrated at hearing the same complaints from new reps year in and year out. I remember one year we had an hour-long discussion about the extra cost of using Federal Express as opposed to some other overnight carrier. It got a little out of control, but at least it showed that players were taking their jobs seriously.

Far from being the thief that I thought he was, I began to see the real Gene Upshaw. This was a man who had guided the players to their greatest position of strength in the history of the league. This was a man who had gone without pay in order to keep his union afloat. This was a man who had the courage to stand by his beliefs when so many around him doubted his motives and his effectiveness. I've come to realize that Gene's job is not that different from any other elected official's. The bottom line is that you need to make decisions based on the best interests of your constituency; you can't just concern yourself with popularity or trying to appease the masses. You can't get everyone to agree with all of the decisions you make, so you must act in a way that you feel is best for all. There will always be nay-sayers who base their objections on half-truths and innuendo, but the great leader sees past this and has the courage of his or her convictions. It was the union representatives of the past and leaders like Gene who paved the way for the current free agency system in the league. To understand why players get paid what they do, you must first understand a little about the specifics of this system.

First, it should be understood that players' salaries are based on league revenues. People talk as if salaries are arbitrarily set. This is not true. Teams pay salaries based on a percentage of what is called "defined gross revenue." Defined gross revenue, or DGR, consists predominately of gate receipts and television contracts. This is the bulk of the money that flows into the league. The league total is added up for a given year and then divided up equally among the 32 teams. This revenue sharing is one of the main reasons that the NFL is as healthy financially as it is; smaller market teams get the same share as large market teams. From this point, a team must spend a minimum of 50 percent of that revenue on players (including benefits) and spend no more than that year's salary cap percentage number, which varies from year to year. That percentage has remained in the mid 60s throughout this newest Collective Bargaining Agreement. So teams basically spend between 50 and 65 percent of DGR on player costs. The beautiful part about this system for players is the fact that this cap is not a "hard" ceiling on the amount of actual dollars that a team may spend; the cap really is just an accounting tool. Teams can spend more actual dollars than the cap would allow because signing bonuses are amortized over the length of a given contract. For example, let's say a team signs a player to a five-year deal with a $10 million signing bonus. The player may receive all of that money in the first year, but only $2 million of it counts for each of the five years of the contract. In this way, teams find themselves exceeding the cap in "real" dollars.

This system allows teams to be creative in the way they structure deals, enabling them to sign players regardless of their cap situation. Of course, the owners try to blame this system when it comes time to part with veterans, but it's just another example of misinformation. If a team really wants to re-sign a player, it usually can find a way; it's just more convenient, and better PR, for them to blame it on the system. This new system has been a windfall for the players. Prior to the new system's inception in 1993, the league was controlling 70 percent of total revenue, and the players 30 percent. Today those numbers are reversed. The 1990s also saw a huge jump in the league's television contracts, along with a corresponding jump in salaries.

People decry the high salaries of athletes without realizing that they themselves are the real reason salaries are higher. Television contracts are the lifeblood of league revenue. And this is a great thing for players because it seems that America just can't get enough of sports on television. The advertisers and networks are well aware of the viewing habits of the public, and sports are the one sure thing when it comes to securing viewers. People love the drama of live professional sports and they spend many hours every week watching them. Networks know that they must compete with cable, the Internet, and other forms of enter-tainment, and they are willing to pay billions to ensure that professional sports stay on their channels. People think that it is the demands of players that drive up salaries. The truth of the matter is that it's the public's demand for sports that causes the elevation of salaries. Some individuals may get more or less than they deserve, but, as a whole, play-ers can only make the money that the league receives in revenue. And, yet, people still complain. In response to my letter, some fans said that it took a lot of nerve to blame the fans for driving up salaries. They pointed to the fact that high ticket prices made it almost financially impossible for the average fan to take a family to a game. Well it's also hard for the average family to afford a trip to a concert or a movie.

People say that athletes shouldn't get paid all of that money for just playing a sport, but what do they think the players should be paid? Are they proposing some sort of limit? Where do they think that rev-enue should go? Shouldn't the players benefit from the popularity of their sport? And what does "just" a sport really mean? Is an author getting paid "just" to write? Is Oprah getting paid "just" to talk? We live in a free-market economy and the people who work in lucrative fields should reap the benefits. Some actors make more for one movie than I made in my entire career. It doesn't bother me, though, because I know there's a huge demand for their product.

People always use the teacher line, but I bet that most of them make more than teachers, too. The reason is clear: Teaching is a govern-ment job that is paid by tax revenue. Who do you think makes more, a defense attorney hired by a defendant or a prosecutor hired by the state? If you want to complain about salaries, complain about lawmakers in Congress (who make far more than teachers) and state legislatures that decide how much compensation teachers receive.

These money issues always come up when people discuss topics relating to professional sports. The latest uproar has surrounded the building of new stadiums. People say, "Why should we help to pay for stadiums?" Former Minnesota Governor Jesse Ventura said it didn't make sense for a city or state to help pay for a stadium when it didn't get free entertainment, like it does from libraries. Well, how many libraries bring in millions of dollars of revenue for a city or state? Professional sports teams can revitalize entire cities and create thousands of jobs. Unfortunately, many Americans see themselves as the victims of some nefarious plot by forces beyond their control—especially when they identify those forces as a nebulous group referred to as "the rich."

Fans feel as if they have lost touch with athletes because of what they call athletes' outrageous salaries. The only thing that's outrageous about these salaries is the priorities of the society that drives them up. Our society is obsessed with wealth, and those that don't have it accuse those that do of trying to manipulate our society. This is particularly true when it comes to legal issues.

CHAPTER ELEVEN

PROS OR CONS?

I'm a respectable enough citizen, a multiple felon perhaps, but certainly not dangerous.

—Hunter S. Thompson

To alcohol, the cause of and solution to all of life's problems.

—A line from Homer J. Simpson
in an episode of *The Simpsons*

Just because you're paranoid, doesn't mean they're not out to get you

—Unknown

The roots of language are very interesting. Most of the words in the English language have Latin or Greek roots. However, you can change the meaning of words dramatically just by adding different prefixes. The prefix "re" is one of the most common. It generally means "again." If you add a hyphen, it changes things significantly. If I didn't **re**sign in 2001, I would have been in a position to **re**-sign with the Vikings. "Pro" and "con" generally mean "for" and "against." The point is that they are opposites. So if they're opposite terms, does this mean that **con**gress is the opposite of **pro**gress? But, I **di**gress.

In 1999, the sports world was shocked by the release of *Pros and Cons: The Criminals Who Play in the NFL*. It documented some criminal cases, including police reports and testimony, of players and coaches who had played or were still in the NFL. This book basically proclaimed that the league was nothing short of a reservoir for some of the most dangerous criminals in the nation. One of the most "shocking" revelations was that approximately one in five players had been charged with some serious crime—from fraud to murder. When I first heard about the book from some guys in the locker room, I was pretty amused. Minnesota was well represented in the book, so we did have some laughs about it. The more I thought about it, though, the angrier I got. Now, there's no denying that the league has some guys who've gotten into hot water, but this book paints a picture that doesn't accurately represent the complete world of the NFL. You have to remember that there are about 1,800 players in the NFL from year to year and it only makes sense that some of those guys are going to get into trouble. At its best, this book portrays players as spoiled prima donnas who think that they can get away with anything. At its worst, this book insinuates that football players are animals, incapable of controlling their rage.

A reporter for the *Columbus Dispatch* wrote an article last year that chastised athletes for believing they are above the law. His article referenced a college player who had been arrested in a drunken driving incident. The writer said that athletes try to get away with things that the rest of the public would never dream of attempting. To listen to this guy, you would think that athletes were the only people who had ever committed crimes. Barely a day goes by without there being a story in the paper or on television about some athlete getting into trouble. But do you really think that this means that athletes are more prone to criminal behavior or do you think that this is just a case of these incidents being blown out of proportion? Surely there must be some people besides athletes committing all those crimes out there. The NFL is well aware of the perception held by many in the public and does its best to help players avoid these incidents.

Each year during training camp, the league sends representatives out to warn players about some of the legal pitfalls that they could face. I don't know if all teams did this, but Denny Green would supplement the league presentation with a series of seminars. Training camp is a very appropriate time to do this, not just because there's more time during the day, but also because of the high number of incidents that seem to occur with players during this time of year. This is especially true for the rookies. This is their first real taste of the NFL and they like to let off steam when they get the opportunity. We don't get much time off during training camp, but when we do, the rookies hit the town in full force. Training camp locations are usually in small towns, so the entire area gets a "buzz" about it as training camp approaches. They know we're around and they like to hang out in the same places. This can cause some problems. Athletes + alcohol + enthusiastic fans = potentially dangerous situations. Some of the players get caught up in these environments, with the fans buying them drinks and telling them how great they are. They may have one or two (or five or six) too many and then start making some questionable decisions. Evil may have money at its roots, but it definitely has alcohol as one of its prime sources of nourishment.

If you read about a player getting into trouble on a particular night, you can almost bet the house that alcohol was somehow involved. Excessive alcohol use is bad enough for you by itself, but it's the problems that can occur after heavy drinking that are most dangerous. I don't think a week goes by when you don't hear about an athlete at some level of sports getting a DUI. In one of our seminars, an attorney came in and discussed the best way to handle these types of situations. The first thing that they tell you is that you need to be polite with the officers. This sounds like a no-brainer, but I'm sure it's not always easy. People say that athletes always get off easy, but not every cop is a sports fan. You get some cop who makes $40,000 a year pulling over some athlete who makes millions, and he's not going to be very sympathetic. The Vikings had our fair share of players who had DUIs. Most of the guys on the team would be quick to crack jokes about the unfortunate players who had suffered the embarrassment of the dreaded DUI; I wasn't one of them.

First of all, I know that I've been in bad enough shape behind the wheel myself to have gotten a DUI if I had been pulled over. The truth is that just about anyone who's had something to drink in his life has been behind the wheel when he shouldn't have. It's the bad part about alcohol and drunk driving—your judgment gets clouded when you drink, and you believe that you aren't as drunk as you really are. Even if you do think you've had too much, you believe that you're not going to be the one to get caught. One of my drinking friends says that we're statistical anomalies because we haven't been caught yet. I do try to stay safe behind the wheel, but I know I don't always do the right thing when it comes to this—and I know I'm not alone.

Between 40 and 50 percent of all traffic fatalities involve alcohol. Nobody who gets behind the wheel after drinking wants to kill someone, but it is a very real possibility. DUIs are much more common than you would think. According to MADD.org, almost 15 percent of all men will get a DUI at some point in their life. There were 1.5 million DUI arrests in 1999. The truth is that drunk driving is a problem in our entire society—not just in pro football. People always use the phrase: "drugs and alcohol," but make no mistake about it, alcohol is a drug, a socially acceptable drug, no doubt, but a drug nonetheless.

Far from ignoring or condoning the behavior, the NFL responds quickly when a player is involved in an alcohol related incident. The player is first placed in an evaluation period in which he is tested randomly for all drugs—including alcohol. The player will meet with counselors during this period, and it will be determined whether there needs to be some sort of continuing treatment after the initial evaluation. Normally, players are only tested once a year for "street" drugs. A positive test results in the same evaluation period mentioned above. Players face possible fines and/or suspensions if there are further infractions of the drug policy. The perception of the general public is that athletes just get slapped on the wrist for these offenses, but it's simply not true. I know for a fact that people in "normal" jobs get away with multiple DUI offenses. I don't think people should necessarily be fired from a job just because they've been convicted of some offense. Obviously, a pattern of this type of behavior may indicate some deeper issues, but that should be the decision of the employer, not the public.

I came close to being caught for smoking marijuana one year. Normally, we would be tested annually at training camp. No sweat, just stop smoking a few weeks before camp and you've got no problems. But there was a clause in the rules that allowed teams to test as early as mini-camp that they had not enforced up to that year. We got into the locker room for mini-camp that year and they told us that players were going to be tested the following day. There I was, the team's union representative and one of the locker room's most respected leaders and I was about to get caught with THC in my system. Luckily for me, they decided to test the defensive players that year. A lot of guys got caught that time. Some players smoked marijuana occasionally (myself included), but I don't think it ever got excessive. I know it's illegal to do (for now at least), but I really think people have demonized marijuana unfairly. There are no studies that show it's any more harmful than nicotine or alcohol. It all boils down to what drug the majority wants to accept. There was, after all, a time in our own country when alcohol was illegal.

It's hard to believe, but for 14 years it was illegal for anyone to consume alcohol in America (prohibition.history.ohio-state.edu). "The Noble Experiment" was definitely a failure. Crime actually increased during Prohibition and then dropped significantly after its repeal. You have to wonder if the same wouldn't be true with marijuana, and it has been shown that decriminalization hasn't dramatically increased its use (http://www.mpp.org/adolescents.html). We could be spending our resources in much more useful ways than by arresting, prosecuting, and incarcerating non-serious drug offenders.

Say what you will about marijuana and its dangers, but alcohol causes far more problems in our society. Alcohol has definitely been given protected status in our country. They've banned cigarette commercials and decried the tobacco industry for targeting our youth, but it's alcohol advertising that dominates our airwaves, particularly in sports programming. You think kids aren't influenced when they see a bunch of models dancing around half-naked in beer commercials in between seeing their favorite athletes? It's ironic that alcohol causes so many problems for athletes and at the same time provides the bulk of advertising dollars that pays their salaries. But DUI's aren't the only problems that can arise from drinking. Athlete + alcohol + adoring female fans = potential for more serious trouble.

Women love athletes. And why not? They're young, talented, wealthy, and have status. It was way too easy to find a young woman willing to spend some time with you. This is a topic that was covered early and often during training camp and throughout the season. Denny Green would warn us every time we had a night off to be careful when it came to women in the city. They knew where we hung out, and it didn't even matter if their husbands or boyfriends were with them, which could cause problems of another sort. Of course, the real problems can start when it's time to go home after inhibitions have been lowered. Denny would always warn us by saying, "Remember, no means no!"

Each year, we would have a woman come in to speak to us during training camp about some issues involving women. The topic of sexual consent always came up. This can be a very tricky issue. She told us that a drunk "yes" from a woman was really the same thing as no. I understand the spirit of that statement, but who's to say when someone is incapable of making decisions? Should men have contracts that women must sign before having sex? Should men give breathalyzers before having sex? How many times have you had sex after a night of drinking? How many of us were conceived under those very circumstances? If it's rape to have sex with a drunk woman, then there are a hell of a lot of us that wouldn't be here if it weren't for "rape." Now, I understand that you shouldn't have sex with some woman who can barely stand or is passed out, but the gray area has caused confusion and placed some people in precarious legal positions. The woman who gave these seminars cautioned us to be careful about what positions we placed ourselves in. We had to see ourselves as potential targets of these women. Some of these women want to use you. They may want to get pregnant to get money out of you, or they may want to make their boyfriends jealous. I know one of my teammates was charged with rape by a woman who had a boyfriend. She ended up admitting that she had lied about the incident because she didn't want her boyfriend to know that she had voluntarily cheated on him. This kind of scenario scared me. I would try to make sure that I didn't deal with women like that, but how could you know for sure? The public so readily believes women who make these types of accusations that you don't really have a fair chance to keep your name clean. The accusations are front-page news; the retraction is buried on page 22.

We also received advice on domestic violence issues. This, too, can be a tricky area for male athletes. In some states, the mere fact that a call to the police has been made means that the man is going directly to jail. Growing up in a home in which domestic violence occurred, I understand the need to protect women who have to deal with that terror. But laws like this are simply unfair. Men are not the only ones that cause domestic incidents. Women get angry, too, and they sometimes provoke their partners through their own violent actions. The woman counseling us told us to just leave when things seemed to be getting out of control, but it's not always that easy. I had an ex-girlfriend jump into my truck to try to keep me from leaving. I told her to get out and let me go, but she insisted. What was I supposed to do, grab her and risk hurting her? I felt my only option was to call the police and have them escort her from my car. There was nothing else that made sense. I wasn't just going to sit there and have the situation escalate. You have to be aware of your public status when situations like that arise. If one of the neighbors had called the police because she was screaming and crying, I may have been taken to jail and had my name all over the news. Once again, though, it's not just athletes who get into this type of trouble, it's just the stories about public figures that make headlines. It's not just today's athletes that have gotten into trouble for issues of domestic violence or crimes in general. Take a look at Jim Brown's rap sheet online sometime. His arrest record is longer than his list of rushing records. This is another case where today's athlete is scrutinized to a greater degree than his predecessors. This is also a case where our society really needs to examine itself more closely instead of pretending that this is only someone else's problem.

Cybergrrl (www.cybergrrl.com) reports that some 500,000 women are battered annually in America. You may only hear about the high profile cases involving athletes and entertainers, but this is a problem that extends to all areas of our society. Any attack is bad enough by itself, but the disturbing truth is that they often lead to further attacks and even murder. Attitudes in this country about domestic violence definitely have changed for the better, though. Just think about the way that domestic violence used to be treated as a joke. Ralph Cramden would threaten his wife Alice with a shaking fist and a promise "to send her to the moon." This was on one of the most popular prime-time network shows of all time. What do you think they'd say about a similar joke now? We live in a violent society, and it takes vigilance by all to make sure that things don't get out of control. We are somewhat desensitized to violence by television and video games, but this can't be the only reason we're so violent. Television, books, and movies have contained, and even praised, violence for years. I remember a Bugs Bunny cartoon in which some rabbits shot themselves in the head because they made a mistake. When I see that cartoon now, they've cut that scene out. I think we need to be more aware of what our children watch, but we also need to be more involved in general with the lives of our youth. We need to stop blaming violence on movies and video games, and start realizing that the "real-world" violence that children experience and witness with their own families is far more significant. The league automatically puts players into anger management when they have any type of incident involving violence. Once again, the league is trying to ensure that its players are good citizens and have the resources available to get help when they need it. The rest of our society would do well to follow the league's example.

Socio-economic issues are usually ignored in the evaluation of athletes and crime. Most professional athletes are from lower income homes and many had troubles with the law before they ever made it to the pros but, once again, people believe what they want to believe and ignore common sense in favor of their own pre-conceived ideas. It's also difficult to even define the demographic of professional athletes. How many people grow up poor and end up becoming millionaires in their early twenties? Some athletes abuse their position, but you have to take their age into account as well. Young people commit more crimes in all segments of our society. You need to take all of these factors into account when you consider these issues of crime. I think part of the problem is that our population has a general distrust of our legal system. They feel that people with high status or money get away with crimes more often. Part of this is related to the cost of defending yourself in our country. Wealthy individuals can afford better lawyers, so it makes sense that they would fair better in some legal cases. But you can't blame the wealthy or athletes for the way our legal system is set up. People have said that athletes are getting away with murder, literally and figuratively, and a couple of high profile cases seemed to confirm this belief.

The Baltimore Ravens' Ray Lewis and the Carolina Panthers' Rae Carruth were charged in separate murder cases in 1999 and 2000, respectively. Ray Lewis and two of his friends (they were not athletes) were charged for the murder of two men who were involved in a fight following an evening at a nightclub. Ray was uncooperative initially in the investigation but eventually plea-bargained down to an obstruction of justice charge in exchange for his testimony against the other two defendants. As it turned out, Ray wasn't even involved in the fight that resulted in the death of the two young men. He testified that he saw his friends hitting the victims but that he did not see any weapons (the men were stabbed to death) being used. There's no question in my mind that Ray was implicated in this case because of who he is. The people in the area recognized him and gave his name to the police just because they knew who he was. This is an issue that people oftentimes overlook. A famous person often gets charged in these types of incidents just because they get recognized. You really have to be careful about the types of crowds you hang out with. You have far more to lose than most, and a much greater potential for being singled out when these incidents occur. A lot of guys are jealous of the attention that athletes get, and they try to start fights to prove their own masculinity. You have to keep your eyes open when you're out and try to avoid the trouble that seems to develop so frequently when beer muscles start to develop during the course of an evening.

I'm definitely not defending Ray for his behavior early in the investigation, but everyone seemed to focus on him and his involvement rather than the facts of the case. I feel bad for the families of the victims, but they, too, directed their anger at the wrong person. They attacked Ray for his lack of cooperation early in the trial and then attacked him further after the trial ended without a conviction for either of the other two men that were initially charged in the murder. I understand their frustration, but it wasn't Ray's fault that no one was convicted in this case. People always say that athletes are getting away with these crimes, but they have to remember that these cases are decided by juries, not the athletes involved. Does an athlete or celebrity's status have an impact on some of these juries? Yes, probably, but who's fault is that? People get away with crimes all of the time, and it's obviously not just athletes. Rae Carruth didn't get away with his crime, but the impact of his trial was devastating for the image of the NFL.

Rae was charged with murder in the death of his pregnant girlfriend. The trial revealed that Rae had hired a hit man to kill his girlfriend so he could avoid paying child support. Rae was driving a car in front of his girlfriend as the hit man and a driver pulled up alongside her, shooting her in the chest and abdomen. She later died from the gunshot wounds. Rae was found not guilty of murder, but was convicted on conspiracy charges and sentenced to 19 to 24 years in prison. People cried foul at this lighter charge, but did they really think that this jury was acting in favor of Rae Carruth? Facts are facts in a case, but a jury is composed of people who must make decisions based on their interpretation of those facts. We sometimes feel that justice hasn't been served in cases like this, but cases are decided on law, not emotion or our loosely defined sense of what's "right." These athletes were sentenced the way they were because a jury made those decisions, not because there's some conspiracy in this country to go easy on athletes and other celebrities. It's not just our nation's belief that athletes are criminals who get away with their crimes that's at play here, though. Our country harbors other more insidious stereotypes that also apply here. It was the "trial of the century" involving O.J. Simpson's murder charges that brought some of these issues from the depths of our collective conscience.

CHAPTER TWELVE

THE RACE, CREED, AND COLOR CARDS

That's what they told us today; in other words, you're still a slave. No matter how much money you got, you still ain't shit!

——Dr. Dre

Why can't we brothers protect one another? No one's serious and it makes me furious!

——Curtis Mayfield

The O.J. Simpson trial was a case study in some of the most contentious issues in our nation today: domestic violence, money, privilege, fame, and, most pointedly, race. The people of the United States are very uncomfortable talking about race, but the issue was unavoidable in this trial. You had a famous black, ex-professional athlete being accused in the murder of his white, ex-wife. All of the other issues were important, but race played a leading role from day one. The *Time* magazine cover that showed O. J's mug shot was purposely darkened and the pundits were off to the races. They did have one thing right, though: White America believes that blacks are more dangerous individuals than whites, and this murder case, along with all of the other crimes reported about black athletes and blacks in general, confirmed the issue in the minds of many white people. There can be no separation between the way in which this society views athletes and celebrities and the way it views race.

To many white people in America, their favorite black entertainer or athlete is somehow different from the blacks they encounter in the rest of the world. As I stated in the first chapter, things were made easy for me because I was an athlete. People tend to look past color more easily when the individual they see is an athlete or entertainer. When a person becomes frustrated with an athlete or entertainer, however, I think it's easier for them to break them down because those latent racial tensions rise to the surface. They are no longer the "hero" that won the big game, they're just the "dumb nigger" who dropped the ball and ruined the team's chances. America is in denial about its racial issues, but they are as important in forming our opinions on certain issues as any other factor. This is especially true when it comes to athletes, race, and crime. This is no different than any of the other issues I've touched on: It's perception, not reality, that matters most.

The major professional leagues (excluding hockey) have a majority of black players. Whites are convinced that black men, especially young black men, are more capable of crime than any other segment of our society; and, in a sense, they have a justification for that belief. Blacks do commit a disproportionate number of crimes in this country as compared to their overall percentage of the population. So when they see a story about a black athlete being accused of a crime, it's not much of a leap for them to assume that athlete's guilt. "O.J. beat his wife? That's no surprise to me—that's what black men do." But what's really behind the statistics on crime?

Yes, blacks do commit more crime on a percentage basis, but so do people of lower education. Blacks have been in poor school districts for years, so it's no surprise that more of them would have a lower level of education. This leads to worse jobs and to generally worse conditions in life, which also contribute to crime. In 1997, only 51 percent of state prison inmates had a high school degree (http://www.seisummit.org/ Downloads/aspd/ProjectLearnLiteracyData.PDF) as compared to 71 percent of the general population. Only 2.7 percent of those inmates graduated from college, and when you consider that only 56 percent of blacks graduated from high school nationally in 1998 (Jay P. Green, PhD), the picture starts to become clearer. Once again, we need to stop focusing on the problems of athletes, or black athletes in this case, and start looking at some social problems that are being ignored by our country. Another more disturbing statistic is that among juveniles, blacks are six times more likely to be "convicted" for crimes against people, four times more likely for property damage, and thirty times more likely for drugs (William Raspberry, *Washington Times*). The real issue in America isn't whether wealthy athletes are being coddled in court; it's whether our legal system is being administered fairly in terms of race.

You don't hear about brutality cases perpetrated by blacks against whites. I'm sure it's happened at some time, but there's no question that blacks have been attacked on numerous occasions by white officers. Rodney King and Abner Luoima are two of the most well known incidents, but there have been others that have sparked riots and protests in recent years. Both of those high-profile cases also showed the lengths that cops will go to protect themselves and each other, even if it means breaking the laws they swore to uphold. The Los Angeles police force seems to be particularly adept at evidence tampering and cover-ups. Recent revelations about some of those cases have caused the reversal of some convictions. The veracity, or lack thereof, of the L.A. police definitely played a major role in the acquittal of O.J. It amazes me that someone such as Mark Furman, who perjured himself in a capital murder trial, is still respected as an author and pundit in some recent legal cases (I guess it took someone like Geraldo Rivera to make that possible). I don't know what really happened the night Nicole Simpson and Ron Goldman were killed, but I'd have to say that the police work alone in that case provided some reasonable doubt. If you're black in America, you almost certainly have had some unpleasant run-in with a law enforcement agent.

I was 13 the first time I went to jail. I had been inside most of the evening and then I decided to go out into the neighborhood to see what my brother and some of the other guys were doing. As it turned out, they had been running around the neighborhood scaring people with a Halloween mask. The police showed up right after I joined the group.

They had been called about a disturbance with a mask and they questioned us about it. They saw that one of us had a mask and decided to take us all in. The other guys tried to tell them that I wasn't involved, but it was too late: I was guilty by association. I don't think we were charged, but they held us for a few hours to shake us up. It worked on me. I was stunned that I could be locked up for no other reason than being suspected of being involved in a crime. Of course, at the time we didn't have the full citizenship privileges of an adult, so we didn't have to be formally charged, and we didn't have the right to call an attorney. "Young, black male" is often associated with "criminal" in this society, and I was a victim of this stereotype that night.

Since then, I've had a few incidents that I would fit into the DWB category—or "driving while black." Recently, I was pulled over while I was driving a new Hummer, hauling my boat down the freeway. A female officer came up to the car and said that my plates didn't match my vehicle. She was right. I had just purchased the new truck and they had put the plates from my previous vehicle on this one, a common practice. However, both of the vehicles were registered in my name, so there shouldn't have been a problem. I asked the officer why she had run my plates in the first place. She said she did it because it was a new vehicle. That was the best she could come up with? Does she run the plates on every new vehicle that goes down the road? Besides, what kind of speeding getaway would I have been making hauling a boat? She said I should just consider myself lucky that she was doing her job. In her estimation, until I proved otherwise, I was a thief or a drug dealer. In situations like that, you just have to try to stay calm, because she could have come up with any charge to cause me trouble. I'm not saying that all cops are bad or that all of them are prejudiced, but a lot of it goes on. Most blacks simply don't trust the police—and I think the feeling is mutual.

How many times do you hear or see some story about blacks committing crime on television? There is simply more time spent covering crimes committed by blacks. This is especially true when the crime is against a white person. What do you think the media spin would have been if Bernhard Goetz (he was the so called "subway vigilante" who shot four unarmed black youths on a subway because he felt threatened) was black, and he shot four white kids? Conversely, if a white child is missing, the media spends much more time covering the story than if it's a black child. Just look at the story about the young black girl who went missing from Florida's foster care system. Heard much about her lately? The movies are no better. If a black person can even find a job in a movie, they're usually stuck with some demeaning role as a thief or drug dealer. Some of that has begun to change with actors such as Denzel Washington and Samuel L. Jackson, but it's difficult to find many black actors in major Hollywood movies. Furthermore, how many movies show the tired *Dangerous Minds* theme in which some white person comes in and saves young black people from themselves—as if blacks couldn't make it without whites intervening. Part of the problem here is that our nation never has come to terms with its racial past. It wasn't that long ago that blacks weren't even allowed to eat in the same restaurants as whites. It was only a couple of years ago when a school principal in Georgia threatened to cancel the prom because there were going to be inter-racial couples. My parents had to face this same discrimination when they wanted to get married in the late 1960s. There may be some improvements in racial issues in this country, but it still bothers many Americans to see inter-racial couples.

Most of white America was very angry that O.J. had gotten away with murder, but long before that, many of them were upset that he had the nerve to date white women. I know it bothers some people to see inter-racial couples and I know that it can add to a person's frustration with an athlete. Who does he think he is dating a white girl? There are plenty of examples. I'm one of them. Most of the women I've dated in my life have been white. You see a lot of black athletes with white women, but I think people read too much into this. Believe me, this works both ways. There were as many blacks who were upset with O.J. for dating a white woman as there were whites upset with him. A person shouldn't be criticized for who they choose to date, but race is such a divisive issue that it's almost inevitable. Some blacks see this as an attempt by the person to "abandon" his or her race. I remember seeing some of the talk shows about O.J. that mentioned his appearance and behavior. They said that O.J. had given up his black roots once he became famous. One man even said that the fact that O.J. didn't wear facial hair meant that he wasn't really "black." That's the most ridiculous thing I've ever heard!

Too many black Americans have bought into the idea that there's a "right" and a "wrong" way to be black in America. We're starting to buy into the stereotypes we once despised. It used to be that blacks wanted to get out of the ghetto and find a better life for themselves. Now, if you don't act "ghetto" or like a "thug," you can't get respect, especially in the sports or entertainment world.

The truth is that you don't have to wear "ice" to be black. The truth is that you aren't a "house nigger" if you speak proper English. The truth is that it's good to be intelligent and an independent thinker. The schools should do a better job teaching young black people about "real" role models from the black community, but part of that responsibility lies with the black community itself. A man like Dr. Ben Carson is a prime example. Ben Carson is black, and he's the head of pediatric neurosurgery at Johns Hopkins University. Black kids should be taught about role models like Ben Carson and should be given the opportunity to learn about other black heroes more than just during Black History Month. This is not to say that you leave the ghetto and never look back. We should do things to try to uplift our own people, but we need to start focusing our youth in positive, realistic ways. Drugs, sports, and rap aren't the only ways for a black person to earn a good living in this country. But if all they're taught is "to get rich or die tryin,'" then what real chance do they have?

There needs to be more open dialogue in this country about race, but part of the problem is that some black people won't allow the conversation to be truly open. If you bring up slavery every time someone wants to talk honestly about race, then things will never progress. It's just like Jewish people and the Holocaust. Past transgressions against your people don't give you unlimited license to say and do what you choose. If you say things like "black people can't be racist," when the topic of race comes up then you're doing the entire process a disservice.

Black people can't technically be racist, but they can be prejudiced and they can act as foolish as anybody. We as a black community need to be honest with ourselves and not defend every black person's actions just because they are black. Just look at the way Maurice Green and the other members of our Olympic 4X100 meter relay team behaved after winning the gold medal in Sydney. They put on a shameful display of arrogance that was a disservice to our nation and the black community. Similar displays by Terrell Owens have done the same. You don't have to disrespect your opponent to "keep it real." And now every time someone accuses a black person of some impropriety, Jesse Jackson and Al Sharpton come out and call it a racial conspiracy. I had to deal with one of these incidents in my duties as an agent disciplinary committee member.

The NFL Players Association certifies and regulates all agents who want to represent NFL players in contract negotiations with clubs. From time to time, agents violate the regulations and the union steps in to file a complaint against that agent. A disciplinary committee, comprised of three to four current players and an ex-player (in my case), hear the facts of the cases and make determinations on any discipline that might need to be imposed. In the summer of 1999, we brought charges against an agent named Tank Black. The charges against him included fraud and money laundering. He was stealing millions of dollars from his players through various schemes and bogus investments. We had never had a case that involved such egregious misuse of a position of trust. We ended up de-certifying him to keep him from financially harming any new players.

Now, Tank happens to be black, and Jesse Jackson came out and attacked the union for what he saw as prejudicial treatment. We had never de-certified someone so quickly, but it was because of his danger to other players, not because he was black. Jesse accused the union of racist behavior, disregarding the fact that the union head, Gene Upshaw, is black himself. Believing that all accused blacks are innocent is as ridiculous as assuming that all blacks are criminals. There are too many "real" cases that deserve a man like Jesse's attention. I think he's done some great things for black people, but he needs to be careful about who he chooses to endorse and when he calls an action "racist." As the boy who called wolf, this becomes a case of "the reverend who calls racism." Racism still exists in this country, but it diminishes legitimate causes to cry racism every time a black is accused of wrongdoing. Jesse even called for a boycott of the movie "Barber Shop," because it made statements that called into question some of the more sacredly held views of black heroes; I'm sure that the fact that one of the characters said "fuck Jesse Jackson" had something to do with his feelings towards the film. A black actor, Cedric the Entertainer, in a black film said some in the black community feel you should never question the black establishment. This also keeps open dialogue from occurring. Some people are reluctant to say what's on their minds because they're scared to be labeled as a racist.

Our age of political correctness has gone too far. We'll never be able to make advances in race relations if we can't say what's on our minds and if we're not open to opposing views. There needs to be an attempt by all sides to be sensitive to the other, but there also needs to be honesty when all sides evaluate themselves. This doesn't just apply to race. By nature, we're suspicious of those who are different than us, whether that difference is as simple as skin color or something more personal, like religion. As with skin color, there's an arrogance that develops when one is a member of a majority, making one believe that his or her views are correct.

Reggie White gave a speech in front of the Wisconsin legislature in 1998 that stunned a lot of people into silence. He made some controversial comments about race and homosexuality. He threw out some stereotypes about various races and cursed the evil of gay lifestyles. He said that his comments were an attempt to identify all races as a "reflection" of God and homosexuality as a sin that was taking America further from God. A reporter asked me about Reggie's statements and I replied that I thought they were "ignorant." People mistakenly assume that the word ignorant means stupid. It actually refers to one's lack of knowledge on a subject, and I thought that that's just what Reggie exhibited with his statements. Far from bringing people together, statements such as his perpetuate archaic beliefs that can only keep our society hope-lessly divided. Reggie's a minister, so I understand how he thought that he had cornered the market on truth. Religious and racial arrogance may seem like different issues, but they're not. Christians make up nearly 90 percent of our American population. Problems can develop when Chris-tians try to impose their views on those who have different religious beliefs. We don't all pray to the same God and some of us don't pray or even believe in a God. I happen to be one of those people. It made me angry to hear Reggie say those things because he was making the as-sumption that everyone believed in "his" God. However, this is an as-sumption a lot of people make in this country.

People look at me as if I have two heads when I tell them I'm an atheist. It seems inconceivable to them that someone wouldn't believe in God, but they can no more prove that a God exists than I can prove that one doesn't. They certainly can't prove that their religion is any more valid than any other. Christians don't even realize how offensive their assumptions about the world can be. We would pray the Lord's Prayer before every game. I would kneel and hold hands with my teammates, but I would remain silent. Not only do prayers like this assume that one believes in God, but this particular prayer ends with a reference to "Christ," obviously a Christian term. There are Jewish players in the league, as well as Muslims (others I'm sure, too), that might take offense to such prayers, but they are never considered. I just don't think religion belongs in the locker room. Religion should be personal, and assump-tions should not be made about the religious make-up of a team. I just think that some players have gotten out of hand with religious state-ments. Sean Gilbert is a prime example. He made some comments that he held out during contract negotiations because God had given him a number he should wait for. (He actually ended up signing for more than that number. I guess Sean would have us believe that God doesn't make a good agent.) You see these athletes and entertainers literally wearing their religion and you begin to realize why the world's other cultures and religions don't think much of Americans. Jesus' teachings are about hu-mility and simplicity. What do you think he would have thought of people wearing diamond-studded crucifixes in his honor?

The very way in which Christians celebrate their biggest holidays might seem offensive to other religions. Jewish and Muslim holidays are marked by fasting and solemn observance. Christian holidays are marked by presents, bunnies, and gorging. I'm not trying to say that Christians are wrong for having celebrations around religious holidays. I just think it illustrates some of the views that the rest of the world has about us as a nation. Many in the world see us as arrogant and hedonistic, and the style of our religious observances is indicative of this. This boils down to perception once again. Not all Muslims are terrorists and not all Christians are good people. We need to be aware of how the world views us, especially since we have become inextricably tied to world politics.

What is even more troubling about our religious arrogance is the problems that it can bring to our domestic issues. It seems that religious sentiment has begun to creep into the political arena, a place it most certainly doesn't belong. Our government readily acknowledges our freedom of worship, but it seems to forget that "not worshiping" is also a legitimate option. I don't feel like less of an American because I don't believe in the term "under God." Our nation may have been founded under some religious principles, but there's a reason the founding fathers wanted a separation between church and state. Some are perplexed when people complain about religious symbols on public property, but they fail to realize the rights of others. Some of these symbols can be incredibly offensive. If you're a Muslim or Jew (or any other religion— or an atheist), you don't want to see a cross or a nativity scene displayed as if it were a part of the only "true" faith. It's similar to displaying other secular symbols that some find offensive. Confederate flags are offensive to most blacks. Say what you want about representing southern heritage, but to many blacks the flag represents slavery and racist sentiments. Some might argue that the Nazi flag could represent German heritage, but that's not they way their government sees it; the Nazi flag has been outlawed by the German government. I don't think we should go as far as outlawing the Confederate flag, but I think state governments should realize that it is a divisive symbol that has no place on state property, especially not on a state flag.

Religion has also intruded in some of our most controversial public issues. It doesn't belong in our public schools. Whether it's a display of the Ten Commandments or a discussion on creationism, religion simply is out of place in our public school system. It does not belong in our court system either. The people who support religion in these venues are forgetting that not everyone agrees with their religious views, let alone whether or not these views belong in secular discussions.

The religious views on gays hit home for the NFL when Esera Tualo came out in 2002. I played with Esera for a few years and it never occurred to me that he was gay. I knew he liked to sing and that he was a bit effeminate, but neither of those things mean that someone is gay. I remember hearing some guys in the locker room talking about gays before Esera made his announcement. They said that they would disown their own kids if they found out they were gay. With a culture that feels this way about gays, it's not surprising that many gays feel threatened by society and ashamed of their sexual orientation.

I had no problem talking with Esera after I found out he was gay. A lot of guys shunned him after his announcement. It's the manly culture of the NFL, combined with some narrow religious sentiment.

The church has never been known for its sense of humor, or its willingness to accept challenges to its power. However, its power is based on faith, and not all believe the same about the world. Giordano Bruno was an Italian astronomer who expressed his belief that the earth revolved around the sun. This contradicted the belief, expressed by the church (these beliefs are based on passages in the Bible that state that the Earth "does not move"), that the Earth was the center of the universe and was immovable. Bruno was turned over to the inquisition for this "heresy" and was burned at the stake after refusing to recant. The same fate would have befallen Galileo had he not changed his tune.

People use religion very inconsistently, but this arises partly from contradictions that exist in the Bible itself. People say convicted murderers should die because of passages in the Old Testament ("an eye for an eye"), but they disregard passages in the New Testament that call for forgiveness ("turn the other cheek"). The death penalty is simple revenge and has no place in a civilized society. The mere fact that so many have been found to be innocent after being executed is reason enough to eliminate the practice. People always point to the fact that we would all want these "monsters" killed if our own family members were victims, but laws should not be based on revenge. There have also been an inordinate number of blacks killed, especially for killing white victims. This really is a complicated issue because there are so many factors that come into play—money, race, privilege, and religion are among them.

We sometimes get lost in our own pre-conceived notions about the world around us. We forget or fail to realize how much our opinions get affected by outside factors such as the media. We have to do our best to understand the world and people around us. It's harmful to be rigid in your thoughts and beliefs. Many of the views that people express about the sports world are tied to the misunderstandings that they have about the world in general. We judge those who are different from us more severely than those with whom we share similarities.

Athletes aren't perfect, but the rest of the world isn't, either. We need to stop focusing on just the "high profile" problems of our society and start taking a closer look at our society itself. It's about changing the way you look at the world. It's about widening your narrow view and seeing a new, more complete reality. Until we do this, we'll be stuck with our eyes focused on the surface...unable to see the truth that lies beneath.